Pseudo-Gregory of Nyssa:
Testimonies against the Jews

Society of Biblical Literature

Writings from the Greco-Roman World

John T. Fitzgerald, General Editor

Editorial Board

David Armstrong
Elizabeth Asmis
Brian E. Daley, S.J.
David G. Hunter
David Konstan
Michael J. Roberts
Johan C. Thom
Yun Lee Too
James C. VanderKam

Number 8

Pseudo-Gregory of Nyssa:
Testimonies against the Jews

Volume Editors
David Konstan and John T. Fitzgerald

Pseudo-Gregory of Nyssa:
Testimonies against the Jews

Translated with an Introduction and Notes by
Martin C. Albl

Society of Biblical Literature
Atlanta

PSEUDO-GREGORY OF NYSSA: TESTIMONIES AGAINST THE JEWS

English translation and notes, introduction, appendix, and index copyright © 2004, by the Society of Biblical Literature.

All rights reserved.

No part of this work may be reproduced or transmitted in any form or by any means, electronic or mechanical, including photocopying and recording, or by means of any information storage or retrieval system, except as may be expressly permitted by the 1976 Copyright Act or in writing from the publisher. Requests for permission should be addressed in writing to the Rights and Permissions Department, Society of Biblical Literature, 825 Houston Mill Road, Suite 350, Atlanta, GA 30329, USA.

Library of Congress Cataloging-in-Publication Data

Gregory, of Nyssa, Saint, ca. 335-ca. 394.
  [Selections. English. 2004]
  Pseudo-Gregory of Nyssa : testimonies against the Jews / translated with an introduction and notes by Martin C. Albl.
      p. cm. — (Society of biblical literature writings from the Greco-Roman world ; v. 8)
  Includes bibliographical references and index.
    ISBN: 1-58983-092-X (pbk. : alk. paper)
    1. Gregory, of Nyssa, Saint, ca. 335-ca. 394. I. Albl, Martin C. II. Title. III. Series: Writings from the Greco-Roman world ; v. 8.

BR65.G74E53 2004
239'.2–dc22   2004021310

04 05 06 07 08 09 10 11 — 5 4 3 2 1

The book is printed in the United States of America
on recycled, acid-free paper.

To Julian Hills,
teacher, mentor, meticulous scholar,
who first suggested this project

Table of Contents

Preface ix

Abbreviations xi

Introduction xiii
    The *Testimonia* Hypothesis xiii
    Ps.-Gregory and Other *Testimonia* Literature xvi
    Author and Date of Composition xvii
    Text xviii
    Place within the *Adversus Judaeos* Literature xix
    Purpose of This Study xxi

Outline of the Testimonies xxiii

Ps.-Gregory of Nyssa Testimonies: *Text and Translation* 1

Notes to the Text and Translation 62

Commentary 83

Appendix: Analysis of the Quotations 137

Bibliography 143

Indices
    Index of Biblical and Other Ancient Sources 153
    Index of Modern Authors 171

Preface

This translation and commentary have their origin in studies for my doctoral dissertation, "'And Scripture Cannot Be Broken': The Form and Function of the Early Christian *Testimonia* Collections," completed at Marquette University in 1997 under the direction of Julian V. Hills.

Ps.-Gregory's *Testimonies* have long been recognized as an important example of the Christian scriptural *testimonia* genre, and have played an important role in the research and thinking of some of the great scholars of early Christian scriptural exegesis. Beyond their relevance in the specialized field of *testimonia* research, however, the *Testimonies* offer a precious glimpse into a widespread Christian didactic tradition that supported basic Christian beliefs with proofs from scripture. It is my hope that this translation will facilitate further study in this important aspect of early Christian catechesis.

I am grateful to the Editorial Board of the Society of Biblical Literature's Writings from the Greco-Roman World series for accepting this work. Specifically, I wish to acknowledge the editorial expertise of Professors John T. Fitzgerald (notes) and David Konstan (translation). It has been a great pleasure working with them.

My greatest debt is owed to Julian Hills. He first encouraged me to undertake this project many years ago, and I am happy to dedicate (at last!) the finished work to him.

Martin C. Albl
Aberdeen, South Dakota
November 1, 2004
Feast of All Saints

Abbreviations

All abbreviations follow Patrick H. Alexander, et. al., eds., *The SBL Handbook of Style for Ancient Near Eastern, Biblical, and Early Christian Studies* (Peabody, Mass.: Hendrickson, 1999) except for the following:

Alt. Sim.	Evagrius. *Altercatio Legis inter Simonem Iudaeum et Theophilum Christianum*
Basil *Spirit*	*On the Holy Spirit*
Ps.-Basil *Eunom.*	*Adversus Eunomium IV-V*
Commodian *Carm.*	*Carmen Apologeticum*
Cyril of Alexandria *Jul.*	*Contra Julian*
Cyril of Jerusalem *Cat.*	*Catechetical Lectures*
Dial. AZ	*Dialogue of Athanasius and Zacchaeus*
Dial. TA	*Dialogue of Timothy and Aquila*
Ps.-Epiphanius *Test.*	*A Pseudo-Epiphanius Testimony Book*
Novatian *Trin.*	*De trinitate*
TC	*testimonia* collection
UQ	uncertain quotation
trans.	transpose

For biblical MSS and versions, I follow the abbreviations in Academia Litterarum Gottingensis. *Septuaginta: Vetus Testamentum Graecum* (Göttingen: Vandenhoeck & Ruprecht, 1931-).

Introduction

In terms of form, Ps.-Gregory's *Testimonies against the Jews* belongs to the scriptural *testimonia* genre, a genre employed by both Jews and Christians.[1] This genre may be defined as a collection of scriptural proof-texts, organized under specified headings, that function as "witnesses" or "proofs" of particular beliefs.[2] In terms of content, the *Testimonies* belong to the *adversus Judaeos* literature, an apologetic and/or polemical genre that sought to define basic Christian identify and beliefs over against Jewish objections.

THE *TESTIMONIA* HYPOTHESIS

The so-called *testimonia* hypothesis is a scholarly attempt to show that the earliest Christians collected, edited, and gave authoritative status to discrete collections of Old Testament excerpts. In many cases, according to this argument, Christians quoted not from biblical MSS directly, but rather from such *testimonia* collections (TCs). Further, the hypothesis claims that the process of gathering and commenting upon these *testimonia* was not simply a technical activity, rather it lay at the heart of the development of the earliest Christian theology worked out on the basis of certain central scriptural passages.[3]

J. Rendel Harris articulated the classic form of the hypothesis.[4] He posited the existence of a single, authoritative

---

[1] For an overview of this genre, see my "*And Scripture Cannot Be Broken*": *The Form and Function of the Early Christian Testimonia Collections* (NovTSup 96; Leiden: Brill, 1999).

[2] I distinguish between "extract collections" (general collections of excerpted materials) and "*testimonia* collections" (excerpts that function as forensic proofs of particular theses).

[3] This latter point is clearly expressed in the title of C. H. Dodd's book *According to the Scriptures: The Sub-Structure of New Testament Theology* (London: Nisbet, 1952).

[4] Harris, *Testimonies* (2 vols.; Cambridge: Cambridge University Press, 1916–20). See now Alessandro Falcetta, "Testimonies: The Theory of James Rendel Harris in the Light of Subsequent Research" (Ph.D. diss., University of

"Testimony Book" that was compiled before the earliest NT writings. This Book consisted of two general categories of proof-texts: christological (e.g., scriptural proofs showing that Jesus' suffering and death were predicted in scripture) and anti-Jewish (e.g., that God had rejected the Jewish people because of their disbelief and instead was establishing a new covenant with the Gentiles).[5]

Harris relied on two major pieces of evidence for his thesis. Firstly, he considered extant TCs, such as Cyprian's *To Quirinus* and Ps.-Gregory's *Testimonies*. Secondly, he noted peculiar features of New Testament and early Christian quotations of scripture that pointed towards the use of scriptural collections rather than direct MSS.

Harris and others looked to the first two books of Cyprian's *To Quirinus* (written in 248) as the classic example of the *testimonia* genre. The first book consists of twenty-four anti-Jewish TCs, bearing such headings as "That the Jews have fallen under the heavy wrath of God because they have departed from the Lord and have followed idols." The second is composed of thirty christological TCs, "proving" such theses as "that Christ is the First-born, and that He is the Wisdom of God, by whom all things were made."

I summarize below Harris's criteria for detecting early Christian use of TCs as developed and refined by subsequent scholars. Even a cursory overview of the commentary section of this current translation will reveal how often these indications are found in Ps.-Gregory's work:

(1) quotations that deviate considerably from known scriptural texts (e.g., LXX or LXX recensions, MT)
(2) composite quotations
(3) false attributions (e.g., a quotation of Isaiah is attributed to Jeremiah)
(4) use of the same series of texts in independent authors
(5) editorial or interpretive comments indicative of a collection

Birmingham, 2001); *ibid.*, "The Testimony Research of James Rendel Harris," *NovT* 45 (2003): 280–99.

[5] One should note that although Harris is best known for championing the existence of a single Testimony Book, he at times used more flexible language (e.g., speaking of testimony books). See Falcetta, "Theory of James Rendel Harris," 20–22; *ibid.*, "Testimony Research of James Rendel Harris," 286–87.

(6) evident lack of awareness of the biblical context of a quotation
(7) use of the same exegetical comments in independent authors.[6]

The *testimonia* hypothesis underwent a major modification with the work of C. H. Dodd, who accepted the general thesis that early Christians drew on a specific body of OT texts, and that these texts were highly influential in the development of early Christian theology.[7] Dodd, however, rejected Harris's model of a single "Testimony Book," arguing instead that it was within the early Christian oral tradition that these texts were isolated and reflected upon. Dodd identified three major categories of *testimonia*: "apocalyptic-eschatological" scriptures (e.g., Zech 9–14); "scriptures of the New Israel" (e.g., Jer 31); and "scriptures of the Servant of the Lord and the righteous Sufferer" (e.g., Ps 22; Isa 53). Barnabas Lindars filled out many of the details of Dodd's theory, showing how the *testimonia* were employed in an apologetic context as Christians responded to a variety of Jewish challenges.[8]

The hypothesis underwent further revision with the discovery of the Dead Sea Scrolls and with continuing research in patristic literature. Among the Scrolls, documents such as 4QTestimonia present concrete evidence that written scriptural excerpt collections were in use at a time contemporary with earliest Christianity. In the patristic field, studies of the *Epistle of Barnabas* and of Justin's *First Apology* and *Dialogue with Trypho* have established that these second-century works made use of extensive, sophisticated, and authoritative written *testimonia* collections.[9] These recent developments have revived the possibility

---

[6] Criteria from Albl, *Early Christian Testimonia*, 66–67.

[7] Dodd, *According to the Scriptures*.

[8] Lindars, *New Testament Apologetic: The Doctrinal Significance of the Old Testament Quotations* (Philadelphia: Westminster, 1961).

[9] On *Barnabas*, see Pierre Prigent, *Les testimonia dans le christianisme primitif: L'Épître de Barnabé 1–16 et ses sources* (Ebib; Paris: Gabalda, 1961). On Justin, see Oskar Skarsaune, *The Proof from Prophecy: A Study in Justin Martyr's Proof-Text Tradition. Text-Type, Provenance, Theological Profile* (NovTSup 56; Leiden: Brill, 1987). Jean Daniélou provides a series of studies on patristic *testimonia*; see his *Études d'exégèse judéo-chrétienne* (*Les Testimonia*) (ThH 5; Paris: Beauschesne, 1966).

that the earliest Christians made use of smaller, written collections. Such collections would have been employed not only in an apologetic context, but also as an essential method used in teaching (catechesis) and missionary work.

Recent scholarship continues to breathe new life into the *testimonia* hypothesis. Enrico Norelli has shown convincingly the presence of a TC (drawn from Christian catechesis on the Passover) underlying Justin's claims that Jewish teachers had "removed" passages from the scriptures (see *Dial.* 71–73 and 120); in other studies he demonstrates how TCs form the basis for both canonical and non-canonical accounts of Jesus' infancy.[10] Alessandro Falcetta has extended and deepened the work of the master *testimonia* scholar Harris.[11] My own work has been an attempt to synthesize and update the *testimonia* hypothesis.[12]

PS.-GREGORY AND OTHER *TESTIMONIA* LITERATURE

Ps.-Gregory's *testimonia* show a literary relationship with several strands of the *testimonia* tradition. The Commentary that accompanies the following translation traces the main lines of these relationships, providing at the same time several examples of detailed parallels. Yet I make no claim to be exhaustive: tracing the precise literary relationships between Ps.-Gregory and other works in the *testimonia* genre would require several individual studies. One can categorize the main lines of the *testimonia* literature in this way:

---

[10] Enrico Norelli, "Il *Martirio di Isaia* come *testimonium* antigiudaico?" *Henoch* 2 (1980): 37–57; *idem*. "Due *testimonia* attribuiti a Esdra,"*Annali di storia dell' esegesi* 1 (1984): 231–82; *idem*., "Avant le canonique et l'apocryphe: Aux origines des récits de la naissance de Jésus," *RTP* 126 (1994): 305–24. See also Norelli's overview of the *testimonia*, "Il dibattito con il giudaismo nel II secolo. Testimonia; Barnaba; Guistino," in *La Bibbia nell'antichità cristiana. I: Da Gesù a Origene* (ed. E. Norelli; La Bibbia nella storia 15/1; Bologna: EDB, 1993): 199–233.

[11] Falcetta, "Theory of James Rendel Harris"; *idem*., "A Testimony Collection in Manchester: Papyrus Rylands Greek 460," *BJRL* 83 (2001): 3–19; *idem*., "The Logion of Matthew 11:5–6 Par. from Qumran to Agbar," *RB* 110 (2003): 222–48; *idem*., "Research of James Rendel Harris."

[12] Albl, *Early Christian Testimonia*.

1. The Early Greek Tradition. Several of Ps.-Gregory's TCs show a close relationship with *testimonia* in *Barnabas*, Irenaeus's *Against Heresies* and *Proof of the Apostolic Preaching,* and Justin's *1 Apology* and *Dialogue with Trypho.*
2. The Latin Tradition. Ps.-Gregory closely parallels the *testimonia* of Tertullian, Cyprian, Lactantius, and Commodian.
3. The Later Greek Tradition. Ps.-Gregory parallels many passages and exegetical comments found in Eusebius's work (especially the *Proof of the Gospel* and the *Prophetic Selections*); Ps.-Basil's *Against Eunomius*; and Ps.-Epiphanius's *Testimonies.*
4. The Dialogue Tradition. Especially to be noted are Ps.-Gregory's connections with the *Dialogue of Athanasius and Zacchaeus,* the *Dialogue of Timothy and Aquila,* and the *Dialogue of Simon and Theophilus.* These in turn of course follow closely in the exegetical tradition of Justin's *Dialogue with Trypho.*
5. The Creedal Tradition. Often the *testimonia* served as proofs for particular creedal statements. Creedally arranged *testimonia* sources can already be traced in Justin. Cyril of Jerusalem's *Catechetical Lectures* and Rufinus's *Commentary on the Creed* are largely composed of scriptural proofs supporting creedal beliefs.

AUTHOR AND DATE OF COMPOSITION

Ps.-Gregory drew on a variety of earlier TCs, and thus his entire collection is difficult to date. His clear awareness of the Sabellian controversy (especially in chapter 1) locates him in the second half of the fourth century. A. Lukyn Williams places the work after 400 in view of its attribution to Gregory of Nyssa (d. 395).[13] The pseudonymous nature of the *Testimonies* is widely accepted.[14]

---

[13] Williams, *Adversus Judaeos: A Bird's-Eye View of Christian Apologiae until the Renaissance* (London: Cambridge University Press, 1935), 124.

[14] The Migne editors include it under *Dogmatica Dubia*; Williams states categorically, "No one believes that the treatise entitled *Selected Testimonies from the Old Testament against the Jews* was written by Gregory of Nyssa" (*Adversus Judaeos*, 124). Otto Bardenhewer finds the document too weakly attested to be authentic (*Geschichte der altkirchlichen Literatur* [5 vols.; 2nd ed.; Freiburg:

TEXT

I have used the text printed in J.-P. Migne's *Patrologia graeca* (PG 46:193–234). The Migne editors took the text from volume 6 of Andreas Gallandi, *Bibliotheca veterum patrum antiquorumque scriptorum ecclesiasticorum graecorum* (14 vols.; Venice: J. B. Albritius Hieron Fil., 1765–81). Gallandi himself had used the edition of Lorenzo Alessandro Zacagni, *Collectanea monumentorum veterum Ecclesiae* (Rome: Sacred Congregation for the Propagation of the Faith, 1698), 288–329. The Migne edition reproduces Zacagni's notes and Latin translation. I have viewed Zacagni's edition, noting any discrepancies between it and the Migne text; in a few cases I have used Zacagni to correct the Migne text.

Zacagni's text is based on two Vatican codices: 451 (14th century) and 1907 (12th or 13th century); he relies on the readings in Codex 1907 as more original. Codex 1907 lacks the beginning chapter and part of the second chapter, beginning with the words καὶ πάλιν, Στήσονται οἱ πόδες (*PG* 46:201a, line 15). Codex 451 breaks off with the phrase ἐν τῇ ἡμέρᾳ ἐκείνῃ λέγει κ[ύριος] (PG 46:232a line 3); some unrelated material follows.

Zacagni's notes also refer to a Latin translation by Laurentius Sifanus [Siphanus] that closely follows Codex 451 (Sifanus breaks off at the same place as this codex), and to comments on the quotations (primarily on textual form and parallels in other patristic authors) by Flaminius Nobilius (Flaminio Nobili) (1532–1590). I have compared the Sifanus translation (*Divi Gregorii episcopi Nysseni Opera* [Basel: Per Nic. Episcopium iuniorem, 1562], 315–331) to Zacagni's readings and noted any

---

Herder, 1913–1932], 3:202). On (quite weak) evidence for its authenticity (a parallel between a reading in Gregory's *Life of Moses* 2.270 and Ps.-Gregory *Test.* 7), see Jean Daniélou, "Bulletin d'histoire des origines chrétiennes," *RSR* 44 (1956): 621.

discrepancies.[15] The Sifanus translation in general is quite faithful to the Greek wording; occasionally, however, explanatory expansions are made.

All references to variant readings in Codices 451 and 1907 are taken from Zacagni's notes. I have not reproduced the notes from Nobilius's work, although I have incorporated some of his references into my notes and commentary when appropriate.

PLACE WITHIN THE *ADVERSUS JUDAEOS* LITERATURE

Ps.-Gregory's work forms part of the so-called *adversus Judaeos* literature.[16] Two major anti-Jewish themes in this literature are: (1) God's rejection of the Jews as the chosen people and God's election of the Gentiles; (2) the obsolescence of Jewish Law and cult, which had served merely to foreshadow Christian belief and practice.[17] A related theme is the christological interpretation of the Jewish scripture: "proofs" are adduced in support of Christian beliefs about Jesus (and explicitly or implicitly against Jewish interpretations), including prophecies of various details of Jesus' life recorded in the Gospel tradition. To a lesser extent, prophecies concerning the church and Christian life are also presented.

Ps.-Gregory follows the main lines of this literature:

(1) *Testimonia* of Jesus' life: Chaps. 1–2 (pre-existence and incarnation); Chaps. 3–9 (birth to ascension); Chaps. 19–21 (miscellaneous events in Christ's life).

---

[15] Sifanus usually omits Ps.-Gregory's specific attributions before quotations (e.g., "Moses:," "Amos:," "David:"), but in most cases refers to the source in a marginal note. Sifanus always translates introductory phrases such as "and again." I have thus not indicated Sifanus' omissions of these specific attributions in the textual notes.

[16] On this literature, see Rosemary Radford Ruether, "The *Adversus Judaeos* Tradition in the Church Fathers: The Exegesis of Christian Anti-Judaism," in *Aspects of Jewish Culture in the Middle Ages* (ed. Paul E. Szarmach; Albany: State University of New York Press, 1979):27–50; repr. in *Essential Papers on Judaism and Christianity in Conflict: From Late Antiquity to the Reformation* (New York: New York University Press, 1990): 174–89; Williams, *Adversus Iudaeos*; and Heinz Schreckenberg, *Die christlichen Adversus-Iudaeos-Texte und ihr literarisches und historisches Umfeld (1.–11. Jh.)* (3rd ed.; European University Studies, Series 23, Theology, vol. 172; Frankfurt: Peter Lang, 1995).

[17] Ruether, *Adversus Judaeos*, 30.

(2) God's rejection of the Jewish law and choosing of Christians: Chaps. 11–13, 16.
(3) *Testimonia* to specific Christian beliefs: Chaps. 10, 14–15, 17–18, 22.

Though clearly anti-Jewish, Ps.-Gregory lacks the unmitigated hostility of other patristic writers. For example, while Ps.-Gregory certainly regards the practice of circumcision as currently obsolete, he gives it a positive interpretation in its earlier context: God commanded it in order to keep the Jewish people from mixing with other peoples before the birth of the Messiah (*Test.* 11). Justin and Tertullian also interpret circumcision as a "sign" to separate Jews from other nations, but apply it to the exclusion of the Jewish people from Jerusalem under Hadrian's decree (*Dial.* 16.2; *Adv. Jud.* 3). Ps.-Gregory also offers a non-polemical reason for God's institution of the system of sacrifice: it was a means for the tribe of the Levites to earn a living without having to work (*Test.* 14).

Given the paucity of our knowledge regarding authorship, time, place, and circumstances of composition, the question of whether Ps.-Gregory's *Testimonies* is directed towards an actual Jewish audience, or whether it simply employs the Jew as a "straw man" to work out Christian beliefs, must remain open. However, in view of Ps.-Gregory's use of traditional, stereotypical *testimonia* collections and arguments, and his clear intra-Christian Trinitarian polemic in chapter one, one may reasonably conclude that Ps.-Gregory is not debating a live Jewish audience. Rather, the *Testimonies* seem to belong to the Christian "discourse of self-definition" that used "the Jews" as a convenient foil in working out particular Christian stances.[18]

---

[18] On modern scholarship's distinction between actual Jewish-Christian debates in a concrete social setting on the one hand, and the Christian "discourse of self-definition" on the other, see Guy G. Strousma, "From Anti-Judaism to Antisemitism in Early Christianity?" in *Contra Iudaeos: Ancient and Medieval Polemics between Christian and Jews* (ed. Ora Limor and Guy G. Strousma; Texts and Studies in Medieval and Early Modern Judaism 10; Tübingen: Mohr-Siebeck, 1996): 3, 10–16. Strousma sees this distinction as overly simplistic.

PURPOSE OF THIS STUDY

I do not intend a detailed study of every aspect of Ps.-Gregory's *Testimonies*. I do not comment on every passage, for example, and my discussion of the christological controversies evident in chapter one of the *Testimonies* is circumscribed. The main focus of the study is instead to place the *Testimonies* within the larger context of the early Christian *testimonia* literature. In this sense, I comment not so much on Ps.-Gregory itself, but rather on Ps.-Gregory as a witness to this early Christian *testimonia* activity. It is my conviction that the *testimonia* played an essential role in early Christian catechesis and developing self-definition, and I hope to shed some light on the role that the *testimonia* preserved in Ps.-Gregory's collection played in that process.

To this end, a major technique of the commentary is to cite parallels to the *Testimonies* from other early Christian authors, concentrating on authors who are themselves using *testimonia* collections. I often include some discussion of the specific relationship between Ps.-Gregory and these other witnesses (especially comparing the form and function of the quotations). Limitations of time and space, however, preclude a thorough study of these relationships. More detailed studies would be able to map out major lines of early Christian exegesis, teaching, and self-definition running through the extensive *testimonia* literature.

Outline of Ps.-Gregory's *Testimonies*

NOTE: Chapter headings (except for the first, untitled, chapter) translate Ps.-Gregory's headings; sub-headings are my own additions.

Chapter 1: Proofs of the Trinity
- 1.1. Introduction: A paradigmatic reference to the Trinity
  - Ps 32:6
  - John 1:1 and John 15:26 (allusions)
- 1.2. God sends out the Word and the Spirit
  - Ps 147:7
  - Ps 106:20
  - Ps 103:30
- 1.3. Proof of the subsistence of the Word
  - Jer 23:18
- 1.4. Wisdom's role in creation
  - Uncertain quotation
  - 1 Cor 1:24
  - Prov 8:27a, 30
  - Isa 40:13 (cf. Rom 11:34)
- 1.5. Trinitarian references in the Genesis creation account
  - Gen 1:2
  - Gen 1:26a–27
  - Gen 3:22
  - Gen 1:6–16 (summary)
- 1.6. Theophany of the Trinity: Appearance to Abraham at Mamre
  - Gen 18:1–10
- 1.7. Conversations between Father and Son, including Father "begetting" the Son
  - Gen 11:7
  - Ps 109:3
  - Ps 71:17
  - Ps 2:7–8
  - 2 Kgdms 7:14
- 1.8. References to plurality within the Godhead

1.8.1. Paradigmatic reference to two Lords
   Gen 19:24
1.8.2. Passages in which God speaks, referring to a God or Lord different from himself
   Gen 9:6
   Exod 34:4–6
   Gen 31:13
   Deut 32:43 (cf. Heb 1:6)
   Exod 9:5
   Hag 2:4–5
   Exod 19:10–11
   Joel 2:28–32 (cf. Acts 2:17)
1.8.3. Further references to "two powers in heaven" passages
   Ps 101:20–22
   Ps 2:4
   Ps 29:9
   Amos 4:11
   John 12:41
   Isa 53:1

Chapter 2: Other [proofs] by the same [author], concerning the parousia of the Incarnate Lord
   2.1. Various references to manifestations of the divine
      Bar 3:36–38
      Ps 49:2–3
      Ps 83:8
      Ps 117:27
   2.2. References to Jesus' entry into Jerusalem (and the Temple)
      Mal 3:1
      Zech 9:9 (cf. Matt 21:5)
      Zech 2:10–11
      Mal 3:1 / Exod 23:20 (cf. Matt 11:10)
      Zech 14:4
   2.3. Reference to the two *parousias* of Christ
      Zech 3:1–8
   2.4. Further references to manifestations of the divine
      Isa 65:1
      Uncertain quotation (cf. Isa 33:17)

Zeph 2:11
Isa 65:1
Ps 79:2–3
Ps 71:6
2.5. References to the Davidic Messiah and a "prophet like Moses"
Mic 5:2 (cf. Matt 2:6)
Deut 18:15–19 / Lev 23:29 (cf. Acts 3:22–23)
2.6. Excursus on Jesus' divine authority
Matt 8:3 (par.); Luke 7:14; John 11:43; Mark 4:39
Deut 12:32 (allusion)
Isa 40:10
2.7. Davidic descent of the messiah
Ps 131:11
Ps 88:4–5
1 Chr 17:11–14
3 Kgdms 8:26–27
2.8. Miscellaneous texts on the Incarnation
Jer 17:9
Amos 4:12–13
Mic 1:2–3
2.9. A messianic cluster: Gen 49:10–11, Num 24:17, and Isa 11:1–10
Gen 49:10
Num 24:17–18
Isa 10:33–11:10
2.10. Further references to "two powers in heaven" passages
Ps 44:7–8
Heb 3:1 (allusion)
Ps 101:26–28

Chapter 3: Concerning his birth from a virgin
Isa 7:14 (cf. Matt 1:23)
Isa 8:4
Wis 8:19–20
Isa 9:5–6
Uncertain quotation (*Apocr. Ezek.* Frag. 3)
Isa 7:15
Isa 45:14–15

Ezek 44:1–2
Isa 49:1–2
Dan 2:34–35
Isa 1:2–3
Isa 8:1–3
Luke 2:23
Ps 86:5

Chapter 4: Concerning the miracles which the Lord was destined to perform when he became incarnate
Isa 49:6–9 (false attribution)
Bar 3:36
Isa 35:3–4
Isa 40:9–10
Isa 35:5–6
Isa 61:1 (cf. Luke 4:18)

Chapter 5: Concerning [his] betrayal
Ps 40:10

Chapter 6: Concerning [his] passion
6.1. Concerning Jesus' trial before the Jewish and Roman authorities
Isa 3:12–14
Ps 2:1–2
Lam 4:20
6.2. References to the Suffering Servant
Isa 53:4–9
Isa 53:12
Isa 50:6
Isa 53:2–3
Isa 53:8
6.3. Further references to the passion
Ps 21:17–19
Jer 11:19a
Jer 11:19b
Zech 11:12–13; Jer 32:6–9 (cf. Matt 27:9–10)

Chapter 7: Concerning the cross and the darkness that occurred
Deut 28:66–67
Amos 8:9

Jer 15:9
Isa 65:2
Isa 62:10
Uncertain quotation (cf. 4 Ezra 5:5)
Zech 14:6–7
Ps 68:21–22
Ps 87:7
Zech 13:7 (cf. Matt 26:31)
Zech 14:20

Chapter 8: Concerning the resurrection of Christ
Ps 43:24
Ps 3:8
Ps 43:27
Ps 81:8
Isa 33:10–11
Hos 5:15–6:3
Ps 15:10
Ps 87:5
Phil 2:8 (allusion)
Isa 28:16 (cf. 1 Pet 2:6)
Ps 117:22–23 (allusion)

Chapter 9: Concerning the ascension
Ps 46:6
Dan 7:9
Dan 7:13–14
Ps 109:1

Chapter 10: Concerning the glory of the church
Ps 44:10

Chapter 11: Concerning circumcision
Jer 38:31–32
Jer 9:26
Uncertain quotation (cf. Jer 4:4 and Deut 10:16)
Jer 4:3 / Deut 10:16
Jer 4:4

Chapter 12: Concerning sacrifices
Jer 7:22
Jer 7:22 (false attribution)
Isa 1:11–14

Isa 1:16
Ps 49:13
Ps 49:9
Ps 49:14
Amos 5:21–23
Mal 1:10b–11

Chapter 13: Concerning keeping the sabbath
Exod 20:9–10

Chapter 14: Concerning sealing with the sign of the cross
Ps 4:7
Ps 85:17
Ps 59:6
Ezek 9:4
Ezek 9:2, 5–6

Chapter 15: Concerning the Gospel
Ps 67:12
Isa 52:7 (cf. Rom 10:15)

Chapter 16: Concerning the unbelief of the Jews, and concerning the church of the nations
Isa 48:8
Mal 1:11
Mic 4:1–2
Jer 1:9b–10
Ps 17:44–46
Gen 12:3
Deut 32:20–21
Isa 53:9
Isa 65:1a
Isa 65:1b
Ps 68:9
Ps 21:23
Isa 52:5
Mal 1:10b–12
Ps 2:8
Uncertain quotation (cf. Exod 32:10 and Deut 9:14)
Isa 1:10
Isa 1:13–16
Ps 64:2

　　　　　Zeph 2:11
　　　　　Mal 1:11
　　　　　Isa 65:15–16
　　　　　Ps 21:32
　　　　　Ps 67:7
　　　　　Isa 11:9
　　　　　Ps 21:28–29
　　　　　Matt 21:43
　　　　　Ps 110:3
　　　　　Ps 109:1
　　　　　Isa 45:1
　　　　　Isa 45:1–3
　　　　　Isa 42:6–7
　　　　　Isa 49:6

Chapter 17: That before the second parousia of the Lord Elijah will come
　　　　　Mal 4:4–5 (3:23–24)

Chapter 18: That we will be called "Christians"
　　　　　Isa 62:2
　　　　　Isa 65:15–16
　　　　　Uncertain quotation (false attribution; cf. Hos 14:10)

Chapter 19: That Herod will be troubled, and all those with him
　　　　　Jer 4:9

Chapter 20: Concerning baptism
　　　　　Ezek 47:8–9
　　　　　Jer 29:20

Chapter 21: Concerning the descent of the Lord into Egypt
　　　　　Isa 19:1
　　　　　Isa 19:21

Chapter 22: Concerning the Holy Spirit
　　　　　Isa 48:16
　　　　　Num 11:16 (false attribution)
　　　　　Ps 50:12–14
　　　　　Ps 138:7
　　　　　Job 33:4

Job 32:8
Job 27:2–3
Hag 2:4–5 (false attribution)
Wis 1:7
Isa 63:10
Mic 2:7
Joel 2:28 (cf. Acts 2:17)
Isa 61:1
Isa 11:2–3 (allusion)
Isa 62:14
Exod 31:3–11 (summary)
4 Kgdms 2:9–11 (summary)
Isa 57:16
Isa 42:1 (cf. Matt 12:18)
Isa 30:1
Isa 34:15–16
Ps 103:29–30

Ps.-Gregory of Nyssa,
Testimonies against the Jews
Text and Translation

ΤΟΥ ΕΝ ΑΓΙΟΙΣ ΓΡΗΓΟΡΙΟΥ ΕΠΙΣΚΟΠΟΥ ΝΥΣΣΗΣ

ΕΚΛΟΓΑΙ ΜΑΡΤΥΡΙΩΝ ΠΡΟΣ ΙΟΥΔΑΙΟΥΣ

ΑΠΟ ΤΗΣ ΠΑΛΑΙΑΣ

Μετά τινος ἐπεξεργασίας περὶ τῆς ἁγίας Τριάδος·
ὅτι Λόγον καὶ Πνεῦμα ἔχει ὁ Θεός, κατὰ τὰς Γραφάς·
Λόγον ἐνυπόστατον καὶ ζῶντα, καὶ Πνεῦμα ὡσαύτως.

Λέγει Δαβὶδ ἐν δευτέρῳ καὶ τριακοστῷ ψαλμῷ· «Τῷ Λόγῳ Κυρίου οἱ οὐρανοὶ ἐστερεώθησαν, καὶ τῷ Πνεύματι τοῦ στόματος αὐτοῦ πᾶσα ἡ δύναμις αὐτῶν.» Οὐ Λόγος οὖν ὑπάρχει ἀέρος τύπωσις σημαντικὴ διὰ φωνητικῶν ὀργάνων ἐκφερομένη, οὔτε Πνεῦμα στόματος ἀτμός, ἐκ τῶν ἀναπνευστικῶν μερῶν ἐξωθούμενος, ἀλλὰ Λόγος μὲν ὁ πρὸς Θεὸν ἐν ἀρχῇ, καὶ Θεὸς ὤν· Πνεῦμα δὲ στόματος Θεοῦ, τὸ Πνεῦμα τῆς ἀληθείας, ὃ παρὰ τοῦ Πατρὸς ἐκπορεύεται. Τρία τοίνυν νόει, τὸν προστάττοντα Κύριον, τὸν δημιουργοῦντα Λόγον, τὸν στερεοῦντα, τουτέστι τὸ Πνεῦμα· τὴν γὰρ στερέωσιν τὸν ἁγιασμὸν εἶπε καὶ τὴν συμπλήρωσιν. Ἵνα δὲ μάθῃς ὅτι οὐ τούτῳ λέγει τῷ προφορικῷ, ἀλλὰ τῷ ἐνυποστάτῳ, ὁ αὐτὸς ἀλλαχοῦ λέγει· «Ἀποστελεῖ τὸν Λόγον αὐτοῦ, καὶ τήξει αὐτά· πνεύσει τὸ Πνεῦμα αὐτοῦ, καὶ ῥυήσεται ὕδατα.» Λόγος δὲ ἀνυπόστατος οὐκ ἀποστέλλεται. Καὶ πάλιν· «Ἀπέστειλε τὸν

SAINT GREGORY

BISHOP OF NYSSA

SELECTIONS FROM THE TESTIMONIES AGAINST THE JEWS

FROM THE OLD TESTAMENT

With some elaboration concerning the holy Trinity: God has Word and Spirit according to the scriptures; a Word subsistent and living and a Spirit likewise.

Chapter 1: Proofs of the Trinity[1]

1.1. Introduction: A paradigmatic reference to the Trinity

David says in the thirty-second Psalm,
"By the word of the Lord the heavens were established, and by the spirit of his mouth their every power" (Ps 32:6).[2]
Now "Word" is not a meaningful impression of air brought forth by speech-producing organs, nor is "Spirit" a vapor of the mouth expelled from the respiratory regions; rather "Word" is he who was with God in the beginning, since he is indeed God (cf. John 1:1). "Spirit" is from the mouth of God, "the Spirit of truth, who goes forth from the Father" (John 15:26). Recognize therefore three persons: the commanding Lord, the creating Word, and the establishing one, that is, the Spirit. For he called the establishment [of the universe] its sanctification and completion.

1.2. God sends out the Word and the Spirit

So that you might learn that he means not "by this spoken word," but rather "by the subsistent word," he himself [i.e., David] says elsewhere,
"He will send out his word, and he will melt them. He will breathe his spirit and waters will flow" (Ps 147:7).[3]
An unsubsistent word is not sent out.
And again:

Λόγον αὐτοῦ, καὶ ἰάσατο αὐτούς, καὶ ἐρρύσατο αὐτοὺς ἐκ τῶν δια-
φθορῶν αὐτῶν.» | Καὶ πάλιν· «Ἐξαποστελεῖς τὸ Πνεῦμά σου, καὶ
κτισθήσονται, καὶ ἀνακαινιεῖς τὸ πρόσωπον τῆς γῆς.» «Τίς ἔστη ἐν
ὑποστηρίγματι Κυρίου, καὶ εἶδε τὸν Λόγον αὐτοῦ;» Λόγος δὲ ἀνθρώπου οὐ θεωρεῖται. Ὁρᾶς, ὅτι οὐκ ἀκουστόν, ἀλλ' ὁρατὸν Λόγον λέγει,
δῆλον τὸν ἐνυπόστατον, ὁπότε κατὰ τὸν εἰκότα λογισμόν, οὐδὲ χώραν
ἔχει ἐπὶ Θεοῦ τὸ τοῦ ἀνυποστάτου λόγου. Ἡμᾶς γὰρ ἐκόσμησεν ὁ Δη-
μιουργὸς λόγῳ, διὰ τὰς πρὸς ἀλλήλους συνουσίας, καὶ τὸ γινώσκειν
ἡμᾶς τὰ ἀλλήλων διὰ τοῦ λόγου. Συντελεῖ δὲ ἡμῖν καὶ τὸ πνεῦμα πρὸς
τὴν τοῦ σώματος σύστασιν, διὰ τὸ προσίεσθαι, καὶ πάλιν ἀπωθεῖσθαι
αὐτό· ἐπὶ δὲ Θεοῦ, τοῦ καὶ μόνου ἀσωμάτου, οὐ δυνατὸν ὑπολαβεῖν
ταῦτα. «Ἔτη τελεῖς, ὁ Θεός, τῇ δυνάμει σου. Χριστὸς δὲ Θεοῦ δύναμις, καὶ Θεοῦ σοφία.» Ἐκ προσώπου τῆς Σοφίας, τουτέστι τοῦ Υἱοῦ·
«Ἡνίκα ἡτοίμαζε τὸν οὐρανόν, συμπαρήμην αὐτῷ· καὶ ἐγὼ ἤμην, ᾗ
ἔχαιρε· καθ' ἡμέραν ηὐφραινόμην τῷ προσώπῳ αὐτοῦ.»
Ποίαν οὖν ἔχει χώραν ταῦτα, εἰ μὴ ἦν ἐνυπόστατον πρόσωπον; Οὐ
γάρ ἐστιν ἄλλος, πρὸς ὃν διαλεχθῇ· «Τίς γὰρ ἔγνω νοῦν Κυρίου, ἢ
τίς σύμβουλος αὐτοῦ ἐγένετο;» Ἀλλ' ἤρκεσεν αὐτῷ μόνη βούλησις
εἰς τὴν τῶν πάντων δημιουργίαν. Εἴρηται γάρ· «Καὶ Πνεῦμα Θεοῦ
ἐπεφέρετο ἐπάνω τῶν ὑδάτων.» Τὸ ἐνυπόστατον τοῦ ἁγίου Πνεύματος θάλποντος καὶ ζωογονοῦντος εἰς τὴν μέλλουσαν γονὴν τὰ πάντα,

"He sent out his word, and healed them, and rescued them from their corruption" (Ps 106:20).[4]

And again:

"You will send out your spirit, and they will be created, and you will renew the face of the earth" (Ps 103:30).[5]

1.3. Proof of the subsistence of the Word

"Who stood in the foundation of the Lord, and saw his word?" (Jer 23:18).[6]

Now the word of a human being is not seen. You see that he means, not an audible, but a visible Word; clearly, the subsistent Word, since, following proper reasoning, that which pertains to an unsubsistent word has no place in God's presence.

For the Creator equipped us with speech for the sake of living in community with one another, and so that, through speech, we might know one another's concerns. He perfects in us also breath for the sustenance of the body, through its being drawn in and expelled again. But it is not possible to assume these things in the case of God, who alone is incorporeal.

1.4. Wisdom's role in creation

"You complete the years, O God, by your power."[7]

"But Christ is the power of God and the wisdom of God" (1 Cor 1:24).[8]

[Speaking] in the person of Wisdom, that is, the Son, "When he was preparing heaven, I was present with him. And I was she, in whom he rejoiced. Daily I was happy in his presence" (Prov 8:27a, 30).[9]

How are these things possible, unless he was a subsistent person?

For there is not another about whom one might say,

"For who has known the mind of the Lord, or who was his adviser?" (Isa 40:13; cf. Rom 11:34).[10]

But his will alone was sufficient for the creation of all things.

1.5. Trinitarian references in the Genesis creation account

For it is said,

"And the spirit [breath] of God was carried above the waters" (Gen 1:2), scripture thereby indicating the subsistence of the Holy Spirit, inasmuch as it nurtures and gives life to all things for the coming generation.[11]

τῆς Γραφῆς δηλούσης. Ὧν οὕτως ἐχόντων, σαφὴς ἡ τῆς ἁγίας Τριάδος, Πατρός, φημί, καὶ Υἱοῦ, καὶ ἁγίου Πνεύματος ἀπόδειξις. Αὕτη γοῦν πρὸς ἑαυτὴν ἡ ἁγία καὶ ὁμοούσιος Τριὰς τό: «Ποιήσωμεν ἄνθρωπον κατ' εἰκόνα ἡμετέραν καὶ καθ' ὁμοίωσιν. Καὶ ἐποίησεν ὁ Θεὸς τὸν ἄνθρωπον· κατ' εἰκόνα Θεοῦ ἐποίησεν αὐτόν.» Μεμορφώμεθα γὰρ νοητῶς πρὸς τὴν εἰκόνα τοῦ Μονογενοῦς. Καὶ πάλιν· «Ἰδοὺ Ἀδὰμ γέγονεν ὡς εἷς ἐξ ἡμῶν.» Ὅτι δὲ διὰ τοῦ Λόγου τὰ πάντα ἐδημιούργησεν ὁ Θεός, σαφὲς ἀφ' ὧν ἐπὶ ἑκάστου τῶν δημιουργημάτων γέγραπται τό: «Καὶ εἶπεν ὁ Θεός· Γενηθήτω,» τῆς Γραφῆς σημαινούσης τὴν διὰ τοῦ Λόγου δημιουργίαν· εἰ γὰρ μὴ τοῦτο ἦν, ἤρκει εἰπεῖν· Καὶ ἐποίησεν ὁ Θεὸς οὐρανόν, καὶ γῆν, καὶ τὰ λοιπά· καὶ πάλιν· Προστάξαντος τοῦ Θεοῦ ἐγενήθη τὸ στερέωμα· καὶ πάλιν, Διεχώρισεν ὁ Θεός. Καὶ ὅταν ἀκούσῃς τό: «Εἶπεν ὁ Θεός,» εὐθὺς τῇ ἐννοίᾳ σύναγε τὸν ἀκούσαντα τοῦ εἰπόντος· «Καὶ εἶπεν ὁ Θεός· Γενηθήτωσαν φωστῆρες. Καὶ ἐποίησεν ὁ Θεὸς τοὺς φωστῆρας.» Τίς εἶπε, καὶ τίς ἤκουσε; Καὶ ἐπὶ πλείοσι τόποις τῆς Παλαιᾶς ἔστιν εὑρεῖν, ἠρέμα ὑποδεικνυμένης τῆς ἁγίας Τριάδος τὴν ὑπόστασιν καὶ τὸ ὁμοούσιον αὐτῆς· οἷον ὡς ἐπὶ τοῦ Ἀβραάμ· «Ὤφθη» γάρ, φησίν: «αὐτῷ ὁ Θεὸς πρὸς τῇ δρυῒ τῇ Μαμβρῇ, καθημένου | αὐτοῦ ἐπὶ τῆς θύρας τῆς σκηνῆς αὐτοῦ μεσημβρίας. Ἀναβλέψας δὲ τοῖς ὀφθαλμοῖς, εἶδε· καὶ ἰδοὺ τρεῖς ἄνδρες παρειστήκεισαν ἐπάνω αὐτοῦ· καὶ ἰδοὺ προσέδραμεν εἰς συνάντησιν αὐτῶν, καὶ προσεκύνησεν ἐπὶ τὴν γῆν. Καὶ εἶπε· Κύριε, εἰ εὗρον χάριν ἐναντίον σου, μὴ παρέλθῃς τὸν παῖδά σου.» Καὶ μεθ' ἕτερα· «Εἶπε δὲ πρὸς αὐτόν· Ποῦ Σάρρα ἡ γυνή σου; Ὁ δὲ εἶπεν· Ἰδοὺ ἐν τῇ σκηνῇ. Εἶπε δέ· Ἐπαναστρέφων ἥξω πρὸς σέ, κατὰ τὸν

Since these things are so, the proof of the holy Trinity—I mean, the Father, the Son, and the Holy Spirit—is clear.

This holy and consubstantial Trinity, indeed, [spoke] to itself,

"Let us make humankind in our image and in our likeness. And God made humankind; in God's image he made them" (Gen 1:26a–27).[12]

For we have been formed spiritually into the image of the only-begotten.

And again:

"Look! Adam has become like one of us" (Gen 3:22).[13]

That God created all things through the Word is clear from what has been written in the case of each of the created things, namely, "And God said, 'Let there be,'" scripture thereby signaling creation through the Word. For if this were not the case, it would have been sufficient to say, "And God made heaven and earth and all the rest."

And again:

"After God commanded, the firmament came into being" (Gen 1:6).[14] And again, "God divided" (Gen 1:4 etc.). And whenever you hear the phrase, "God said," immediately call to mind the one hearing the speaker, "And God said, 'Let there be lights.' And God made the lights" (Gen 1:14–16).

Who spoke, and who heard?

1.6. Theophany of the Trinity: Appearance to Abraham at Mamre

And it is possible to find [such things] in many places of the Old Testament (since the holy Trinity quietly hints at its subsistence and its consubstantiality); for example, as [in the passage] concerning Abraham:

For, "God appeared," it says, "to him at the oak in Mamre while he was sitting by the door of his tent at midday. Raising his eyes, he saw. And look! Three men stood before him. And look! He ran to meet them, and prostrated himself upon the ground. And he said, 'Lord, if I have found favor before you, do not pass by your servant'" (Gen 18:1–3).[15]

And later on:

"He said to him, 'Where is Sara your wife?' He said, 'Look! There in the tent.' He said, 'When I return, I will come to you

καιρὸν τοῦτον εἰς ὥρας, καὶ ἕξει υἱὸν Σάρρα ἡ γυνή σου.» Ἰδοὺ δὴ
φησὶν ὀφθῆναι μὲν αὐτῷ τὸν Θεόν, εἶναί γε μὴν τρεῖς ἄνδρας τοὺς ἑωραμένους· αὐτὸν δὲ πάλιν οὐχ ὡς τρισὶν εἰπεῖν· Κύριοι, εἰ εὕρηκα χάριν ἐναντίον ὑμῶν, μὴ παρέλθητε τὸν παῖδα ὑμῶν. Κύριον δὲ μοναδικῶς τοὺς τρεῖς ὀνομάζοντα, καὶ ὡς ἕνα καταίρειν ἀξιοῦντα, καὶ ὡς εἷς φωνεῖ· Ἥξω. Ὅρα οὖν τοὺς ὀφθέντας τρεῖς μὲν ὄντας, καὶ ὑφεστῶτας ἰδιοσυστάτως ἕκαστον· τῷ γε μὴν τῆς ὁμοουσίας λόγῳ συνειλημμένους εἰς ἕνα, καὶ τὰς διαλέξεις ποιησαμένους. Τίς δὲ πρὸς τίνα ἔλεγεν· «Δεῦτε, καταβάντες συγχέωμεν τὴν γλῶσσαν αὐτῶν;» Ἢ δῆλον πρὸς ὃν εἶπεν· «Ἐκ γαστρὸς πρὸ ἑωσφόρου ἐγέννησά σε·» καί: «Πρὸ τοῦ ἡλίου τὸ ὄνομα αὐτοῦ, καὶ πρὸ τῆς σελήνης·» καὶ πάλιν· «Κύριος εἶπε πρός με· Υἱός μου εἶ σύ, ἐγὼ σήμερον γεγέννηκά σε. Αἴτησαι παρ' ἐμοῦ, καὶ δώσω σοι ἔθνη τὴν κληρονομίαν σου, καὶ τὴν κατάσχεσίν σου τὰ πέρατα τῆς γῆς·» καὶ πάλιν: «Ἐγὼ ἔσομαι αὐτῷ εἰς Πατέρα, καὶ αὐτὸς ἔσται μοι εἰς Υἱόν;» Τί δὲ τό: «Ἔβρεξε Κύριος πῦρ καὶ θεῖον παρὰ Κυρίου;» Τί δὲ τὸ ἐκ προσώπου τοῦ Θεοῦ: «Καὶ πᾶς ὁ ἐκχέων

during this time in future seasons, and Sara your wife will have a son'" (Gen 18:9–10).[16]

Notice: it says that God appeared to him, yet there were three men who were seen; he did not speak in turn as if to three, "Lords, if I have found favor before you [plural], do not pass by [second person plural] your [plural] servant."

But to [Abraham], when he calls the three "Lord" in the singular, and sees fit to ask [them] to come down as one [person], [the Lord] declares also as one [person], "I will come." See then that those who appeared were three, each one subsisting as its own entity, yet truly gathered together into one by the principle of consubstantiality,[17] and holding conversations.

1.7. Conversations between Father and Son, including Father "begetting" the Son

Who said to whom,

"Come, let us go down and confuse their language"? (Gen 11:7).[18]

Isn't it clear to whom he said, "From the womb before the morning star I brought you forth" (Ps 109:3),[19]

and:

"His name was before the sun and before the moon" (Ps 71:17 / 71:5),[20]

and again:

"The Lord said to me, 'You are my son, today I have brought you forth. Ask of me, and I will give you the nations as your inheritance, and the ends of the earth as your possession'" (Ps 2:7–8),[21]

and again:

"I will be to him as a father, and he will be as a son to me"? (2 Kgdms 7:14).[22]

1.8. References to plurality within the Godhead

1.8.1. Paradigmatic reference to two Lords: Gen 19:24

What about:

"The Lord rained fire and brimstone from the Lord" (Gen 19:24)?[23]

1.8.2. Passages in which God speaks, referring to a God or Lord different from himself

What about the following passage [spoken] in the person of God:[24]

αἷμα, ἀντὶ τοῦ αἵματος αὐτοῦ ἐκχυθήσεται, ὅτι ἐν εἰκόνι Θεοῦ ἐποίησα
τὸν ἄνθρωπον;» Ὁρᾶς ὅτι ὁ Θεὸς *ἐν εἰκόνι τοῦ Θεοῦ ἐποίησε*;
Τὸ δὲ ἐν τῇ Ἐξόδῳ πῶς νοητέον· «Καὶ ὀρθρίσας Μωϋσῆς ἀνέβη εἰς
τὸ ὄρος τὸ Σινᾶ, καθότι συνέταξεν αὐτῷ Κύριος. Καὶ ἔλαβε Μωϋσῆς
τὰς πλάκας τὰς λιθίνας. Καὶ κατέβη Κύριος ἐν νεφέλῃ, καὶ παρέστη
ἐκεῖ, καὶ ἐλάλησε τῷ ὀνόματι Κυρίου. Καὶ παρῆλθε Κύριος ἀπὸ προσώπου Κυρίου.» Ποῖος ἄρα ἐλάλησε Κύριος ἐν ὀνόματι Κυρίου; καὶ
ποῖος παρῆλθε Κύριος ἀπὸ προσώπου Κυρίου; Τί δὲ τὸ πρὸς Ἰακὼβ
[200] εἰρημένον: «Ἐγώ εἰμι ὁ ὀφθείς σοι ἐν | τόπῳ Θεοῦ;» Πῶς δὲ τό·
«Προσκυνησάτωσαν αὐτῷ πάντες ἄγγελοι Θεοῦ;» Τίνι, καὶ ποίου
Θεοῦ; Λέγει Μωϋσῆς· «Καὶ ἔδωκε Κύριος ὅρον, λέγων· Ἐν τῇ αὔριον ἡμέρᾳ ποιήσει Κύριος τὸ ῥῆμα τοῦτο ἐπὶ τῆς γῆς·» καὶ πάλιν·
«Ἴσχυε, Ζοροβάβελ, διότι ἐγὼ μεθ' ὑμῶν εἰμι, καὶ ὁ Λόγος μου ὁ
ἀγαθός, καὶ τὸ Πνεῦμά μου ἐν μέσῳ ὑμῶν.» Τίς οὖν χρεία τριῶν μνη-
σθῆναι, εἰ μὴ ἕκαστον ἐν ἰδίᾳ ὑποστάσει; Καὶ πάλιν· «Καὶ εἶπε Κύριος
πρὸς Μωϋσῆν· Καταβὰς διαμάρτυραι τῷ λαῷ, καὶ ἅγνισον αὐτοὺς
σήμερον καὶ αὔριον, καὶ πλυνάτωσαν τὰ ἱμάτια αὐτῶν, καὶ ἔστωσαν
ἕτοιμοι εἰς τὴν ἡμέραν τὴν τρίτην. Τῇ γὰρ ἡμέρᾳ τρίτῃ καταβήσεται
Κύριος ἐπὶ τὸ ὄρος τὸ Σινᾶ, ἐναντίον παντὸς τοῦ λαοῦ.» Καὶ οὐκ εἶ-
πε· Καταβήσομαι. «Καὶ ἔσται ἐν ταῖς ἐσχάταις ἡμέραις, λέγει Κύριος,

"And everyone who sheds [a person's] blood, instead of that blood shall [his own blood] be shed,[25] for I created humankind in the image of God"? (Gen 9:6)[26]

Do you see that God created humankind in the image of "God"?

How then is the passage in Exodus to be understood?

"And Moses, having awakened before dawn, ascended Mount Sinai, as the Lord commanded him. And Moses took the stone tablets. And the Lord descended in a cloud, and stood near there, and spoke in the name of the Lord. And the Lord passed by from the face of the Lord" (Exod 34:4–6).[27]

What kind of "Lord," therefore, spoke in the name of the Lord? And what kind of "Lord" passed by from the face of the Lord?

And what about what was said to Jacob,[28]

"I am the one who appeared to you in the place of God"? (Gen 31:13).[29]

How, then, [should we understand]:

"Let all the angels of God worship him" (Deut 32:43; cf. Heb 1:6)?[30]

[Worship] whom, and of what kind of "god"?

Moses says,

"And the Lord set a limit, saying, 'Tomorrow the Lord will perform this action upon the land'" (Exod 9:5),[31]

and again:

"Be strong, Zerubbabel, for I am with you, and my good word, and my spirit in your midst" (Hag 2:4–5).[32]

What need is there to mention three, unless each one exists in its own subsistent entity?

And again:

"And the Lord spoke to Moses, 'Go down and warn the people, and sanctify them today and tomorrow, and let them wash their clothes, and let them be prepared for the third day. For on the third day the Lord will descend upon Mount Sinai, before all the people" (Exod 19:10–11).[33]

Now he did not say, "I will descend."

"And it will happen in the last days," says the Lord, "that I will pour out from my spirit upon every person, and your sons will prophesy, and your daughters will dream dreams" (Joel 2:28; cf. Acts 2:17).[34]

ἐκχεῶ ἀπὸ τοῦ Πνεύματός μου ἐπὶ πᾶσαν σάρκα, καὶ προφητεύσουσιν
οἱ υἱοὶ ὑμῶν, καὶ αἱ θυγατέρες ὑμῶν ἐνύπνια ἐνυπνιασθήσονται.» Καὶ
μετά τινα· «ὁ ἥλιος μεταστραφήσεται εἰς σκότος, καὶ ἡ σελήνη εἰς
αἷμα, πρὶν ἐλθεῖν τὴν ἡμέραν Κυρίου τὴν μεγάλην καὶ ἐπιφανῆ.» Οὐκ
εἶπε· Τὴν ἡμέραν μου. «Καὶ ἔσται, ὃς ἂν ἐπικαλέσηται τὸ ὄνομα Κυρίου, σωθήσεται.» Καὶ οὐκ εἶπε· Τὸ ὄνομά μου. Καὶ πάλιν· «Κύριος
ἐκ τοῦ οὐρανοῦ ἐπὶ τὴν γῆν ἐπέβλεψε, τοῦ ἰδεῖν τὸν στεναγμὸν τῶν
πεπεδημένων, τοῦ λῦσαι τοὺς υἱοὺς τῶν τεθανατωμένων, τοῦ ἀναγ-
γεῖλαι ἐν Σιὼν τὸ ὄνομα Κυρίου.» Οὐκ εἶπε· Τὸ ὄνομα αὐτοῦ. Καὶ
πάλιν· «Ὁ κατοικῶν ἐν οὐρανοῖς ἐκγελάσεται αὐτούς, καὶ ὁ Κύριος
ἐκμυκτηριεῖ αὐτούς.» Καὶ πάλιν· «Πρὸς σέ, Κύριε, κεκράξομαι, καὶ
πρὸς τὸν Θεόν μου δεηθήσομαι.» Τίς οὖν ὁ Κύριος παρὰ τῷ Θεῷ; Ἐκ
προσώπου τοῦ Θεοῦ· «Κατέστρεψα ὑμᾶς, καθὼς κατέστρεψεν ὁ Θεὸς
Σόδομα καὶ Γόμορρα, ὅτε εἶδε τὴν δόξαν αὐτοῦ. Κύριε, τίς ἐπίστευ-
σεν τῇ ἀκοῇ ἡμῶν; καὶ ὁ βραχίων Κυρίου, τίνι ἀπεκαλύφθη;» Οὐκ
εἶπε· Καὶ ὁ βραχίων σου. Ἰδοὺ ἀποδέδεικται σὺν Θεῷ διὰ πλειόνων
τῆς ἁγίας καὶ ὁμοουσίου Τριάδος αἱ ὑποστάσεις.

And after a bit:

"The sun will be turned into darkness, and the moon into blood, before the great and glorious day of the Lord comes" (Joel 2:31).³⁵

He did not say, "my day."

"And it will happen that whoever calls on the name of the Lord will be saved" (Joel 2:32).³⁶

And he did not say, "my name."

1.8.3. Further references to "two powers in heaven" passages

And again:

"From heaven the Lord looked upon the earth to see the groaning of those in chains, to release the sons of those condemned to death, to announce in Zion the name of the Lord" (Ps 101:20b–22a).³⁷

He did not say, "his name."

And again:

"The one living in the heavens will laugh at them, and the Lord will mock them" (Ps 2:4).³⁸

And again:

"To you, O Lord, I will cry, and to my God I will plead" (Ps 29:9).³⁹

Who is "the Lord" alongside God?

[Speaking] in the person of God,

"I destroyed you, as God destroyed Sodom and Gomorrah" (Amos 4:11),⁴⁰

"when he saw his glory" (John 12:41).⁴¹

"Lord, who has believed our report, and the arm of the Lord, to whom has it been revealed?" (Isa 53:1).⁴²

He did not say, "And your arm."

See, with God ['s help], the subsistent entities of the holy and consubstantial Trinity have been demonstrated by many [proofs].

Β'. *Τοῦ αὐτοῦ ἕτερα περὶ τῆς ἐνσάρκου τοῦ Κυρίου παρουσίας.*

«Οὗτος ὁ Θεὸς ἡμῶν· οὐ λογισθήσεται ἕτερος πρὸς αὐτόν. Ἐξεῦρε πᾶσαν ὁδὸν ἐπιστήμης, καὶ ἔδωκεν αὐτὴν Ἰακὼβ τῷ παιδὶ αὐτοῦ, καὶ Ἰσραὴλ τῷ ἠγαπημένῳ αὐτοῦ. Μετὰ δὲ ταῦτα ἐπὶ τῆς γῆς ὤφθη, καὶ τοῖς ἀνθρώποις συνανεστράφη.» «Ὁ Θεὸς ἐμφανῶς ἥξει, ὁ Θεὸς ἡμῶν, καὶ οὐ παρασιωπήσεται.» Καὶ πάλιν· «Ὀφθήσεται ὁ Θεὸς τῶν θεῶν ἐν Σιών.» | Καὶ πάλιν: «Θεὸς Κύριος καὶ ἐπέφανεν ἡμῖν.» «Ἐξαίφνης ἥξει εἰς τὸν ναὸν ἑαυτοῦ Κύριος, ὃν ὑμεῖς ζητεῖτε, καὶ ὁ Ἄγγελος τῆς διαθήκης, ὃν ὑμεῖς θέλετε.» «Χαῖρε σφόδρα, θύγατερ Σιών· κήρυσσε, θύγατερ Ἰερουσαλήμ. Ἰδοὺ ὁ Βασιλεύς σου ἔρχεταί σοι πραΰς, καὶ ἐπιβεβηκὼς ἐπὶ ὑποζύγιον καὶ πῶλον ὄνου.» Τίς δέ ποτε τῶν βασιλέων, ὄνῳ καθήμενος, εἰς Ἰερουσαλὴμ εἰσῆλθε; Καὶ πάλιν: «Τέρπου καὶ εὐφραίνου, θύγατερ Σιών, διότι ἐγὼ ἔρχομαι, καὶ κατασκηνώσω ἐν μέσῳ σου, λέγει Κύριος. Καὶ καταφεύξονται ἔθνη πολλὰ ἐπὶ τὸν Κύριον ἐν τῇ ἡμέρᾳ ἐκείνῃ, καὶ ἔσονται αὐτῷ εἰς λαόν.» Καὶ πάλιν: «Ἰδοὺ ἐγὼ ἀποστέλλω τὸν ἄγγελόν μου πρὸ προσώπου σου, ὃς κατασκευάσει τὴν ὁδόν σου ἔμπροσθέν σου.» Καὶ πάλιν: «Στήσονται οἱ πόδες αὐτοῦ ἐν τῇ ἡμέρᾳ ἐκείνῃ ἐπὶ τὸ ὄρος τῶν Ἐλαιῶν, τὸ κατέναντι Ἰερουσαλὴμ ἐξ ἀνατολῶν.» Καὶ μετὰ βραχέα: «Ἔδειξέ μοι Κύριος τὸν Ἰησοῦν, τὸν ἱερέα τὸν μέγαν, ἑστῶτα πρὸ προσώπου ἀγγέλου Κυρίου· καὶ ὁ διάβολος εἱστήκει ἐκ δεξιῶν αὐτοῦ

Chapter 2: Other [proofs] by the same [author], concerning the *parousia* of the Incarnate Lord

2.1. Various references to manifestations of the divine

"This is our God, no other will be reckoned as anything beside him. He discovered every path of knowledge and gave it to Jacob his servant and to Israel his beloved. After these things he appeared on the earth, and lived among humans" (Bar 3:36–38).[43]

"God will come visibly, our God, and he will not keep silent" (Ps 49:2–3).[44]

And again:

"The God of gods will appear in Zion" (Ps 83:8).[45]

And again:

"God is the Lord, and he has appeared to us" (Ps 117:27).[46]

2.2. References to Jesus' entry into Jerusalem (and the Temple)

"The Lord, whom you seek, will come suddenly into his temple, and the angel of the covenant, whom you desire" (Mal 3:1b).[47]

"Rejoice greatly, daughter of Zion! Proclaim, daughter of Jerusalem! See, your king is coming to you, gentle, and mounted upon a beast of burden, and the foal of a donkey" (Zech 9:9; cf. Matt 21:5).[48]

Which of the kings, seated on a donkey, ever came into Jerusalem?

And again:

"'Be happy and rejoice, daughter of Zion, for I am coming, and I will settle in your midst,' says the Lord. And many nations will flee for refuge to the Lord in that day, and they will be his people" (Zech 2:10–11).[49]

And again:

"See, I am sending my messenger before you; he will prepare your way before you" (Mal 3:1 / Exod 23:20; cf. Matt 11:10).[50]

And again:[51]

"On that day, his feet will stand on the Mount of Olives, which faces Jerusalem from the east" (Zech 14:4).[52]

2.3. Reference to the two parousias of Christ

And after a short bit:

"The Lord showed me Jesus, the high priest, standing before the angel of the Lord. And the devil stood at his right to oppose

τοῦ ἀντικεῖσθαι αὐτῷ. Καὶ εἶπε Κύριος πρὸς τὸν διάβολον· Ἐπιτιμήσαι Κύριος ἐν σοί, διάβολε. Καὶ διεμαρτύρατο ὁ ἄγγελος Κυρίου πρὸς τὸν Ἰησοῦν, λέγων· Τάδε λέγει Κύριος παντοκράτωρ· Ἐὰν ταῖς ὁδοῖς μου πορεύσῃ, καὶ ἐὰν τὰ προστάγματά μου φυλάξῃ, καὶ σὺ διακρινεῖς τὸν οἶκόν μου.» Καὶ πάλιν: «Ἄκουε δή, Ἰησοῦς, ὁ ἱερεὺς ὁ μέγας.» Ἡσαΐας: «Ἐμφανὴς ἐγενόμην τοῖς ἐμὲ μὴ ζητοῦσι, καὶ εὑρέθην τοῖς ἐμὲ μὴ ἐπερωτῶσι.» (Καὶ πάλιν: «Καὶ βασιλέα μέγαν ὄψεσθε.» Θεὸν δὲ οὐδεὶς ὁρᾷ.) Καὶ πάλιν· «Ἐπιφανήσεται Κύριος ἐπ' αὐτούς, καὶ ἐξολοθρεύσει πάντας τοὺς θεοὺς τῶν ἐθνῶν.» Καὶ πάλιν· «Ἰδοὺ πάρειμι τῷ ἔθνει, οἳ οὐκ ἐπεκαλέσαντο τὸ ὄνομά μου.» Δαβίδ: «Ὁ καθήμενος ἐπὶ τῶν χερουβὶμ ἐμφάνηθι. Ἐξέγειρον τὴν δυναστείαν σου, καὶ ἐλθὲ εἰς τὸ σῶσαι ἡμᾶς.» Καὶ πάλιν: «Καταβήσεται ὡς ὑετὸς ἐπὶ πόκον.» Τὸ ἀτάραχον καὶ ἄνευ ψόφου τῆς καταβάσεως σημαίνων· ἐπὶ γὰρ τὴν γῆν ὑετὸς καταβαίνων, ψόφον ποιεῖ· ἐπὶ δὲ πόκον ἐρίου καταβαίνων, οὐ ποιεῖ. Μιχαίας: «Καὶ σύ, Βηθλεὲμ γῆ Ἰούδα, οὐδαμῶς ἐλαχίστη εἶ ἐν τοῖς ἡγεμόσιν Ἰούδα· ἐκ γὰρ σοῦ ἐξελεύσεταί μοι ἡγούμενος, ὃς ποιμανεῖ τὸν λαόν μου τὸν Ἰσραήλ· καὶ | ἔξοδοι αὐτοῦ ἀπ' ἀρχῆς ἀφ' ἡμερῶν αἰῶνος.» Μωσῆς: «Προφήτην ὑμῖν ἀναστήσει Κύριος ὁ Θεὸς ἡμῶν ἐκ τῶν ἀδελφῶν ὑμῶν ὡς ἐμέ· αὐτοῦ ἀκούσεσθε κατὰ πάντα, ὅσα ἂν λαλήσει πρὸς ὑμᾶς· καὶ ἔσται, ὃς ἂν μὴ ἀκούσῃ τοῦ προφήτου ἐκείνου, ἐξολοθρευθήσεται.»

him. And the Lord said to the devil, 'May the Lord rebuke you, devil'" (Zech 3:1–2a).[53]

"And the angel of the Lord testified to Jesus, saying, 'The Lord Almighty says this: 'If you go in my ways,[54] and if you keep my commands, you will indeed judge my house'" (Zech 3:6–7).[55]

And again:

"Listen, Jesus, high priest" (Zech 3:8).[56]

2.4. Further references to manifestations of the divine

Isaiah:

"I became manifest to those who were not seeking me, and I was found by those who were not asking for me" (Isa 65:1a).[57]

(And again: "You will see the great king" [Uncertain quotation; cf. Isa 33:17].

Yet no one sees God.)[58]

And again:

"The Lord will appear to them, and he will utterly destroy all the gods of the nations" (Zeph 2:11).[59]

And again:

"See, I am near to a nation who did not call upon my name" (Isa 65:1b).[60]

David:

"You who sit upon the cherubim, show yourself! Stir up your power, and come to save us" (Ps 79:2c–3).[61]

And again:

"He will come down like rain upon a fleece" (Ps 71:6a) signifies the unperturbed and soundless nature of his descent.[62] For rain falling on the ground makes a noise, but rain falling on a woolen fleece does not.

2.5. References to the Davidic Messiah and a "prophet like Moses"

Micah:

"But you, Bethlehem, land of Judah, are not at all least among the rulers of Judah. For from you will come forth for me a ruler who will shepherd my people Israel. And his going forth was from the beginning, from the days of old" (Mic 5:2; cf. Matt 2:6).[63]

Moses:

"The Lord our God will raise up for you a prophet like me from your brothers. Listen to him in all things that he will say to you. And it will be, that whoever does not listen to that prophet

Πολλοί ανέστησαν προφήται. Ἆρα περί ποίου αυτών λέγει; Οὗτος δὲ ὁ
ἀναστησόμενος, ἆρα τὰ Μωσέως διδάξει, ἢ ἕτερα; Εἰ μὲν τὰ Μωσέως,
τί τὸ περίεργον, ἄλλον ἀναστῆναι ἀρκοῦντος Μωσέως; Εἰ δὲ ἕτερα, εἰ-
πάτωσαν, καὶ ποῖα ἦν τὰ διδάγματα αὐτοῦ, καὶ τίς ὁ προφήτης; τῶν
γὰρ νενομισμένων οὐδεὶς ἔξωθεν ἢ ἐδίδαξεν ἢ ᾔτησε παρ' αὐτῶν τι.
Καὶ αὐτὸς δὲ ὁ τῶν ὅλων Θεὸς ἐκύρωσε τὴν περὶ ἑαυτοῦ προφητείαν,
εἰπών· «Ὀρθῶς πάντα ἐλάλησαν· Προφήτην αὐτοῖς ἀναστήσω ἐκ μέσου τῶν ἀδελφῶν αὐτῶν, ὥσπερ σέ· καὶ δώσω τὸ ῥῆμά μου ἐν τῷ
στόματι αὐτοῦ.» Σκόπει οὖν τὴν δύναμιν τοῦ ῥητοῦ. Οὐδὲ γὰρ ἄλλῳ
προφήτῃ εἶπε δεδωκέναι ῥῆμα· αὐτοὶ γὰρ δουλοπρεπῶς διακονοῦντες
ἔλεγον· «Τάδε λέγει Κύριος.» Αὐτὸς δὲ κατὰ τὸ πατρικὸν ἀξίωμα,
ἔλεγε τῷ λεπρῷ· «Θέλω, καθαρίσθητι.» Τοῖς τεθνεῶσι· «Νεανίσκε,
σοὶ λέγω, ἐγέρθητι·» καί· «Λάζαρε, δεῦρο ἔξω.» Τῇ θαλάσσῃ ἐπιτι-
μᾷ, καὶ τοῖς πνεύμασιν ἐν ἐξουσίᾳ, λέγων· «Σιώπα, πεφίμωσο.» Τί δὲ
τό· «Προφήτην ὥσπερ σέ;» Ἀντιπαραθέντες τὰ Μωσέως τοῖς Χριστοῦ εὑρήσομεν ἐπὶ σχολῆς, καὶ αὐτὸ δὲ τὸ εἰρημένον ὑπὸ Μωσέως
ἐν τῷ νόμῳ, ὅτι οὐκ ἔστιν ἐπ' αὐτῶν προσθεῖναι, καὶ οὐκ ἔστιν ἀπ'
αὐτῶν ἀφελεῖν. Εἶτα καὶ εἰπών· «Αὐτοῦ ἀκούσεσθε κατὰ πάντα, ὅσα
ἂν λαλήσῃ πρὸς ὑμᾶς,» σημαίνει τὸ ὑπέροχον τοῦ προφητευομένου.
Ἡσαΐας· «Ἰδοὺ ὁ Θεὸς ἡμῶν· ἰδοὺ Κύριος μετὰ ἰσχύος ἔρχεται, καὶ
ὁ βραχίων μετὰ κυρίας.» Δαβίδ· «Ὤμοσε Κύριος τῷ Δαβὶδ ἀλήθειαν,
καὶ οὐ μὴ ἀθετήσει αὐτήν· Ἐκ καρποῦ τῆς κοιλίας σου θήσομαι ἐπὶ

will be completely destroyed" (Deut 18:15–19 / Lev 23:29; cf. Acts 3:22–23).[64]

Many prophets arose. Concerning which one of them does he speak? This one who will arise, will he teach the things of Moses, or other things? If the teachings of Moses, why the superfluity of another arising, when Moses was sufficient? If other teachings, let them say both what his instructions were and who the prophet was. For no one either taught beyond the things that are customarily accepted [i.e., in the Law of Moses] or asked about anything besides them.

But the God of all himself confirmed the prophecy concerning himself,[65] saying, "They spoke everything rightly. I will raise up a prophet like you for them from the midst of their brothers. And I will place my word in his mouth" (Deut 18:17–18).[66] Observe the power of what is said. For he did not say, "I have given a word to another prophet."

For, while serving in a slavish manner, they were saying, "The Lord says this."

2.6. Excursus on Jesus' divine authority

But he himself, on the basis of the rank given by the Father, said to the leper, "I do will [to cleanse you], be made clean!" (Matt 8:3 par.). To those who had died, "Young man, I say to you, arise" (Luke 7:14)[67] and "Lazarus, come out here!" (John 11:43). With authority he rebuked the sea and the spirits, saying, "Be silent, be still!" (Mark 4:39).[68] What about "a prophet like you"? If we compare the teachings of Moses with those of Christ[69] we will find at our leisure the very same thing said by Moses in the law, that one may not add to them, and one may not take away from them [cf. Deut 12:32]. And then saying, "Listen to him in all things that he may say to you," signifying the excellence of the one about whom it is prophesied.[70]

Isaiah:[71]

"See, our God.[72] See, the Lord comes with power, and his arm with authority" (Isa 40:9b–10).[73]

2.7. Davidic descent of the Messiah

David:

"The Lord swore the truth to David, and he will not annul it, 'I will place on your throne [someone] from the fruit of your loins'" (Ps 131:11). [74]

τοῦ θρόνου σου.» Καὶ πάλιν: «Διεθέμην διαθήκην τοῖς ἐκλεκτοῖς μου. Ὤμοσα Δαβὶδ τῷ δούλῳ μου· Ἕως τοῦ αἰῶνος ἑτοιμάσω τὸ σπέρμα σου, καὶ οἰκοδομήσω εἰς γενεὰν καὶ γενεὰν τὸν θρόνον σου.» Ἐν τοῖς Παραλειπομένοις· «Καὶ ἔσται ὅταν πληρωθῶσιν αἱ ἡμέραι σου, καὶ κοιμηθήσῃ μετὰ τῶν πατέρων σου. Καὶ ἀναστήσω τὸ σπέρμα σου μετὰ σέ, ὃ ἔσται ἐκ τῆς κοιλίας σου, καὶ ἑτοιμάσω τὴν βασιλείαν αὐτοῦ. Αὐτὸς οἰκοδομήσει μοι οἶκον· καὶ | ἀνορθώσω τὴν βασιλείαν αὐτοῦ εἰς τὸν αἰῶνα. Ἐγὼ ἔσομαι αὐτῷ εἰς Πατέρα, καὶ αὐτὸς ἔσται μοι εἰς Υἱόν, καὶ τὸ ἔλεός μου οὐκ ἀποστήσω ἀπ' αὐτοῦ, καθὼς ἀπέστησα ἀπὸ τῶν ἔμπροσθέν σου. Καὶ πιστώσω αὐτὸν ἐν οἴκῳ μου· καὶ ἡ βασιλεία αὐτοῦ ἕως αἰῶνος· καὶ ὁ θρόνος αὐτοῦ ἔσται ἀνωρθωμένος ἕως αἰῶνος.» Σολομών: «Καὶ νῦν, Κύριε ὁ Θεὸς Ἰσραήλ, πιστωθήτω δὴ τὸ ῥῆμά σου τῷ Δαβὶδ τῷ Πατρί μου· εἰ ἀληθῶς κατοικήσει ὁ Θεὸς μετὰ ἀνθρώπων ἐπὶ τῆς γῆς.» Ἱερεμίας: «Καὶ ἄνθρωπός ἐστι, καὶ τίς γνώσεται αὐτόν;» Ἀμώς· «Ἐπικαλεῖστο τὸν Θεόν σου· ἑτοιμάζου, Ἱερουσαλήμ, ὅτι ἐγὼ στερεῶν βροντήν, καὶ κτίζων πνεῦμα, καὶ ἀποστέλλων εἰς ἀνθρώπους τὸν Χριστόν μου, ποιῶν ὄρθρον, καὶ ὁμίχλην, καὶ ἐπιβαίνων ἐπὶ τὰ ὑψηλὰ τῆς γῆς.» Μιχαίας: «Ἀκούσατε, λαοὶ πάντες, λόγον, καὶ προσεχέτω ἡ γῆ, καὶ πάντες οἱ κατοικοῦντες ἐν αὐτῇ· καὶ ἔσται Κύριος ἐν ἡμῖν εἰς μαρτύριον, Κύριος ἐκ ναοῦ ἁγίου αὐτοῦ, διότι ἰδοὺ Κύριος ἐκπορεύεται ἐκ τοῦ τόπου αὐτοῦ, καὶ καταβήσεται ἐπὶ τὰ ὑψηλὰ τῆς γῆς.»

Ὁ Ἰακὼβ ἐν ταῖς ἐντολαῖς: «Οὐκ ἐκλείψει ἄρχων ἐξ Ἰούδα καὶ ἡγούμενος ἐκ τῶν μηρῶν αὐτοῦ, ἕως οὗ ἔλθῃ ᾧ ἀπόκειται. Καὶ αὐτὸς προσδοκία ἐθνῶν.» Βαλαάμ: «Ἀνατελεῖ ἄστρον ἐξ Ἰακώβ, καὶ ἄνθρωπος

And again:

"I established a covenant with my chosen ones. I swore to David my servant, 'I will prepare your seed forever, and I will build your throne for generations and generations'" (Ps 88:4–5).[75]

In Chronicles:

"And it will happen, when your days are fulfilled, that you will sleep with your fathers. And I will raise up your seed after you, which will be from your loins, and I will prepare his kingdom. He himself will build a house for me. And I will establish his kingdom forever.[76] I will be as a father to him, and he will be as a son to me. And I will not remove my mercy from him, as I removed [it] from those before you. And I will confirm him in my house, and his kingdom will be forever. And his throne will be established forever" (1 Chr 17:11–14).[77]

Solomon:[78]

"And now, Lord God of Israel, let your word to David my father be confirmed, if God truly will live with humans on the earth" (3 Kgdms 8:26–27).[79]

2.8. Miscellaneous texts on the Incarnation

Jeremiah:

"And he is a human, and who will know him?" (Jer 17:9).[80]

Amos:

"Call your God. Prepare, Jerusalem, because I am the one who strengthens thunder, and creates the wind, and sends my anointed to humans, making the morning and the darkness, and going against the high places of the land" (Amos 4:12b–13).[81]

Micah:

"Hear, all you peoples, a word, and let the earth pay attention, and all who dwell in it. And the Lord will be among us to bear witness, the Lord out of his holy Temple, for behold the Lord goes out from his place, and he will descend upon the high places of the earth" (Mic 1:2–3).[82]

2.9. A messianic cluster: Gen 49:10–11, Num 24:17, and Isa 11:1–10

Jacob [says] in the commandments:

"A ruler will not be lacking from Judah, and a leader from his thighs, until the time when he shall come for whom it is reserved. For he is the expectation of the nations" (Gen 49:10).[83]

Balaam:

ἐξ Ἰσραήλ, καὶ θραύσει τοὺς ἀρχηγοὺς Μωάβ, καὶ προνομεύσει τοὺς
υἱοὺς Σήθ· καὶ ἔσται Ἐδὼμ κληρονομία ἐθνῶν.» Δαβὶδ δὲ τούτων οὐ
περιεγένετο. Εἰ δὲ περὶ τῶν ἐξ αὐτοῦ ἔδει εἰπεῖν, Ἀνατελοῦσιν ἄστρα
ἐξ Ἰακώβ, καὶ ἡγούμενοι ἐξ Ἰσραήλ. Ἡσαΐας: «Ἰδοὺ ὁ δεσπότης Κύριος Σαβαὼθ συνταράξει τοὺς ἐνδόξους μετὰ ἰσχύος, καὶ οἱ ὑψηλοὶ τῇ
ὕβρει συντριβήσονται, καὶ ταπεινωθήσονται οἱ ὑψηλοί, καὶ πεσοῦνται
μαχαίρᾳ. Ὁ δὲ Λίβανος σὺν τοῖς ὑψηλοῖς πεσεῖται. Καὶ ἐξελεύσεται
ῥάβδος ἐκ τῆς ῥίζης Ἰεσσαί, καὶ ἄνθος ἐκ τῆς ῥίζης ἀναβήσεται, καὶ
ἀναπαύσεται ἐπ' αὐτὸν πνεῦμα Θεοῦ, πνεῦμα σοφίας καὶ συνέσεως,
πνεῦμα βουλῆς καὶ ἰσχύος, πνεῦμα γνώσεως καὶ εὐσεβείας· ἐμπλήσει
αὐτὸν πνεῦμα φόβου Θεοῦ. Οὐ κατὰ τὴν δόξαν κρινεῖ, οὐδὲ κατὰ τὴν
λαλιὰν ἐλέγξει· ἀλλὰ κρινεῖ ταπεινῷ κρίσιν, καὶ ἐλέγξει τοὺς ἐν|δόξους
τῆς γῆς, καὶ πατάξει τὴν γῆν τῷ λόγῳ τοῦ στόματος αὐτοῦ, καὶ ἐν
Πνεύματι διὰ χειλέων ἀνελεῖ ἀσεβῆ· καὶ ἔσται δικαιοσύνη ἐζωσμένος
τὴν ὀσφὺν αὐτοῦ, καὶ ἀλήθειαν ἠλειμμένος τὰς πλευρὰς αὐτοῦ.» Καὶ
μετ' ὀλίγα· «Καὶ ἔσται ἐν τῇ ἡμέρᾳ ἐκείνῃ ἡ ῥίζα τοῦ Ἰεσσαί, καὶ ὁ
ἀνιστάμενος ἄρχειν ἐθνῶν· ἐπ' αὐτῷ ἔθνη ἐλπιοῦσι, καὶ ἔσται ἡ ἀνά-
παυσις αὐτοῦ τιμή.» Δαβίδ: «Ὁ θρόνος σου, ὁ Θεός, εἰς τὸν αἰῶνα
τοῦ αἰῶνος· ῥάβδος εὐθύτητος, ἡ ῥάβδος τῆς βασιλείας σου. Ἠγάπη-
σας δικαιοσύνην καὶ ἐμίσησας ἀνομίαν, διὰ τοῦτο ἔχρισέ σε ὁ Θεός,
ὁ Θεός σου, ἔλαιον ἀγαλλιάσεως περὶ τοὺς μετόχους σου.» Ὁρᾷς ὅτι
ὁ Θεὸς χρίεται παρὰ τοῦ Θεοῦ· ἐνανθρωπίσας γὰρ γέγονεν ἀρχιερεύς,
καὶ ἀπόστολος τῆς ὁμολογίας ἡμῶν. Καὶ μετ' ὀλίγα: «Καὶ σύ, Κύριε,
τὴν γῆν ἐθεμελίωσας, καὶ ἔργα τῶν χειρῶν σου εἰσὶν οἱ οὐρανοί. Αὐτοὶ
ἀπολοῦνται, σὺ δὲ διαμένεις· καὶ πάντες ὡς ἱμάτιον παλαιωθήσονται,

"A star will arise from Jacob, and a man from Israel, and he will crush the rulers of Moab, and will plunder the sons of Seth. And Edom will be the inheritance of the nations" (Num 24:17–18a).[84]

Yet David did not overcome these nations.[85] If he had been [referring to] those who descended from himself, he would have had to say: "Stars will arise from Jacob, and leaders from Israel."

Isaiah:

"Behold the master, the Lord of hosts, with his might will throw the esteemed ones into disarray; those exalted in their pride will be crushed, the exalted ones will be humbled, they will fall by the sword. Lebanon will fall with the exalted ones. And a shoot will go forth from the root of Jesse, and a blossom will sprout from the root, and the spirit of God will rest upon him, a spirit of wisdom and understanding, a spirit of counsel and might, a spirit of knowledge and piety. The spirit of the fear of the Lord will fill him fully. He will not judge according to appearance, nor will he reprove according to rumor. But he will render judgment to the one who is humble,[86] and reprove the esteemed ones of the earth, and he will strike the earth with the word of his mouth, and by the breath [spirit] through his lips he will destroy the impious one.[87] And his waist will be girdled with righteousness, and his sides clothed with truth" (Isa 10:33–34; 11:1–5).[88]

And after a bit:

"And in that day there will be the root of Jesse and the one who arises to rule the nations. In him the nations will hope, and his rest will be an honor" (Isa 11:10).[89]

2.10. Further references to "two powers in heaven" passages

David:

"Your throne, O God, is eternal. The scepter of your kingdom is the scepter of righteousness. You have loved righteousness and hated lawlessness; therefore God, your God, has anointed you, with the oil of joy among your companions" (Ps 44:7–8).[90]

You see that God is anointed by "God." For after becoming incarnate, he became "high priest, and apostle of our confession" (cf. Heb 3:1).

And after a bit:

"And you, Lord, founded the earth, and the heavens are the works of your hands. They will pass away, but you remain. And

καὶ ὡσεὶ περιβόλαιον ἑλίξεις αὐτούς, καὶ ἀλλαγήσονται. Σὺ δὲ ὁ αὐτὸς
εἶ, καὶ τὰ ἔτη σου οὐκ ἐκλείψουσιν,» τοῦ χρισθέντος δηλαδή.

Γ'. Περὶ τῆς γεννήσεως αὐτοῦ τῆς ἐκ Παρθένου.

Ἠσαΐας: «Ἰδοὺ ἡ παρθένος ἐν γαστρὶ ἕξει, καὶ τέξεται υἱόν, καὶ καλέσουσι τὸ ὄνομα αὐτοῦ Ἐ[μ]μανουήλ·» ὃ ἑρμηνεύεται, *Μεθ' ἡμῶν ὁ Θεός·* «Καὶ πρὶν ἐπιγνῶναι πατέρα ἢ μητέρα, λήψεται δύναμιν Δαμασκοῦ, καὶ τὰ σκῦλα Σαμαρείας ἔδεται.» Καὶ Σολομὼν προφητικῶς: «Παῖς ἤμην εὐφυής, ψυχῆς τε ἔλαχον ἀγαθῆς· μᾶλλον δὲ ἀγαθὸς ὤν, ἦλθον εἰς σῶμα ἀμίαντον.» (Τίς οὖν πρὸ γεννήσεως ἦν ἀγαθός; καὶ τίς ἦλθεν εἰς σῶμα ἀμίαντον;) Ἠσαΐας: «Καὶ θελήσουσιν εἰ ἐγενήθησαν πυρίκαυστοι. Ὅτι παιδίον ἐγεννήθη ἡμῖν, υἱὸς καὶ ἐδόθη ἡμῖν, οὗ ἡ ἀρχὴ ἐπὶ τοῦ ὤμου αὐτοῦ, καὶ καλεῖται τὸ ὄνομα αὐτοῦ μεγάλης βουλῆς Ἄγγελος, Θαυμαστὸς Σύμβουλος, Θεὸς ἰσχυρός, ἐξουσιαστής, Ἄρχων εἰρήνης, Πατὴρ τοῦ μέλλοντος αἰῶνος.» Καὶ πάλιν: «Ἰδοὺ ἡ δάμαλις τέτοκε, καὶ οὐ τέτοκε.» Τοῦτο δὲ δηλοῖ τὴν Παρθένον. Καὶ πάλιν: «Βούτυρον, καὶ μέλι φάγεται.» Τούτῳ γὰρ ἐτρέφετο κατιούσης τῆς μητρὸς αὐτοῦ ἀπὸ τῆς ἀπογραφῆς· ὕστερον γὰρ εὐπόρησεν γάλακτος. Καὶ πάλιν: «Οὕτως λέγει Κύριος Σαβαώθ· Ἐκοπίασεν Αἴγυπτος, καὶ ἐμπορία Αἰθιόπων· καὶ οἱ Σαβαεὶμ ἄνδρες ὑψηλοὶ ἐπὶ σὲ δια|βήσονται, καὶ σοὶ ἔσονται δοῦλοι, καὶ ὀπίσω σου ἀκολουθήσουσι δεδεμένοι χειροπέδαις, καὶ διαβήσονται πρὸς σέ, καὶ προσκυνήσουσί σοι καὶ ἐν σοὶ προσεύξονται ὅτι ὁ Θεὸς ἐν σοί ἐστι, καὶ οὐκ ἔστι Θεὸς πλὴν σοῦ. Σὺ γὰρ εἶ Θεός, καὶ οὐκ ᾔδειμεν, Θεὸς τοῦ Ἰσραὴλ Σωτήρ.»

they all will grow old like a garment, and you will roll them up like a cloak, and they will be changed. But you are the same, and your years will not fail" (Ps 101:26–28), [the years] of the anointed one, obviously.[91]

Chapter 3: Concerning his birth from a virgin

Isaiah:

"Behold the virgin will conceive, and she will give birth to a son, and they will name him 'Emmanuel'[92] (Isa 7:14), which means 'God is with us' (cf. Matt 1:23).[93] And before he recognizes his father or his mother, he will capture the power of Damascus, and he will devour the spoils of Samaria" (Isa 8:4).[94]

And Solomon [speaking] prophetically:

"I was a clever child,[95] and received a good soul. Even more: since I was good, I came into an undefiled body" (Wis 8:19–20).[96]

(Who, then, was good before his birth? And who came into an undefiled body?)[97]

Isaiah:

"And they will be willing, even if they were burned with fire. For a child was born to us, and a son was given to us, whose rulership is upon his shoulder, and his name will be called 'Messenger of great counsel, wonderful counselor, mighty God, powerful, ruler[98] of peace, father of the coming age'" (Isa 9:5b–6).[99]

And again:

"Look! The heifer has given birth, and has not given birth" (Uncertain quotation; cf. *Apocr. Ezek.* Frag. 3).[100] This signifies the Virgin.

And again:

"Butter and honey he will eat" (Isa 7:15).[101]

For when his mother was returning from the registration he was being nourished on this. For later she had plenty of milk.

And again:

"Thus says the Lord of hosts: 'Egypt has worked hard, and the trade of the Ethiopians. And the proud men of Sabeim will cross over to you and will be your slaves.[102] And they will follow after you, bound in manacles, and they will cross over to you, and they will bow down to you, and they will offer prayers to you because God is in your midst, and there is no God besides you. For you are God, and we did not know, God the Savior of Israel'" (Isa 45:14–15).[103]

Ἰεζεκιήλ: «Καὶ ἐπέστρεψέ με Κύριος κατὰ τὴν ὁδὸν τῆς πύλης τῆς
βλεπούσης κατὰ ἀνατολάς, καὶ αὕτη ἦν κεκλεισμένη· καὶ εἶπε Κύριος
πρὸς μέ· Υἱὲ ἀνθρώπου, ἡ πύλη αὕτη κεκλεισμένη ἔσται, καὶ οὐδεὶς
οὐ μὴ διέλθῃ δι' αὐτῆς, ὅτι Κύριος ὁ Θεὸς Ἰσραὴλ εἰσελεύσεται, καὶ
ἐξελεύσεται δι' αὐτῆς, καὶ ἔσται κεκλεισμένη.» Ἡσαΐας: «Ἐκ κοιλίας
μητρὸς ἐκάλεσα τὸ ὄνομα αὐτοῦ Μάχαιραν ὀξεῖαν.» Δανιήλ: «Ἰδοὺ
ἐτμήθη λίθος ἄνευ χειρῶν, καὶ ἐπάταξε τὸν ἀνδριάντα, καὶ ἐγένετο εἰς
ὄρος μέγα, καὶ ἐπλήρωσε τὴν οἰκουμένην.» Ὁ οὖν τμηθεὶς λίθος ἄνευ
χειρός ἐστιν ὁ γεννηθεὶς ἄνευ σπορᾶς ἀνδρός. Ἡσαΐας πάλιν: «Ἄκουε,
οὐρανέ, καὶ ἐνωτίζου, ἡ γῆ, ὅτι Κύριος ἐλάλησεν· Υἱοὺς ἐγέννησα, καὶ
ὕψωσα, αὐτοὶ δέ με ἠθέτησαν. Ἔγνω βοῦς τὸν κτησάμενον, καὶ ὄνος
τὴν φάτνην τοῦ κυρίου αὐτοῦ· Ἰσραὴλ δέ με οὐκ ἔγνω, οὐδὲ ὁ λαός με
συνῆκε.» Καὶ πάλιν: «Λάβε τόμον καινοῦ χάρτου μεγάλου, καὶ γρά-
ψον ἐν αὐτῷ γραφίδι ἀνθρώπου, τοῦ ὀξέως προνομὴν ποιῆσαι σκύλων.
Καὶ προσῆλθον πρὸς τὴν προφῆτιν, καὶ ἐν γαστρὶ ἔλαβε, καὶ ἔτεκεν
υἱόν· καὶ εἰπέ μοι Κύριος· Κάλεσον τὸ ὄνομα αὐτοῦ, Ταχέως σκύλευ-
σον, Ὀξέως προνόμευσον.» Τόμον οὖν καινὸν νοοῦμεν τὴν Παρθένον·
ὥσπερ γὰρ ὁ χάρτης καινός ἐστι καθαρός, ἄγραφος ὤν, οὕτως καὶ
ἡ Παρθένος ἁγία, ἀμύητος ἀνδρός. Καὶ πάλιν: «Πᾶν ἄρσεν διανοῖγον μήτραν, ἅγιον τῷ Κυρίῳ κληθήσεται.» Οὐδὲν δὲ ἄρσεν διανοίγει
μήτραν, ἀλλ' ἡ κοινωνία ἀνδρὸς πρὸς γυναῖκα. Τὸ γοῦν εἰρημένον περὶ τοῦ Κυρίου νοητέον. Συμβαίνει δὲ πολλοὺς τῶν πρωτοτόκων εἶναι
ἀσεβεῖς, καὶ ἁμαρτωλούς. Πῶς οὖν οὗτοι ἅγιοι τῷ Κυρίῳ, διὰ τοῦτο
καὶ ἄμωμοι; διὰ τί δὲ μὴ καὶ πᾶν θῆλυ; Δῆλον οὖν, ὅτι αὐτὸς ἅγιος καὶ

Ezekiel:

"And the Lord returned[104] me by the way of the gate which faces east, and it was closed. And the Lord said to me, 'Son of man, this gate will be closed, and no one will go through it, because the Lord, the God of Israel will go in, and go out through it, and it will be closed'" (Ezek 44:1–2).[105]

Isaiah:

"From the womb of his mother I named him 'Sharp Sword'" (Isa 49:1–2).[106]

Daniel:

"Look! A stone was cut without hands, and it struck the statue, and became a great mountain, and filled the world" (Dan 2:34–35).[107]

Now the stone cut without a hand is the one born without the seed of a man.

Isaiah again:

"Hear, O heaven, and give ear,[108] O earth, that the Lord said, 'I have given birth to sons, and raised them up, but they rejected me. The ox knows its owner, and the donkey the manger of its master. But Israel has not known me, nor has the people understood me'" (Isa 1:2–3).[109]

And again:

"'Take a roll of large, new papyrus leaf, and write in it with a person's stylus, concerning the swift plundering of the spoils.' And I went into the prophetess, and she conceived, and she gave birth to a son. And the Lord said to me, 'Name him, 'Quickly despoil, swiftly plunder'" (Isa 8:1–3).[110]

We understand "a new roll" to be the Virgin; for as a new papyrus leaf is pure (since it is not written upon), so too the Virgin is holy, uninitiated by a man.

And again:

"Every male opening[111] a womb will be called holy to the Lord" (Luke 2:23).[112] Yet no male opens a womb, rather the intercourse of a man with a woman. One must understand what is said about the Lord. It happens that many of the first born are impious and are sinners. How then are these ones holy to the Lord, and therefore also blameless? Why is not also every female [called holy to the Lord]? It is clear, then, that he alone is holy and blameless.[113]

David:

ἄμωμος μόνος. Δαβίδ· « Μήτηρ Σιὼν ἐρεῖ, Ἄνθρωπος, καὶ ἄνθρωπος ἐγεννήθη ἐν αὐτῇ, καὶ αὐτὸς ἐθεμελίωσεν αὐτὴν ὁ Ὕψιστος.»

Δ'. Περὶ θαυμάτων, ὧν ἔμελλε ποιεῖν ἐνανθρωπίσας ὁ Κύριος.

Ἱερεμίας: «Ἰδοὺ τέθεικά σε εἰς διαθήκην γένους, καὶ εἰς φῶς ἐθνῶν, τοῦ καταστῆσαι τὴν γῆν, | καὶ κληρονομῆσαι κληρονομίαν ἐρήμου, λέγων τοῖς ἐν δεσμοῖς, Ἐξέλθετε· καὶ τοῖς ἐν τῷ σκότει, Ἀνακαλύφθητε.» Καὶ ὅτι οὐ περὶ ψιλοῦ ἀνθρώπου λέγει, αὐτὸς ἦν ὁ εἰπών: « Οὗτος ὁ Θεὸς ἡμῶν, οὐ λογισθήσεται ἕτερος πρὸς αὐτόν.» Ἠσαΐας: « Ἰσχύσατε, χεῖρες ἀνειμέναι καὶ γόνατα παραλελυμένα· παρακαλέσατε, οἱ ὀλιγόψυχοι τῇ διανοίᾳ· ἰσχύσατε, μὴ φοβεῖσθε. Ἰδοὺ ὁ Θεὸς ἡμῶν, ἰδοὺ Κύριος μετὰ ἰσχύος ἔρχεται.» Καὶ πάλιν: « Τότε ἀνοιχθήσονται ὀφθαλμοὶ τυφλῶν, καὶ ὦτα κωφῶν ἀκούσονται· τότε ἁλεῖται, ὡς ἔλαφος, ὁ χωλός, καὶ τρανὴ ἔσται γλῶσσα μογιλάλων.» Καὶ πάλιν: « Πνεῦμα Κυρίου ἐπ᾽ ἐμέ, οὗ εἵνεκεν ἔχρισέ με· εὐαγγελίσασθαι πτωχοῖς ἀπέσταλκέ με, κηρῦξαι αἰχμαλώτοις ἄφεσιν καὶ τυφλοῖς ἀνάβλεψιν.»

Ε'. Περὶ προδοσίας.

Δαβίδ: « Ὁ ἐσθίων ἄρτους μου, ἐμεγάλυνεν ἐπ᾽ ἐμὲ πτερνισμόν.»

ϛ'. Περὶ Πάθους.

« Λαός μου, οἱ μακαρίζοντες ὑμᾶς πλανῶσιν ὑμᾶς, καὶ τὴν τρίβον τῶν ποδῶν ὑμῶν ἐκταράσσουσιν. Ἀλλὰ νῦν καταστήσεται Κύριος εἰς κρίσιν, καὶ στήσει τὸν λαὸν αὐτοῦ εἰς κρίσιν. Αὐτὸς Κύριος εἰς κρίσιν ἥξει

"Mother Zion will say, 'A human, yes a human was born in her, and the Most High himself has established her'" (Ps 86:5).[114]

CHAPTER 4: CONCERNING THE MIRACLES WHICH THE LORD WAS DESTINED TO PERFORM WHEN HE BECAME INCARNATE

Jeremiah:
"Behold, I have established you as a covenant of a people, and as a light of the nations, to set the earth in order, and to receive the inheritance of a desert, saying to those in chains, 'Come out!' and to those in darkness, 'Be revealed!'" (Isa 49:6–9).[115]

And because he [Jeremiah] speaks not of a mere human, he himself was the one who said, "This is our God, no other will be reckoned next to him" (Bar 3:36).[116]

Isaiah:
"Be strong, you slackened hands and you exhausted knees; encourage one another, you discouraged of heart! Be strong, do not fear!" (Isa 35:3–4).[117]

"Behold our God; behold the Lord comes with strength" (Isa 40:9–10).[118]

And again:
"Then the eyes of the blind will be opened, and the ears of the deaf will hear. Then the lame person will leap like a deer, and the tongue of those who speak with difficulty will be articulate" (Isa 35:5–6).[119]

And again:
"The Spirit of the Lord is upon me, because he has anointed me. He sent me to bring good news to the poor, to announce release to the prisoners, and restoration of sight to the blind" (Isa 61:1; cf. Luke 4:18).[120]

CHAPTER 5: CONCERNING [HIS] BETRAYAL

David:
"The one eating my bread increased deceit against me" (Ps 40:10).[121]

CHAPTER 6: CONCERNING [HIS] PASSION

6.1. Concerning Jesus' trial before the Jewish and Roman authorities

"My people, the ones who bless you lead you astray and they greatly disturb the path of your feet. But now the Lord will bring [them] to judgment, and he will bring his people to judgment.[122]

μετὰ τῶν πρεσβυτέρων τοῦ λαοῦ, καὶ μετὰ τῶν ἀρχόντων αὐτῶν.» Δαβίδ: «Ἵνα τί ἐφρύαξαν ἔθνη, καὶ λαοὶ ἐμελέτησαν κενά; Παρέστησαν οἱ βασιλεῖς τῆς γῆς, καὶ οἱ ἄρχοντες συνήχθησαν ἐπὶ τὸ αὐτὸ κατὰ τοῦ Κυρίου καὶ κατὰ τοῦ Χριστοῦ αὐτοῦ.» Ἱερεμίας: «Πνεῦμα προσώπου ἡμῶν Θεὸς Κύριος συνελήφθη ἐν ταῖς διαφθοραῖς αὐτῶν, οὗ εἴπομεν· Ἐν τῇ σκιᾷ αὐτοῦ ζησόμεθα ἐν τοῖς ἔθνεσιν.» Ἡσαΐας: «Αὐτὸς τὰς ἀνομίας ἡμῶν φέρει, καὶ περὶ ἡμῶν ὀδυνᾶται καὶ ἡμεῖς ἐλογισάμεθα αὐτὸν ἐν πόνῳ, καὶ ἐν πληγῇ, καὶ ἐν κακώσει. Αὐτὸς δὲ ἐτραυματίσθη διὰ τὰς ἁμαρτίας ἡμῶν, καὶ μεμαλάκισται διὰ τὰς ἀνομίας ἡμῶν. Παιδεία εἰρήνης ἡμῶν ἐπ' αὐτόν, τῷ μώλωπι αὐτοῦ ἡμεῖς ἰάθημεν. Πάντες ὡς πρόβατα ἐπλανήθημεν· ἕκαστος τὴν ὁδὸν αὐτοῦ ἐπλανήθη. Καὶ Κύριος παρέδωκεν αὐτὸν διὰ τὰς ἁμαρτίας ἡμῶν· καὶ αὐτὸς διὰ τὸ κεκακῶσθαι οὐκ ἀνοίγει τὸ στόμα. Ὡς πρόβατον ἐπὶ σφαγὴν ἤχθη, καὶ ὡς ἀμνὸς ἐναντίον τοῦ κείραντος αὐτὸν ἄφωνος, οὕτως οὐκ ἀνοίγει τὸ στόμα αὐτοῦ ἐν | τῇ ταπεινώσει αὐτοῦ, ὅτι αἴρεται ἀπὸ τῆς γῆς ἡ ζωὴ αὐτοῦ· ἀπὸ τῶν ἁμαρτιῶν τοῦ λαοῦ μου ἤχθη εἰς θάνατον. Καὶ δώσω τοὺς πονηροὺς ἀντὶ ταφῆς αὐτοῦ, καὶ τοὺς πλουσίους ἀντὶ τοῦ θανάτου αὐτοῦ, ὅτι ἀνομίαν οὐκ ἐποίησεν, οὐδὲ εὑρέθη δόλος ἐν τῷ στόματι αὐτοῦ.» Καὶ μετά τινα: «Διὰ τοῦτο αὐτὸς κληρονομήσει πολλούς, καὶ τῶν ἰσχυρῶν μεριεῖ σκῦλα, ἀνθ' ὧν παρεδόθη εἰς θάνατον ἡ ψυχὴ αὐτοῦ, ὅτι ἀνομίαν οὐκ ἐποίησε, καὶ ἐν τοῖς ἀνόμοις ἐλογίσθη· καὶ αὐτὸς ἁμαρτίας πολλῶν ἀνήνεγκε, καὶ διὰ τὰς ἁμαρτίας αὐτῶν παρεδόθη.» Ἐκ τούτων δῆλον ὅτι οὐ περὶ τοῦ λαοῦ τοῦ ἀπαχθέντος ἐν Βαβυλῶνι ὁ Προφήτης λέγει, ὥς τινες ὑπέλαβον. Πῶς γὰρ ἂν ὁ λαός, ἀπὸ τῶν ἁμαρτιῶν τοῦ λαοῦ ἤχθη εἰς θάνατον; ἢ ποῖος λαός, καὶ ποίου λαοῦ; Καὶ πάλιν: «Τὸν νῶτόν μου ἔδωκα εἰς μάστιγας, τὰς

The Lord himself will enter into judgment with the elders of the people, and with their rulers" (Isa 3:12–14).[123]

David:
"Why did the nations rage, and the peoples concern themselves with empty things? The kings of the earth were there, and the rulers were gathered together against the Lord and against his anointed" (Ps 2:1–2).[124]

Jeremiah:
"The spirit of our face, the Lord God, was caught in their corruptions, of whom we said, 'We will live in his shadow among the nations'" (Lam 4:20).[125]

6.2. References to the Suffering Servant

Isaiah:
"He bears our lawlessness, and he suffers for us, and we considered him to be in affliction, in distress, and in misfortune. He was wounded on account of our sins, and he became weak on account of our lawlessness. The discipline for our health was placed upon him; by his bruise we were healed. We all, like sheep, went astray. Each one went astray along his path. And the Lord handed him over for our sins.[126] And he did not open his mouth on account of his suffering. As a sheep to the slaughter he was led, and as a lamb before its shearer he was silent. In this way he did not open his mouth in his humility, because his life is taken away from the earth. Because of the sins of my people he was led away to death. And I will give the wicked ones in return for his burial, and the rich ones for his death, because he did not commit lawlessness, nor was deceit found in his mouth" (Isa 53:4–9).[127]

And after a bit:
"Therefore he will inherit many peoples, and he will divide the spoils of the strong, for whom his soul was handed over to death, since he did not commit lawlessness, yet he was counted among the lawless ones. And he bore the sins of many peoples, and was handed over on account of their sins" (Isa 53:12).[128]

From these things it is clear that the prophet is not speaking about the people led away in Babylon, as some have supposed.[129] How could the people be led to death because of the sins of the people? Which people [were led away], and of which people [were the sins]?

And again:

δὲ σιαγόνας μου εἰς ῥαπίσματα, τὸ δὲ πρόσωπόν μου οὐκ ἀπέστρεψα ἀπὸ αἰσχύνης ἐμπτυσμάτων.» Καὶ πάλιν: «Οὐκ εἶχεν εἶδος, οὐδὲ κάλλος, ἀλλὰ τὸ εἶδος αὐτοῦ ἄτιμον, ἐκλεῖπον παρὰ τοὺς υἱοὺς τῶν ἀνθρώπων.» Καὶ πάλιν ὁ ταῦτα εἰπών, εἶπε: «Τὴν δὲ γενεὰν αὐτοῦ τίς διηγήσεται;» Δαβίδ: «Ὅτι ἐκύκλωσάν με κύνες πολλοί· συναγωγὴ πονηρευομένων περιέσχον με. Ὤρυξαν χεῖράς μου, καὶ πόδας μου· ἐξηρίθμησαν πάντα τὰ ὀστᾶ μου. Αὐτοὶ δὲ κατενόησαν, καὶ ἐπεῖδόν με· διεμερίσαντο τὰ ἱμάτιά μου ἑαυτοῖς, καὶ ἐπὶ τὸν ἱματισμόν μου ἔβαλον κλῆρον.» Ἱερεμίας: «Ἐγὼ δὲ ὡς ἀρνίον ἄκακον ἀγόμενον τοῦ θύεσθαι, οὐκ ἔγνων.» Καὶ πάλιν: «Δεῦτε, καὶ ἐμβάλλωμεν ξύλον εἰς τὸν ἄρτον αὐτοῦ· καὶ ἐκτρίψωμεν αὐτὸν ἀπὸ τῶν ζώντων, καὶ τὸ ὄνομα αὐτοῦ οὐ μὴ μνησθῇ ἔτι.» Ζαχαρίας: «Καὶ ἔλαβον τὰ τριάκοντα ἀργύρια τὴν τιμὴν τοῦ τετιμημένου, ὃν ἐτιμήσαντο ἀπὸ υἱῶν Ἰσραήλ· καὶ ἔδωκαν αὐτὰ εἰς τὸν ἀγρὸν τοῦ κεραμέως, καθὰ συνέταξέ μοι Κύριος.»

Ζ'. *Περὶ τοῦ σταυροῦ, καὶ τοῦ γενομένου σκότους.*

«Ὄψεσθε τὴν ζωὴν ὑμῶν κρεμαμένην ἀπέναντι τῶν ὀφθαλμῶν ὑμῶν, καὶ οὐ μὴ πιστεύσητε, ἐάν τις ἐκδιηγεῖται ὑμῖν. Τὸ πρωῒ ἐρεῖς· Πῶς ἐγένετο ἑσπέρα; καὶ τὸ ἑσπέρας· Πῶς ἐγένετο πρωΐ;» Ἀμώς: «Καὶ ἔσται ἐν τῇ ἡμέρᾳ ἐκείνῃ, λέγει Κύριος ὁ Θεός, Δύσεται ὁ ἥλιος μεσημβρίας, καὶ συσκοτάσει ἐν ἡμέρᾳ τὸ φῶς.» Ἱερεμίας: «Ἐπέδυσεν

"I gave my back to lashes, and my cheeks to blows, I did not turn away my face from the shame of spitting" (Isa 50:6).[130]

And again:

"He did not have form, or beauty, rather his form was dishonorable, falling short of the sons of humans" (Isa 53:2–3).[131]

And again the one who said these things said, "Who will describe his origin?" (Isa 53:8).[132]

6.3. Further References to the Passion

David:

"For many dogs encircled me; a pack of evil-doers surrounded me. They pierced my hands and my feet. All my bones could be counted. They observed and watched me closely. They divided my clothing among themselves, and for my garments they cast lots" (Ps 21:17–19).[133]

Jeremiah:

"Yet I am like an innocent lamb led to the slaughter, not knowing" (Jer 11:19a).[134]

And again:

"Come, and let us cast wood into his bread; and let us rub him out from the living, and let his name no longer be remembered" (Jer 11:19b).[135]

Zechariah:

"And they took the thirty pieces of silver as the price of one on whom a price has been set, on whom some of the sons of Israel set a price. And they gave them for the field of the potter, as the Lord commanded me" (Zech 11:12–13; Jer 32:6–9; cf. Matt 27:9–10).[136]

CHAPTER 7: CONCERNING THE CROSS AND THE DARKNESS THAT OCCURRED

"You will see your life hanging before your eyes, yet you will not believe, even if someone describes it to you fully. In the morning you will say, 'How did the evening come?', and in the evening, 'How did the morning come?'" (Deut 28:66–67).[137]

Amos:

"'And it will happen in that day,' says the Lord God, 'the sun will set at noon, and the light will darken in the day'" (Amos 8:9).[138]

Jeremiah:

ὁ ἥλιος ἔτι μεσούσης τῆς ἡμέρας.» Ἡσαΐας: «Ὅλην τὴν ἡμέραν διεπέτασα τὰς χεῖράς μου πρὸς λαὸν ἀντιλέγοντα καὶ ἀπειθοῦντα.» Καὶ πάλιν: «Ἄρατε σύσσημον εἰς τὰ ἔθνη.» Καὶ πάλιν: «Καὶ τότε ταῦτα συντελεσθήσεται, λέγει Κύριος, ὅταν ξύλον ξύλων κλιθῇ, καὶ ἀναστῇ, καὶ ὅταν ἐκ ξύλου αἷμα | στάξει.» Ζαχαρίας: «Καὶ ἔσται, ἐν τῇ ἡμέρᾳ ἐκείνῃ οὐκ ἔσται φῶς· καὶ ἡ ἡμέρα ἐκείνη γνωστὴ τῷ Κυρίῳ· καὶ οὐχ ἡμέρα, καὶ οὐ νύξ· τὸ πρὸς ἑσπέραν ἔσται φῶς.» Δαβίδ: «Καὶ ὑπέμεινα συλλυπούμενον, καὶ οὐχ ὑπῆρξε, καὶ παρακαλοῦντα, καὶ οὐχ εὗρον· καὶ ἔδωκαν εἰς τὸ βρῶμά μου χολήν, καὶ εἰς τὴν δίψαν μου ἐπότισάν με ὄξος.» Ὧν οὐδὲν ἔχουσι ἐπὶ Δαβὶδ δεῖξαι γενόμενον. Καὶ πάλιν: «Ἔθεντό με ἐν λάκκῳ κατωτάτῳ.» Ζαχαρίας: «Ῥομφαία, ἐξεγέρθητι ἐπὶ τὸν ποιμένα, καὶ ἐπ᾽ ἄνδρα τοῦ λαοῦ μου· πάταξον τὸν ποιμένα μου, καὶ διασκορπισθήσονται τὰ πρόβατα τῆς ποίμνης.» Καὶ πάλιν: «Καὶ ἐν τῇ ἡμέρᾳ ἐκείνῃ, ἔσται τὸ ἐπὶ τὸν χαλινὸν τοῦ ἵππου ἅγιον τῷ Κυρίῳ.»

Η'. Περὶ ἀναστάσεως Χριστοῦ.

Δαβίδ, τὴν ἀνάστασιν αὐτοῦ προορῶν, ἔλεγεν· «Ἐξεγέρθητι, ἵνα τί ὑπνοῖς, Κύριε; ἀνάστηθι, καὶ μὴ ἀπώσῃ εἰς τέλος.» Καὶ πάλιν:

"The sun set when it was still the middle of the day" (Jer 15:9).139

Isaiah:

"The whole day long I spread out my hands to a contradictory and disobedient people" (Isa 65:2).140

And again:

"Raise a sign for the nations" (Isa 62:10).141

And again:

"'And then these things will be accomplished,' says the Lord, 'when the tree of trees is bent, and rises, and when blood drips from the tree.'"142

Zechariah:

"And it will happen that, in that day, there will be no light, and that day is known to the Lord. And there will be no day, nor will there be night. There will be light towards evening" (Zech 14:6–7).143

David:

"And I waited for one to grieve with me, yet there was no one; and for one to comfort me, yet I did not find one. And they gave gall for my food, and for my thirst they gave me vinegar to drink" (Ps 68:21–22).144

But they cannot show that any of these things occurred in the case of David.

And again:

"They placed me in the lowest pit" (Ps 87:7).145

Zechariah:

"Sword, arise against the shepherd, and against a man of my people. Strike my shepherd, and the sheep of the flock will be scattered" (Zech 13:7; cf. Matt 26:31).146

And again:

"And in that day, that which is upon the bridle of the horse will be holy to the Lord" (Zech 14:20).147

CHAPTER 8: CONCERNING THE RESURRECTION OF CHRIST

David, foreseeing his resurrection, said,

"Awaken, why do you sleep, Lord? Arise, and do not reject [us] completely" (Ps 43:24).148

And again:

"Arise, O Lord. Save me, my God" (Ps 3:8a).149

And again:

«Ἀνάστα, Κύριε· σῶσόν με, ὁ Θεός μου.» Καὶ πάλιν: «Ἀνάστα, Κύριε, βοήθησον ἡμῖν, καὶ λύτρωσαι ἡμᾶς ἕνεκεν τοῦ ὀνόματός σου.» Καὶ πάλιν: «Ἀνάστα, Κύριε, κρῖνον τὴν γῆν, ὅτι σὺ κατακληρονομήσεις ἐν πᾶσι τοῖς ἔθνεσι.» Ἡσαΐας: «Νῦν ἀναστήσομαι, λέγει Κύριος, νῦν δοξασθήσομαι, νῦν ὑψωθήσομαι, νῦν ὄψεσθε, νῦν σωθήσεσθε· ματαία ἔσται ἡ ἰσχὺς τοῦ πνεύματος ὑμῶν.» Ὡσηέ: «Καὶ ζητήσουσι τὸ πρόσωπόν μου ἐν θλίψει αὐτῶν, καὶ ὀρθριοῦσι πρός μέ, λέγοντες, Πορευθῶμεν καὶ ἐπιστρέψωμεν πρὸς Κύριον τὸν Θεὸν ἡμῶν, ὅτι αὐτὸς ἥρπακε, καὶ ἰάσεται ἡμᾶς· πατάξει, καὶ μοτώσει ἡμᾶς· | ὑγιάσει ἡμᾶς μετὰ δύο ἡμέρας· ἐν τῇ ἡμέρᾳ τῇ τρίτῃ ἀναστησόμεθα ἐνώπιον αὐτοῦ, καὶ γνωσόμεθα, διώξωμεν τοῦ γνῶναι τὸν Κύριον, ὡς ὄρθρον ἕτοιμον εὑρήσομεν αὐτόν.» Δαβίδ: «Ὅτι οὐκ ἐγκαταλείψεις τὴν ψυχήν μου εἰς ᾅδην, οὐδὲ δώσεις τὸν ὅσιόν σου ἰδεῖν διαφθοράν.» Καὶ πάλιν: «Ἐγενήθην ὡσεὶ ἄνθρωπος ἀβοήθητος, ἐν νεκροῖς ἐλεύθερος.» Τίς δὲ ἐλεύθερος θανάτου, εἰ μὴ ὁ Θεός; Γέγονε γὰρ ὡσεὶ ἄνθρωπος ἀβοήθητος, ταπεινώσας τὴν ἑαυτοῦ σάρκα μέχρι θανάτου, θανάτου δὲ σταυροῦ. Ἡσαΐας: «Ἰδοὺ τίθημι ἐν Σιὼν λίθον ἀκρογωνιαῖον, ἐκλεκτόν, ἔντιμον· καὶ ὁ πιστεύων εἰς αὐτὸν οὐ καταισχυνθήσεται.» Γέγονε γὰρ εἰς κεφαλὴν γωνίας, ἑτέρας δηλαδὴ οἰκοδομῆς τῆς κατὰ τὴν Ἐκκλησίαν, ἥτις ἐστὶ θαυμαστὴ ἐπὶ ὀφθαλμοῖς ἡμῶν.

Θ'. Περὶ τῆς ἀναλήψεως.

Δαβίδ: «Ἀνέβη ὁ Θεὸς ἐν ἀλαλαγμῷ, Κύριος ἐν φωνῇ σάλπιγγος.» Ὅτι δὲ περὶ τοῦ Σωτῆρος ἡμῶν λέλεκται, Δανιὴλ λέγει: «Ἐθεώρουν,»

"Arise, O Lord, help us, and redeem us for the sake of your name" (Ps 43:27).[150]

And again:

"Arise, O Lord, judge the earth, for you will inherit in all the nations" (Ps 81:8).[151]

Isaiah:

"'Now I will arise,' says the Lord, 'now I will be glorified, now I will be raised up, now you will see, now you will be saved. The strength of your spirit is in vain'"[152] (Isa 33:10–11).[153]

Hosea:

"And they will seek my face in their distress,[154] and they will rise early before me, saying, 'Let us go and turn back to the Lord our God, for he has despoiled, yet he will heal us.[155] He will strike, and he will bind us up. He will heal us after two days. On the third day, we will rise up[156] before him, and we will know him; let us pursue knowing the Lord, so that we will find him prepared in the early morning'" (Hos 5:15b; 6:1–3a).[157]

David:

"Because you will not abandon my soul to the underworld, nor will you allow your holy one to see corruption" (Ps 15:10).[158]

And again:

"I became like a helpless person, free among the dead" (Ps 87:5).[159]

Yet who is free from death except God? For he became like a helpless human, humbling his own flesh until the point of death, death on a cross (cf. Phil 2:8).

Isaiah:

"Behold, I am placing in Zion a cornerstone, select and precious. And the one trusting in it will not be put to shame" (Isa 28:16; cf. 1 Pet 2:6).[160]

For he became "the head of the corner," that is, clearly of another building near the church, "which is marvelous in our eyes" (cf. Ps 117:22–23).[161]

Chapter 9: Concerning the ascension

David:

"God arose with a loud noise; the Lord with the sound of a trumpet" (Ps 46:6).[162]

That it was said of our Savior, Daniel says:

φησί: «καὶ ἰδοὺ θρόνοι ἐτέθησαν, καὶ Παλαιὸς ἡμερῶν ἐκάθητο.» Καὶ μετά τινα: «Καὶ ἰδοὺ μετὰ τῶν νεφελῶν τοῦ οὐρανοῦ, ὡς Υἱὸς ἀνθρώπου ἐρχόμενος· καὶ ἕως τοῦ Παλαιοῦ τῶν ἡμερῶν ἔφθασε, καὶ προσήχθη· αὐτῷ ἐδόθη ἡ τιμή, καὶ ἡ ἀρχή, καὶ ἡ βασιλεία· καὶ πάντες οἱ λαοί, φυλαί, καὶ γλῶσσαι δουλεύσουσιν αὐτῷ· ἡ ἐξουσία αὐτοῦ, ἐξουσία αἰώνιος, ἥτις οὐ παρελεύσει, καὶ ἡ βασιλεία αὐτοῦ οὐ διαφθαρήσεται.» Καὶ ἀλλαχοῦ Δαβίδ: «Εἶπεν ὁ Κύριος τῷ Κυρίῳ μου· Κάθου ἐκ δεξιῶν μου, ἕως ἂν θῶ τοὺς ἐχθρούς σου ὑποπόδιον τῶν ποδῶν σου.»

Ι'. Περὶ τῆς δόξης τῆς Ἐκκλησίας.

Δαβίδ: «Παρέστη ἡ βασίλισσα ἐκ δεξιῶν σου, ἐν ἱματισμῷ διαχρύσῳ, περιβεβλημένη, πεποικιλμένη.»

ΙΑ'. Περὶ τῆς περιτομῆς.

Ἐροῦσι δὲ πάντες οἱ Ἰουδαῖοι, ὅτι Εἰ τὸν αὐτὸν Θεὸν σέβεσθε, τί μὴ περιτέμνεσθε, ἢ ζῶα προσφέρετε εἰς θυσίαν, ἢ σαββατίζετε, τῶν Γραφῶν περὶ τούτων διαγορευουσῶν; Ἀκούσονται οὖν, ὅτι ἡ περιτομὴ οὐκ ἦν ἐξ ἀρχῆς, ἀλλ' ἐν χρόνῳ ἐγένετο, ὡς καὶ ἐν χρόνῳ παυσομένη· ἔπειτα, ὅτι ὁ Θεὸς διαταξάμενος τοῖς πατράσι τὴν περιτομήν, αὐτὸς εἶπεν: «Ἰδοὺ ἡμέραι ἔρχονται, λέγει Κύριος, καὶ διαθήσομαι τῷ οἴκῳ Ἰσραὴλ διαθήκην καινήν, οὐ κατὰ τὴν διαθήκην, ἣν διεθέμην τοῖς πατράσιν αὐτῶν, ἐπιλαβομένου μου τῆς χειρὸς αὐτῶν, τοῦ ἐξαγαγεῖν αὐτοὺς ἐκ γῆς Αἰγύπτου, ὅτι αὐτοὶ οὐκ ἐνέμειναν τῇ διαθήκῃ μου, κἀγὼ ἠμέλησα αὐτῶν, λέγει Κύριος.» Καὶ πάλιν, αἰτιώμενος τοὺς Ἰουδαίους, λέγει: «Πάντα | τὰ ἔθνη ἀπερίτμητα σαρκί, ὁ δὲ λαὸς οὗτος τῇ καρδίᾳ.» Καὶ πάλιν: «Περιτέμνεσθε τὴν καρδίαν ὑμῶν, καὶ μὴ τὴν σάρκα τῆς ἀκροβυστίας ὑμῶν.» Καὶ πάλιν: «Νεώσατε ἑαυτοῖς

"'I was watching,' he says, 'and look: thrones were set,[163] and the Ancient of Days sat down'" (Dan 7:9).[164]

And after a bit:

"And look! He is coming with the clouds of heaven, like a son of man. He came first to the Ancient of Days, and was presented. To him was given the honor, the rule, and the kingdom. And all the peoples, tribes, and tongues will serve him. His authority is an eternal authority which will not pass away, and his kingdom will not be destroyed" (Dan 7:13–14).[165]

And elsewhere, David:

"The Lord said to my Lord, 'Sit at my right until I place your enemies under your feet'" (Ps 109:1).[166]

Chapter 10: Concerning the glory of the church

David:

"The queen stood at your right, dressed and adorned in clothing interwoven with gold" (Ps 44:10b).[167]

Chapter 11: Concerning circumcision

All the Jews will say, "If you worship the same God, why are you not circumcised, or offer animals in sacrifice, or observe the Sabbath, since the scriptures speak clearly concerning these things?" They will hear, then,[168] that circumcision did not exist from the beginning, but arose in time, just as it will cease in time. Then [they will hear that] God, after having ordained circumcision for the fathers, himself said, "'Behold, the days are coming,' says the Lord, 'and I will make a new covenant with the house[169] of Israel, not on the basis of the covenant that I made with their fathers,[170] when I grasped their hand[171] to lead them out of the land of Egypt. For they did not remain in my covenant, and I have ceased to care for them,' says the Lord" (Jer 38:31–32).[172]

And again, censuring the Jews, he says,

"All the nations are uncircumcised in regard to the flesh, yet this people is uncircumcised in regards to the heart" (Jer 9:26).[173]

And again:

"Circumcise your heart, and not the flesh of your foreskin" (Uncertain quotation; cf. Jer 4:4a and Deut 10:16).[174]

And again:[175]

νεώματα, καὶ μὴ σπείρετε ἐπ' ἀκάνθαις· ἀλλὰ περιτέμνεσθε τὸ σκληρὸν τῆς καρδίας ὑμῶν.» Ἰερεμίας: «Καὶ περιτέμνεσθε τῷ Θεῷ τὴν ἀκροβυστίαν τῆς καρδίας ὑμῶν.» Ὅτι δὲ οὐδένα δικαιοῖ ἡ περιτομή, δῆλον ἐκ τούτων· Ἀβραὰμ ἀπερίτμητος εὐηρέστησε τῷ Θεῷ· πρῶτον γὰρ ὤφθη εὐαρεστῶν, καὶ τότε αὐτῷ τὴν περιτομὴν δίδωσι. Καὶ οἱ ἐν τῇ ἐρήμῳ δὲ γεννηθέντες ἐν τοῖς τεσσαράκοντα ἔτεσιν ἀπερίτμητοι ἦσαν· καὶ οἱ ἀπὸ Ἀδὰμ ὁμοίως ἕως Ἀβραὰμ εὐηρέστησαν τῷ Θεῷ, πάντες ἀπερίτμητοι ἦσαν· διὰ γὰρ τὸ ἐπιμίγνυσθαι τὸν λαὸν εἰς τὰ ἔθνη, ἐδόθη ἡ περιτομή, καὶ ἡ αἰτία δήλη· εἴληφε γὰρ τὴν ἀρχὴν τὰ τῆς περιτομῆς ἐκ τοῦ Ἀβραάμ, ὃν ἀγαπήσας ὑπὲρ πάντας τοὺς τότε ὁ Θεός, ἐξ αὐτοῦ γεννηθήσεσθαι καὶ τὸν Χριστὸν κατὰ σάρκα προέθετο. Ἵνα οὖν ὅπερ ἐβουλήθη καθαρῶς γενέσθαι δυνηθῇ καὶ ἀνοθεύτως, τούτου χάριν ἐδέησε περιτομῆς, καὶ τῆς περὶ τὰ λοιπὰ γένη ἀμιξίας, ἵνα ὥσπερ τι διάφραγμα, τῶν λοιπῶν αὐτοὺς ἀνθρώπων χωρίζῃ ὁ νόμος. Ὅθεν καὶ τεχθέντος τοῦ δι' ὃν ταῦτα γέγονε, λοιπὸν ὡς περιττὰ τῷ Θεῷ τὰ παρὰ τὴν ἀρχαίαν ξενίζοντα κατάστασιν ἐκβέβληνται.

ΙΒ'. Περὶ θυσιῶν.

Ὁμοίως ὁ Θεὸς βοᾷ, λέγων· «Ζῶ ἐγώ, λέγει Κύριος, ὅτι περὶ θυσιῶν, καὶ ὁλοκαυτωμάτων οὐκ ἐνετειλάμην πρὸς τοὺς πατέρας ὑμῶν, ἀφ' ἧς ἡμέρας ἀνήγαγον αὐτοὺς ἐκ γῆς Αἰγύπτου, καὶ ἕως τῆς ἡμέρας ταύτης.» Ἡσαΐας: «Μὴ ἐγὼ ἐνετειλάμην τοῖς πατράσιν ὑμῶν, ἐκπορευομένοις ἐκ γῆς Αἰγύπτου προσενεγκεῖν μοι ὁλοκαυτώματα καὶ θυσίαν;» Καὶ πάλιν: «Τί μοι πλῆθος τῶν θυσιῶν ὑμῶν; λέγει Κύριος· πλήρης εἰμὶ ὁλοκαυτωμάτων κριῶν, καὶ στέαρ ἀρνῶν καὶ αἷμα ταύρων καὶ τράγων οὐ βούλομαι· οὐδ' ἂν ἔρχησθε ὀφθῆναί μοι. Τίς γὰρ ἐξεζήτησε ταῦτα ἐκ τῶν χειρῶν ὑμῶν; πατεῖν τὴν αὐλήν μου οὐ

"Renew for yourself newly plowed fields, and do not sow upon thorns, but rather circumcise the hardness of your hearts" (Jer 4:3b; Deut 10:16).[176]

Jeremiah:[177]

"And circumcise before God the foreskin of your heart" (Jer 4:4a).[178]

That circumcision justifies no one is clear from these things.

Abraham, when he was uncircumcised, was acceptable to God.[179] For first he was seen as acceptable, and then he [God] gives circumcision to him.

And those born in the desert during the forty years were uncircumcised. And similarly those from Adam until Abraham were acceptable to God: all were uncircumcised. For circumcision was given on account of the mixing of the people with the nations; its cause is clear. For the matters involved in circumcision received their beginning from [the time of] Abraham; since God loved him above all others at that time, he determined that Christ too should be born according to the flesh from him.

In order that what he wished might take place purely and without contamination, for this reason there was need of circumcision and lack of mixing with other races, so that, like some barrier, the law might separate them from other humans.[180] Therefore, after he was born for whom these things occurred, the strange things [that prevailed] during the old order were then thrown out as superfluous to God.

CHAPTER 12: CONCERNING SACRIFICES

In the same way God called out, saying:

"'As I live,' says the Lord, 'I did not command your fathers concerning sacrifices and holocausts from the day on which I led them out from the land of Egypt, until this day'" (Jer 7:22).[181]

Isaiah:

"When they were going out from the land of Egypt, did I command your fathers to offer[182] me holocausts and sacrifices?"(Jer 7:22).

And again:

"'What is the heap of your sacrifices to me?' says the Lord. 'I am full of the holocausts of rams; I do not want the fat of lambs and the blood of bulls and goats.[183] Nor shall you come to appear before me. For who sought these things from your hands? You

προσθήσεσθε. Ἐὰν φέρητέ μοι σεμίδαλιν, μάταιον. Θυμίαμα βδέλυγμά μοι ἐστί. Τὰς νεομηνίας ὑμῶν, καὶ τὰ Σάββατα ὑμῶν, καὶ ἡμέραν μεγάλην οὐκ ἀνέχομαι· νηστείαν, καὶ ἀργίαν, καὶ τὰς ἑορτὰς ὑμῶν, μισεῖ ἡ ψυχή μου.» Καὶ πάλιν: «Λούσασθε, καὶ καθαροὶ γίνεσθε, ἀφέλετε | τὰς πονηρίας ἀπὸ τῶν ψυχῶν ὑμῶν.» Δαβίδ: «Οὐ φάγομαι κρέα ταύρων, ἢ αἷμα τράγων πίομαι.» Καὶ πάλιν: «Οὐ δέξομαι ἐκ τοῦ οἴκου σου μόσχους, οὐδὲ ἐκ τῶν ποιμνίων σου χιμάρους.» Καὶ πάλιν: «Θῦσον τῷ Θεῷ θυσίαν αἰνέσεως.» Ἀμώς: «Μεμίσηκα, ἀπῶσμαι τὰς ἑορτὰς ὑμῶν, (καὶ οὐ μὴ ὀσφρανθῶ ἐν ταῖς πανηγύρεσιν ὑμῶν· διότι καὶ ἐὰν ἐνέγκητέ μοι ὁλοκαυτώματα καὶ θυσίας ὑμῶν,) οὐ προσδέξομαι αὐτά, καὶ σωτηρίου ἐπιφανείας ὑμῶν οὐκ ἐπιβλέψομαι. Μετάστησον ἀπ' ἐμοῦ ἦχον ᾠδῶν σου, καὶ ψαλμὸν ὀργάνων οὐκ ἀκούσομαι.» Μαλαχίας: «Οὐκ ἔστι μου θέλημα ἐν ὑμῖν, λέγει Κύριος παντοκράτωρ, καὶ θυσίαν οὐ προσδέξομαι ἐκ τῶν χειρῶν ὑμῶν, διότι ἀπὸ ἀνατολῶν ἡλίου, καὶ ἕως δυσμῶν τὸ ὄνομά μου δεδόξασται ἐν τοῖς ἔθνεσι, καὶ ἐν παντὶ τόπῳ θυμίαμα προσφέρεται τῷ ὀνόματί μου, καὶ θυσία καθαρά· διότι μέγα τὸ ὄνομά μου ἐν τοῖς ἔθνεσι, λέγει Κύριος παντοκράτωρ.»

ΙΓ'. Περὶ τοῦ Σαββατίζειν.

Τὸ Σάββατον ἐδόθη αὐτοῖς, τοῦ καταπαῦσαι τὴν φιλοχρήματον αὐτῶν ἐπιθυμίαν. Τοῦ λαοῦ γὰρ πενομένου, ἐξελθόντος ἐκ τῆς Αἰγύπτου, καὶ μηδὲν ἔχοντος, πλὴν ὧν ἐχρήσαντο παρὰ τῶν Αἰγυπτίων, σπουδὴν ἐποιεῖτο ἕκαστος διὰ τοῦ ἀνενδότου πόνου πλοῦτον ἑαυτῷ περιποιῆσαι. Διὸ λέγει: «Ἓξ ἡμέρας ἐργᾷ· τῇ δὲ ἡμέρᾳ τῇ ἑβδόμῃ οὐ ποιήσεις πᾶν ἔργον ἐν αὐτῇ.» Καὶ τὴν αἰτίαν ἐπιφέρει, ἵνα ἀναπαύσῃ σύ, καὶ ἡ γυνή σου, καὶ ὁ υἱός σου, καὶ ἡ θυγάτηρ σου, καὶ ὁ παῖς σου, καὶ

will not continue to walk in my court. If you bring me fine wheat flour, it is in vain. Incense is an abomination to me.[184] I cannot bear your new moons, and your Sabbaths, and the "great day"! My soul hates your fast, and day of rest, and festivals'" (Isa 1:11–14).[185]

And again:[186]

"Wash yourselves, and be clean. Take away the wickedness from your souls" (Isa 1:16).[187]

David:

"I will not eat the meat of bulls, or drink the blood of goats" (Ps 49:13).[188]

And again:

"I will not accept calves from your house, nor goats from your flocks" (Ps 49:9).[189]

And again:

"Sacrifice to God a sacrifice of praise" (Ps 49:14a).[190]

Amos:

"I have hated, I have rejected your festivals. (And I will not smell in your assemblies. Because even if you bring me your holocausts and sacrifices),[191] I will not accept them, and I will not look upon the outward appearances of your peace-offering.[192] Take away from me the sound of your songs; I will not listen to a psalm of instruments" (Amos 5:21–23).[193]

Malachi:

"'I take no pleasure in you,' says the Lord almighty, 'and I will not accept a sacrifice from your hands, since from the rising of the sun until its setting my name has been glorified among the nations, and in every place incense is offered in my name, along with pure sacrifice, because my name is great among the nations,' says the Lord almighty" (Mal 1:10b–11).[194]

CHAPTER 13: CONCERNING KEEPING THE SABBATH

The Sabbath was given to them in order to check their desire for money.[195] For since they were a poor people when they came out of Egypt, having nothing except that which they borrowed from the Egyptians, each one made an effort, through hard labor, to save up riches for himself.[196] Therefore he says, "Work for six days, but on the seventh day you will not do any work on it" (Exod 20:9–10).[197] And he provides the reason: so that you might rest, and your wife, and your son, and your daughter, and your

ἡ παιδίσκη σου, ὁ βοῦς σου, καὶ τὸ ὑποζύγιόν σου. Ἐπεί τοι τίνος
ἕνεκεν ὁ Ἰησοῦς ὁ τοῦ Ναυῆ κυκλῶν τὴν Ἱεριχὼ μετὰ σαλπίγγων ἐπὶ
ἑπτὰ ἡμέρας, οὐκ ἐσχόλασε τῷ Σαββάτῳ; Πῶς δὲ τῇ ὀγδόῃ ἡμέρᾳ
περιτέμνεται παιδίον; Διὰ τί δὲ ἐν ἡμέρᾳ Σαββάτου τίκτει γυνή; Πῶς
δὲ καὶ οἱ ἱερεῖς πᾶσαν θυσίαν ἐν Σαββάτῳ ποιοῦσι; Πῶς δὲ ἥλιος, καὶ
σελήνη, καὶ ἄστρα τὸν ὡρισμένον δρόμον ἐκτελεῖ καὶ τῷ Σαββάτῳ;

ΙΔ'. Περὶ τοῦ κατασφραγίζεσθαι.

Δαβίδ: «Ἐσημειώθη ἐφ' ἡμᾶς τὸ φῶς τοῦ προσώπου σου, Κύριε.»
Καὶ πάλιν: «Ποίησον μετ' ἐμοῦ σημεῖον εἰς ἀγαθόν· καὶ ἰδέτωσαν
οἱ μισοῦντές με, καὶ αἰσχυνθήτωσαν, ὅτι σύ, Κύριε, ἐβοήθησάς μοι
καὶ παρεκάλεσάς με.» Καὶ πάλιν: «Ἔδωκας τοῖς | φοβουμένοις σε
σημείωσιν, τοῦ φυγεῖν ἀπὸ προσώπου τόξου.» Ἰεζεκιήλ: «Υἱὲ ἀνθρώπου, δίελθε μέσον τὴν Ἱερουσαλήμ, καὶ δὸς τὸ σημεῖον ἐπὶ τὰ μέτωπα
τῶν ἀνθρώπων τῶν στεναζόντων καὶ κατωδυνωμένων ἐπὶ ταῖς ἀδικίαις
ταῖς γινομέναις ἐν μέσῳ αὐτῶν.» Καὶ πάλιν: «Ἓξ ἄνδρες ἤρχοντο
ἀπὸ τῆς πύλης τῆς βλεπούσης πρὸς βορρᾶν, καὶ ἑκάστου ἡ πέλυξ ἐν
τῇ χειρὶ αὐτοῦ· ἀκούοντες πορεύεσθε εἰς τὴν πόλιν, καὶ κόπτετε, καὶ
μὴ φείσασθε τοῖς ὀφθαλμοῖς ὑμῶν, καὶ μὴ ἐλεήσητε· πρεσβύτερον, καὶ
νεανίσκον, καὶ παρθένον, καὶ νήπια, καὶ γυναῖκας ἀποκτείνατε εἰς ἐξ-
άλειψιν· ἐπὶ δὲ πάντας, ἐφ' οὓς ἐστι τὸ σημεῖόν μου, μὴ ἐγγίσητε.»
Περὶ δὲ τοῦ θύειν αὐτοὺς εἴρηται, οὐχ ὅτι ὁ Θεὸς ἐδεῖτο θυσιῶν, ἢ
ὁλοκαυτωμάτων, ἀλλ' ἐπειδὴ ἡ Λευϊτικὴ φυλὴ οὐκ εἶχε κλῆρον ἐν τῇ
γῇ τῆς ἐπαγγελίας, ὅτι αὐτὸς ὁ Θεὸς κλῆρος αὐτῆς, ταύτην ἔδωκεν
αὐτοῖς εἰς τὸ τρέφεσθαι πρόφασιν· οὐκ ἐβούλετο γὰρ αὐτοὺς ἱερατεύον-
τας ἀπὸ πόνου καὶ πραγματείας, ἤγουν καπηλείας, τρέφεσθαι.

male servant and your female servant,[198] your cattle, and your beast of burden. Indeed, for what reason, when Joshua [Jesus], son of Nave, was circling Jericho with trumpets for seven days, did he not rest on the Sabbath? How then is a boy circumcised on the eighth day? Why then does a woman give birth on the day of the Sabbath? How then do the priests perform every sacrifice on the Sabbath? How then do the sun, the moon, and stars complete their appointed course even on the Sabbath?

Chapter 14: Concerning sealing with the sign of the cross

David:[199]

"The light of your face was stamped upon us, O Lord" (Ps 4:7b).[200]

And again:

"Make with me a sign for good. And let the ones who hate me see [it], and let them be ashamed, because you, O Lord, helped me and comforted me" (Ps 85:17).[201]

And again:

"You gave a sign to those who fear you, to flee from the presence of a bow" (Ps 59:6).[202]

Ezekiel:

"Son of man, go through the middle of Jerusalem, and place the sign upon the forehead of those people that groan and grieve for the unrighteous deeds that occur in their midst" (Ezek 9:4).[203]

And again:

"Six men were coming from the gate that faces north, and there was an ax in the hand of each.[204] When you hear, go into the city and strike, do not let your eyes spare [anyone], and do not have mercy. Annihilate completely the elder, and the youth, and the girl, and the infants, and the women.[205] But do not go near all those upon whom my sign lies" (Ezek 9:2, 5–6).[206]

Yet God spoke about their sacrificing, not because he needed sacrifices or holocausts, but because the tribe of the Levites did not have a portion in the land of the promise, since God himself is [the tribe's] portion; he gave this pretext to them for their support. He did not want them, since they were priests, to be supported by toil and business, that is, trading.

ΙΕ'. *Περὶ τοῦ Εὐαγγελίου.*

Δαβίδ: «Κύριος δώσει ῥῆμα τοῖς εὐαγγελιζομένοις δυνάμει πολλῇ.»
Καὶ πάλιν: «Ὡς ὡραῖοι οἱ πόδες τῶν εὐαγγελιζομένων εἰρήνην.»

ΙϚ'. *Περὶ τῆς ἀπιστίας τῶν Ἰουδαίων,
καὶ περὶ τῶν ἐθνῶν Ἐκκλησίας.*

Ἡσαΐας ἐκ προσώπου τοῦ Θεοῦ: «Οὔτε ἔγνως, οὔτε ἠπίστασο, οὔτε ἀπ' ἀρχῆς ἤνοιξά σου τὰ ὦτα· ᾔδειν γάρ, ὅτι ἀπειθῶν ἀπειθήσεις.» Καὶ πάλιν: «Μέγα τὸ ὄνομα αὐτοῦ ἐν τοῖς ἔθνεσι καὶ ἐν παντὶ τόπῳ θυμίαμα προσφέρεται τῷ ὀνόματί μου, καὶ θυσία καθαρά.» Μιχαίας: «Καὶ ἔσται ἐπ' ἐσχάτων τῶν ἡμερῶν ἐμφανὲς τὸ ὄρος Κυρίου, ἕτοιμον ἐπὶ τὰς κορυφὰς τῶν ὀρέων, καὶ μετεωρισθήσεται ὑπεράνω τῶν βουνῶν· καὶ σπεύσουσι πρὸς αὐτὸ λαοί, καὶ πορεύσονται ἔθνη πολλά, καὶ ἐροῦσι, Δεῦτε ἀναβῶμεν εἰς τὸ ὄρος Κυρίου, καὶ εἰς τὸν οἶκον τοῦ Θεοῦ Ἰακώβ· καὶ φωτιοῦσιν ἡμᾶς ταῖς ὁδοῖς αὐτοῦ· ὅτι ἐκ Σιὼν ἐξελεύσεται νόμος, καὶ λόγος Κυρίου ἐξ Ἱερουσαλήμ.» Ἱερεμίας: «Καὶ εἶπε Κύριος πρός με, ἰδοὺ δέδωκα τοὺς λόγους μου ἐν τῷ στόματί σου· ἰδοὺ κατέστησά σε σήμερον ἐπ' ἔθνη, καὶ βασιλεῖς ἐκριζοῦν, καὶ κατακόπτειν, καὶ ἀπολλύειν, καὶ ἀνοικοδομεῖν, καὶ καταφυτεύειν.» Καὶ εἰ ταῦτα περὶ Ἱερεμίου, ποίας βασιλείας ἐξερρίζωσεν, ἢ ποῖα ἔθνη ἀπώλεσεν; Ἀλλὰ περὶ τοῦ Κυρίου εἴρηται, ἐκριζώσαντος ἀπὸ πάσης ψυχῆς πιστευούσης αὐτῷ τὴν βασιλείαν τοῦ Ἀντικειμένου, ὃς κατέστρεψε τὰ οἰκοδομήματα τῆς κακίας, καὶ τῶν μοχθηρῶν δογμάτων, καταφυτεύσας τὰ κρείττονα. Δαβίδ: «Ῥῦσαί με ἐξ ἀντιλογίας λαοῦ,

Chapter 15: Concerning the Gospel

David:

"The Lord will give a word to the ones who announce the good news with great power" (Ps 67:12).[207]

And again:

"How beautiful are the feet of those who announce the good news of peace!" (Isa 52:7; cf. Rom 10:15)[208]

Chapter 16: Concerning the unbelief of the Jews, and concerning the church of the nations

Isaiah, [speaking] in the person of God:

"You did not know, nor did you understand, nor, from the beginning, did I open[209] your ears. For I knew that you would be continually disobedient" (Isa 48:8).[210]

And again:

"His name is great among the nations[211] and in every place incense is offered in my name, and a pure sacrifice" (Mal 1:11).[212]

Micah:

"And in the last days, the mountain of the Lord will be manifest, prepared upon the peaks of the mountains, and it will be raised above the hills. And the peoples will hurry[213] to it, and many nations will go, and will say, 'Come, let us go up to the mountain of the Lord, and into the house of the God of Jacob. And they will enlighten us in his ways. For the law will come forth from Zion, and the word of the Lord from Jerusalem" (Mic 4:1–2).[214]

Jeremiah:

"And the Lord said to me, 'Look! I have placed my words in your mouth. Look! I have appointed you today over the nations, to root out kings, and to cut to pieces, and to destroy, and to build up, and to plant" (Jer 1:9b–10).[215]

And if these things refer to Jeremiah, what kingdoms did he root out,[216] or what nations did he destroy? But it was said concerning the Lord, since he rooted out the kingdom of the Adversary from every soul that believes in him; the one who overturned the edifices of evil and of wicked beliefs[217] while planting better ones.

David:

καταστήσεις με εἰς κεφαλὴν ἐθνῶν. Λαός, ὃν οὐκ ἔγνων, ἐδούλευσέ
μοι· εἰς ἀκοὴν ὠτίου ὑπήκουσέ μου· υἱοὶ ἀλλότριοι ἐψεύσαντό μοι·
υἱοὶ ἀλλότριοι ἐπαλαιώθησαν καὶ ἐχώλαναν ἀπὸ τῶν τρίβων αὐτῶν.»
Μωϋσῆς ἐκ προσώπου τοῦ Θεοῦ πρὸς Ἀβραάμ: «Καὶ ἐνευλογηθήσον
ται ἐν σοὶ πάντα τὰ πέρατα τῆς γῆς.» Καὶ πάλιν: «Ἀποστρέψω τὸ
πρόσωπόν μου ἀπ' αὐτῶν, καὶ δείξω τί ἔσται αὐτοῖς ἐπ' ἐσχάτων, ὅτι
γενεὰ ἐξεστραμμένη ἐστίν. Υἱοὶ οἷς οὐκ ἔστι πίστις ἐν αὐτοῖς· αὐτοὶ
παρεζήλωσάν με ἐπ' οὐ Θεῷ, παρώργισάν με ἐν τοῖς εἰδώλοις αὐτῶν,
κἀγὼ παραζηλώσω αὐτοὺς ἐπ' οὐκ ἔθνει· ἐπ' ἔθνει ἀσυνέτῳ παροργιῶ
αὐτούς.» Καὶ ἀλλαχοῦ: «Δώσει,» φησίν: «τοὺς πονηροὺς ἀντὶ τῆς
ταφῆς αὐτοῦ.» Ἡσαΐας: «Ἐμφανὴς ἐγενόμην τοῖς ἐμὲ μὴ ζητοῦσιν,
εὑρέθην τοῖς ἐμὲ μὴ ἐπερωτῶσιν. (Εἶπα, Ἰδοὺ πάρειμι ἔθνει, οἳ οὐκ
ἐπεκαλέσαντο τὸ ὄνομά μου.») Δαβίδ: «Ἀπηλλοτριωμένος ἐγενήθην
τοῖς ἀδελφοῖς μου, καὶ ξένος τοῖς υἱοῖς τῆς μητρός μου.» Περὶ δὲ τῶν
ἐθνῶν λέγει: «Ἀπαγγελῶ τὸ ὄνομά σου τοῖς ἀδελφοῖς μου, ἐν μέσῳ
Ἐκκλησίας ὑμνήσω σε.» Περὶ Ἰουδαίων: «Δι' ὑμᾶς βλασφημεῖται τὸ
ὄνομά μου διὰ παντὸς ἐν τοῖς ἔθνεσι.» Μαλαχίας: «Οὐκ ἔστι μου θέ
λημα ἐν ὑμῖν, λέγει Κύριος παντοκράτωρ.» (Περὶ Ἐθνῶν δέ: «Ὅτι
ἀπὸ ἀνατολῶν ἡλίου μέχρι δυσμῶν τὸ ὄνομά μου δεδόξασται ἐν τοῖς
Ἔθνεσι, λέγει Κύριος παντοκράτωρ·») «καὶ ἐν παντὶ τόπῳ θυμίαμα

"Rescue me from the conflict of the people; you will appoint me as the head of the nations. A people, whom I did not know, was a slave to me. When they heard, they obeyed me. Foreign sons deceived me.[218] Foreign sons grew old and limped from their paths" (Ps 17:44–46).[219]

Moses, [speaking] in the person of God, to Abraham:
"And all the ends of the earth will be blessed in you" (Gen 12:3).[220]

And again:
"I will turn my face away from them, and I will show what will happen to them in the last [days], because they are a perverse generation." There are sons among them who have no faith. They made me jealous of what is not God, they made me angry with their idols, and I will make them jealous of what is not a nation; I will make them angry with a senseless nation" (Deut 32:20–21).[221]

And elsewhere:
"'He will give' he says, 'the wicked in return for his burial" (Isa 53:9).[222]

Isaiah:
"I became manifest to those who were not seeking me; I was found by those who were not asking for me" (Isa 65:1a).[223]

(I said, "Look! I have come to a nation[224] that did not call upon my name" [Isa 65:1b]).[225]

David:
"I became estranged from my brothers, and a stranger to the sons of my mother" (Ps 68:9).[226]

Yet concerning the nations he says:
"I will announce your name to my brothers, in the midst of the assembly I will sing of you" (Ps 21:23).[227]

Concerning the Jews:
"Because of you my name is blasphemed continually among the nations" (Isa 52:5b).[228]

Malachi:
"'I take no pleasure in you,' says the Lord almighty" (Mal 1:10b).[229]

(But concerning the nations:
"'Because from the rising of the sun until its setting my name has been glorified among the nations,' says the Lord almighty),[230] 'and in every place incense is brought in my name, and my name is great among the nations,' says the Lord almighty" (Mal 1:11).[231]

προσάγεται τῷ ὀνόματί μου, καὶ μέγα τὸ ὄνομά μου ἐν τοῖς Ἔθνεσι, λέγει Κύριος παντοκράτωρ.» (Περὶ δὲ Ἰουδαίων λέγει:) «Ὑμεῖς δὲ βεβηλοῦτε αὐτό.» Δαβίδ: «Αἴτησαι παρ' ἐμοῦ, καὶ δώσω σοι ἔθνη τὴν κληρονομίαν σου, καὶ τὴν κατάσχεσίν σου τὰ πέρατα τῆς γῆς.» Μωϋσῆς: «Ἔασόν με ἐξαλεῖψαι τὸν λαὸν τοῦτον, καὶ δώσω σοι ἔθνος μέγα, καὶ πολύ | μᾶλλον τούτου.» Ἡσαΐας περὶ Ἰουδαίων: «Ἀκούετε λόγον Κυρίου υἱοὶ Σοδόμων· προσέχετε νόμον Θεοῦ, λαὸς Γομόρρας.» Καὶ πάλιν: «Τὰ Σάββατα ὑμῶν, καὶ τὰς νεομηνίας μισεῖ ἡ ψυχή μου· καὶ τὰς εὐχὰς ὑμῶν οὐ προσδέξομαι· λούσασθε, καθαροὶ γίνεσθε· αἱ χεῖρες ὑμῶν μεμολυσμέναι αἵματι.» Καὶ ὅτι τοῦ νόμου σαφῶς διαγορεύοντος τὸ μὴ δεῖν ἔξω Ἱερουσαλὴμ καὶ τοῦ ναοῦ ἑορτάζειν κατὰ τό: «Σοὶ πρέπει ὕμνος, ὁ Θεός, ἐν Σιών· καὶ σοὶ ἀποδοθήσεται εὐχὴ ἐν Ἱερουσαλήμ,» γέγραπται: «Ὅτι προσκυνήσουσι τῷ Κυρίῳ ἐκ τοῦ τόπου αὐτοῦ ἕκαστος.» Καὶ πάλιν ὁ Προφήτης: «Μέγα τὸ ὄνομα αὐτοῦ ἐν τοῖς Ἔθνεσι, καὶ ἐν παντὶ τόπῳ θυμίαμα προσφέρεται τῷ ὀνόματι αὐτοῦ, καὶ θυσία καθαρά.» «Ὑμᾶς δὲ ἀνελεῖ Κύριος· τοῖς δὲ δουλεύουσί μοι κληθήσεται ὄνομα καινόν, ὃ εὐλογηθήσεται ἐπὶ πάσης τῆς γῆς.» Τί δὲ καινότερον τοῦ τῶν Χριστιανῶν ὀνόματος; Καὶ ὁ Δαβίδ: «Ἀναγγελοῦσι τὴν δικαιοσύνην αὐτοῦ λαῷ τῷ τεχθησομένῳ, ὃν ἐποίησεν ὁ Κύριος.» Καὶ ὅτι μὲν τὸ εἰπεῖν τὸν Δαβὶδ τό: «Ὁ Θεὸς κατοικίζει μονοτρόπους ἐν οἴκῳ,» σημαίνει τὸ πρὸς τὰ Ἔθνη τὸ τῶν ὑπὸ νόμον ἄμικτον. Ἡσαΐας: «Πληρωθήσεται πᾶσα ἡ γῆ τοῦ γνῶναι τὸν Κύριον, ὡς ὕδωρ πολὺ κατακαλῦψαι θάλασσαν.» Δαβίδ:

(Concerning the Jews he says:)[232]
"Yet you profane it" (Mal 1:12a).[233]

David:

"Ask of me, and I will give you the nations as your inheritance, and as your possession the ends of the earth" (Ps 2:8).[234]

Moses:

"Let me destroy this people, and I will give you a nation that is great, and much more so than this one" (Uncertain quotation; cf. Exod 32:10 and Deut 9:14).[235]

Isaiah, concerning the Jews:

"Hear the word of the Lord, sons of Sodom.[236] Pay attention to the law of God, people of Gomorrah" (Isa 1:10).[237]

And again:

"My soul hates your Sabbaths and the new moons, and your prayers I will not accept. Wash yourselves, become clean! Your hands are stained with blood" (Isa 1:13b–16).[238]

And as to the law clearly directing that one ought not to celebrate feast days outside of Jerusalem and the Temple, in accordance with the [words], "A hymn is fitting for you, O God, in Zion, and a prayer will be rendered to you in Jerusalem" (Ps 64:2),[239] it is written,

"That they will worship the Lord, each one from his place" (Zeph 2:11b).[240]

And again the prophet:

"Great is his name among the nations, and in every place incense is offered in his name, as well as a pure sacrifice" (Mal 1:11).[241]

"The Lord will destroy you, but those who serve me will be called by a new name, which will be blessed in all the earth" (Isa 65:15–16).[242]

Yet what is newer than the name of the Christians?

And David:

"They will report his righteousness to a people who will be born, whom the Lord has made" (Ps 21:32).[243]

And as to that which David said,[244] "God settles them alone in a house" (Ps 67:7a),[245] signifying the non-mixing of those under the law with the nations,

Isaiah [replies]:

"All the earth will be filled with the knowledge of the Lord, as much water covers the sea" (Isa 11:9b).[246]

«Μνησθήσονται καὶ ἐπιστραφήσονται πρὸς Κύριον πάντα τὰ πέρατα
τῆς γῆς, καὶ προσκυνήσουσιν ἐνώπιον αὐτοῦ πᾶσαι αἱ πατριαὶ τῶν
ἐθνῶν, ὅτι τοῦ Κυρίου ἡ βασιλεία, καὶ αὐτὸς δεσπόζει τῶν ἐθνῶν.»
Καλὸν δὲ καὶ τὸ πυθέσθαι τῶν Ἰουδαίων, τίς ὁ κρατῶν ἐστι νῦν ἄρα,
πότερον ὁ Μωσαϊκὸς νόμος, οὗ παράβασίς ἐστι νῦν, καὶ οὐ τήρησις,
διὰ τὸ μηδὲ τὸν ναόν, ἢ τὸν τόπον εἶναι, ἢ προφήτην προμηνύοντά τι
τῶν μελλόντων, ἢ τὴν κιβωτόν, ἐν ᾗ αἱ πλάκες, καὶ ἡ Δεκάλογος, ἐν
οἷς ἔδει τὰς τρεῖς ἑορτὰς πληροῦν, καὶ οὐκ ἀλλαχοῦ. Καί: «Ὅτι ἀρ-
θήσεται ἀπὸ τῶν Ἰουδαίων ἡ βασιλεία τοῦ Θεοῦ, καὶ δοθήσεται ἔθνει
ποιοῦντι τοὺς καρποὺς αὐτῆς.» Τοῦτο δ' ἂν εἴη τὸ Χριστιανῶν ἔθνος,
τοὺς προσήκοντας καρποὺς τῆς κατὰ Θεὸν πολιτείας ἐπιδεικνύμενον.
Δαβίδ: «Ἐξομολόγησις καὶ μεγαλοπρέπεια τὸ ἔργον αὐτοῦ, καὶ ἡ δικαιοσύνη αὐτοῦ μένει εἰς τὸν αἰῶνα τοῦ αἰῶνος.» Ἐξομολογεῖται δὲ
τῷ Πατρί, οὐ τὰς ἑαυτοῦ ἁμαρτίας ὁ ἄμωμος, ἀλλὰ τὰς τῶν ἐπ' αὐτῷ πιστευόντων· ὅτι τοῦ Δαβὶδ εἰπόντος: «Εἶπεν ὁ Κύριος τῷ Κυρίῳ
μου· Κάθου ἐκ δεξιῶν μου,» καὶ τὰ λοιπά, Ἡσαΐας σαφέστερον λέγει: «Λέγει ὁ Κύριος τῷ Χριστῷ μου Κύρῳ.» Λέγουσι δὲ εἰς Κῦρον
τὸν Πέρσην εἰρῆσθαι ταῦτα. Γελοῖον δέ· ποῦ γὰρ ἁρμόζει Κύρῳ τὰ
λοιπά: «Ἐκράτησα τῆς δεξιᾶς σου· ἐπακούσουσιν ἔμπροσθεν αὐτοῦ
ἔθνη, καὶ ἰσχὺν βασιλέων διαρρήξω· ἀνοίξω ἔμπροσθεν αὐτοῦ πύλας,
καὶ πόλεις οὐ συγκλεισθήσονται· ἔμπροσθέν σου πορεύσομαι, καὶ ὄρη
ὁμαλιῶ· θύρας χαλκᾶς συντρίψω, καὶ μοχλοὺς σιδηροῦς συνθλάσω, καὶ
δώσω σοι θησαυροὺς σκοτεινούς;» Πῶς οὖν ἁρμόσει ταῦτα Κύρῳ, τῷ
μικρὸν ὕστερον εἰς Μασαγέτας αἰσχρῶς ἀναιρεθέντι καὶ εἰς ἀσκὸν ἐκδαρέντι; καὶ μετὰ μικρὸν ἑρμηνεύει αὐτὰ ὁ αὐτὸς προφήτης, λέγων

David:

"All the ends of the earth will remember and turn back to the Lord, and all the families of the nations will worship before him, for the kingdom is the Lord's, and he himself is master of the nations" (Ps 21:28–29).[247]

It is also good to inquire from the Jews who the master is now;[248] whether it was the Mosaic law, from which transgression comes now,[249] and not observance, since the Temple no longer exists, nor its place, nor a prophet foretelling something of the things to come, nor the Ark in which were the tablets and the Decalogue [in which it was necessary to fulfill the three feast days, and not elsewhere].[250]

And:

"That the kingdom of God[251] will be taken away from the Jews and will be given to a nation that produces its fruits" (Matt 21:43).[252]

This would be the nation of Christians, who display the fitting fruits of a community in accord with God.

David:

"Confession and magnificence are his work, and his righteousness remains for ever" (Ps 110:3).[253]

Yet the blameless one [i.e., Jesus] confesses to the father not his own sins, but rather the ones of those who believe in him.

As for David having said:

"The Lord said to my Lord, sit at my right hand" (Ps 109:1)[254] and the rest,

Isaiah says more clearly:

"The Lord says to Cyrus my anointed one" (Isa 45:1).[255]

They say that these things were said to Cyrus the Persian. But that is laughable! For how does the following fit Cyrus: "I grasped your right hand.[256] The nations will be attentive before him, and I will shatter the might of kings. I will open gates before him, and cities will not be shut. I will go before you, and I will level mountains. I will break down brass doors, and I will crush iron bars. And I will give you hidden treasures" (Isa 45:1–3)?[257]

How then will these things fit Cyrus, who a little later was killed shamefully [fighting] against the Massagetes and was flayed into a wineskin? [258]

And after a bit the same prophet explains these same things, saying, in the person of God:

ἐκ προσώπου τοῦ Θεοῦ: «Ἐγὼ Κύριος ὁ Θεὸς ὁ καλέσας σε ἐν δικαιοσύνῃ· ἐκράτησα τῆς χειρός σου, καὶ ἰσχύσω σε, καὶ δώσω σε εἰς διαθήκην γένους, εἰς φῶς ἐθνῶν, ἀνοῖξαι ὀφθαλμοὺς τυφλῶν, καὶ ἐξαγαγεῖν ἐκ δεσμῶν πεπεδημένους, καὶ ἐξ οἴκου φυλακῆς καθημένους ἐν σκότει.» Καὶ πάλιν ὁ αὐτὸς Ἡσαΐας: «Καὶ εἶπέ μοι, Μέγα σοι τοῦτο, κληθῆναι παῖδά μου, καὶ στῆσαι τὰς φυλὰς τοῦ Ἰακώβ, καὶ τὴν διασπορὰν τοῦ Ἰσραὴλ στρέψαι· καὶ τέθεικά σε εἰς διαθήκην γένους, εἰς φῶς ἐθνῶν, τοῦ εἶναί σε εἰς σωτηρίαν ἕως ἐσχάτου τῆς γῆς.»

ΙΖ'. Ὅτι πρὸ τῆς τοῦ Κυρίου δευτέρας παρουσίας ἐλεύσεται Ἠλίας.

Μαλαχίας ὁ προφήτης λέγει: «Ἰδοὺ ἐγὼ ἀποστέλλω ὑμῖν Ἠλίαν τὸν Θεσβίτην, πρὶν ἐλθεῖν τὴν ἡμέραν Κυρίου τὴν μεγάλην καὶ ἐπιφανῆ, ὃς ἀποκαταστήσει καρδίας πατρῶν πρὸς υἱούς, καὶ καρδίαν ἀνθρώπου πρὸς τὸν πλησίον αὐτοῦ, μὴ ἐλθὼν πατάξω τὴν γῆν ἄρδην.»

ΙΗ'. Ὅτι κληθησόμεθα Χριστιανοί.

Ἠσαΐας λέγει: «Ὄψονται ἔθνη τὴν δόξαν σου, καὶ πάντες οἱ βασιλεῖς τὴν δικαιοσύνην σου, καὶ καλέσει σε τὸ ὄνομα τὸ καινόν, ὃ ὁ Κύριος ὀνομάσει αὐτό.» Καὶ πάλιν: «Τοῖς δὲ δουλεύουσί μοι κληθήσεται ὄνομα καινόν, ὃ εὐλογηθήσεται ἐπὶ τῆς γῆς.» Ὡσηέ: «Καὶ ἔσται ἐπ' ἐσχάτου τὸ ὄνομα αὐτοῦ ἐπιφανὲς ἐν πάσῃ τῇ γῇ, καὶ τῷ ὀνόματι αὐτοῦ ἐπικληθήσονται λαοὶ πολλοί, καὶ κατὰ τὰς ὁδοὺς αὐτοῦ πορευθέντες, ζήσονται ἐν αὐταῖς.» |

ΙΘ'. Ὅτι ταραχθήσεται Ἡρώδης, καὶ οἱ μετ' αὐτοῦ πάντες.

Ἱερεμίας φησί: «Ἐν τῇ ἡμέρᾳ ἐκείνῃ, λέγει Κύριος, ἀπολεῖται ἡ

"I am the Lord God who called you in righteousness. I grasped your hand, and I will make you strong, and I will give you as a covenant for the people, as a light for the nations, to open the eyes of the blind, and lead out from their bonds those who are bound,[259] and from the house of prison those sitting in darkness" (Isa 42:6–7).[260]

And again the same Isaiah:

"And he said to me, 'This is a great thing for you, to be called my child, and to raise up the tribes of Jacob, and to reverse the diaspora of Israel. And I have established you as a covenant for the people, as a light for the nations, so that you may be a salvation as far as the end of the earth" (Isa 49:6).[261]

CHAPTER 17: THAT BEFORE THE SECOND *parousia* OF THE LORD ELIJAH WILL COME

Malachi the prophet says:

"Look! I am sending to you, before the great and manifest day of the Lord comes, Elijah the Tishbite,[262] who will reconcile the hearts of the fathers with the sons, and the heart of a person with his neighbor, lest, when I come, I should strike the land completely" (Mal 4:4–5 [3:23–24]).[263]

CHAPTER 18: THAT WE WILL BE CALLED "CHRISTIANS"

Isaiah says:

"Nations will see your glory, and all the kings your righteousness, and he will call you by a new name which the Lord will name" (Isa 62:2).[264]

And again:

"Those who serve me will be called by a new name, which will be blessed upon the earth" (Isa 65:15–16).[265]

Hosea:

"And in the end his name will be manifest in all the earth, and many peoples will be called by his name, and those going along his ways will live in them" (Uncertain quotation).[266]

CHAPTER 19: THAT HEROD WILL BE TROUBLED, AND ALL THOSE WITH HIM[267]

Jeremiah says:

καρδία τοῦ βασιλέως, καὶ ἡ καρδία τῶν ἀρχόντων, καὶ οἱ ἱερεῖς ἐκστήσονται, καὶ οἱ προφῆται θαυμάσονται.»

Κ'. *Περὶ τοῦ Βαπτίσματος.*

Ἰεζεκιήλ: «Καὶ εἶπε Κύριος πρός με· Τὸ ὕδωρ τοῦτο τὸ ἐκπορευόμενον εἰς τὴν Γαλιλαίαν, ἁγιάσει τὰ ὕδατα. Καὶ ἔσται πάσῃ ψυχῇ, ἐφ' ἣν ἂν ἐπέλθῃ τὸ ὕδωρ τοῦτο, ζήσεται καὶ ἰαθήσεται·» Ἱερεμίας: «Ἰδοὺ ὡς λέων ἀναβήσεται ἐκ μέσου τοῦ Ἰορδάνου.»

ΚΑ'. *Περὶ τῆς εἰς Αἴγυπτον τοῦ Κυρίου καθόδου.*

Ἡσαΐας λέγει: «Ἰδοὺ Κύριος κάθηται ἐπὶ νεφέλης κούφης, καὶ ἥξει εἰς Αἴγυπτον, καὶ σεισθήσεται πάντα τὰ χειροποίητα Αἰγύπτου.» Καὶ πάλιν: «Γνωσθήσεται Κύριος τοῖς Αἰγυπτίοις, καὶ φοβηθήσονται Κύριον ἐν τῇ ἡμέρᾳ ἐκείνῃ.»

ΚΒ'. *Περὶ τοῦ ἁγίου Πνεύματος.*

Ἡσαΐας: «Καὶ νῦν Κύριος ἐξαπέσταλκέ με, καὶ τὸ Πνεῦμα αὐτοῦ.» Τῆς Ἐξόδου: «Καὶ εἶπε Κύριος τῷ Μωϋσεῖ· Ἀνάγαγέ μοι ἑβδομήκοντα πρεσβυτέρους, καὶ λήψομαι ἀπὸ τοῦ ἐπὶ σὲ Πνεύματος, καὶ ἐκχεῶ ἐπ' αὐτούς, καὶ ἀντιλήψομαί σε.» Δαβίδ: «Καρδίαν καθαρὰν κτίσον ἐν ἐμοί, ὁ Θεός, καὶ Πνεῦμα εὐθὲς ἐγκαίνισον ἐν τοῖς ἐγκάτοις μου, καὶ τὸ Πνεῦμά σου τὸ ἅγιον μὴ ἀντανέλῃς ἀπ' ἐμοῦ, καὶ Πνεύματι ἡγεμονικῷ στήριξόν με.» Καὶ πάλιν: «Ποῦ πορευθῶ ἀπὸ τοῦ Πνεύματός σου;» Ἰώβ: «Πνεῦμα θεῖον τὸ ποιῆσάν με.» Καὶ πάλιν: «Πνεῦμά

"'In that day,' says the Lord, 'the heart of the king will perish, and the heart of the rulers, and the priests will be astonished, and the prophets will be amazed" (Jer 4:9).[268]

Chapter 20: Concerning baptism

Ezekiel:
"And the Lord said to me, 'This water that flows out into Galilee will sanctify the waters. And it will happen to every soul, upon whom this water comes, that he will live and will be healed'" (Ezek 47:8–9).[269]

Jeremiah:
"Behold, he will go up from the midst of the Jordan as a lion" (Jer 29:20).[270]

Chapter 21: Concerning the descent of the Lord into Egypt

Isaiah says:
"Behold, the Lord sits upon a light cloud, and he will come into Egypt, and all the idols of Egypt will be shaken" (Isa 19:1).[271]

And again:
"The Lord will be known to the Egyptians, and they will fear the Lord in that day" (Isa 19:21).[272]

Chapter 22: Concerning the Holy Spirit

Isaiah:
"And now the Lord has sent me out, and his spirit" (Isa 48:16)[273]

From Exodus:
"And the Lord[274] said to Moses, 'Bring me seventy elders, and I will take from the spirit upon you, and I will pour it out upon them, and I will help you" (Num 11:16–17).[275]

David:
"Create a clean heart in me, O God, and renew an honest spirit within my entrails, and do not take away your holy spirit from me, and support me with [your] guiding spirit" (Ps 50:12–14).[276]

And again:
"Where could I go away from your spirit?" (Ps 138:7a).[277]

Job:
"The divine spirit which made me" (Job 33:4).[278]

ἔστιν ἐν βροτοῖς, πνοὴ δὲ Παντοκράτορός ἐστιν ἡ διδάσκουσά με.» Καὶ
πάλιν: «Ζῇ Κύριος, ὃς οὕτω με κέκρικε, καὶ ὁ Παντοκράτωρ, ὁ πικράνας μου τὴν ψυχήν. Πνεῦμα δὲ θεῖον τὸ περιόν μοι ἐν ῥισί.» Ζαχαρίας:
«Ἐγώ εἰμι ἐν ὑμῖν, καὶ τὸ Πνεῦμά μου ἐφέστηκεν ἐν μέσῳ ὑμῶν.»
Σολομών: «Πνεῦμα Κυρίου πεπλήρωκε τὴν οἰκουμένην.» | Ἡσαΐας·
«Παρώξυναν τὸ Πνεῦμα τὸ ἅγιον, καὶ ἐστράφη αὐτοῖς εἰς ἔχθραν.
Ὁ οἶκος τοῦ Ἰακὼβ παρώξυναν τὸ Πνεῦμα Κυρίου.» Ἰωήλ· «Καὶ
ἔσται ἐν ταῖς ἐσχάταις ἡμέραις, ἐκχεῶ ἀπὸ τοῦ Πνεύματός μου ἐπὶ
πᾶσαν σάρκα,» δηλαδὴ τὴν πιστεύουσαν: «καὶ ἐπὶ τοὺς υἱοὺς ὑμῶν,
καὶ ἐπὶ τὰς θυγατέρας ὑμῶν,» καὶ τὰ ἑξῆς. Ἡσαΐας· «Πνεῦμα Κυρίου ἐπ' ἐμέ, οὗ εἵνεκεν ἔχρισέ με,» καί: «Ἐπαναπαύσεται ἐπ' αὐτὸν
ἑπτὰ πνεύματα.» Καί: «Κατέβη Πνεῦμα Κυρίου, καὶ ὡδήγησεν αὐτούς.» Καί: «Πνεῦμα ἐπιστήμης ἔπλησε Βεσελεὴλ τὸν ἀρχιτέκτονα
τῆς σκηνῆς· Πνεῦμα παροξυνόμενον, καὶ Πνεῦμα ἐξᾶραν Ἠλίαν ἐν ἅρματι, καὶ ζητηθὲν παρ' Ἐλισσαίου διπλάσιον.» Καί: «Πνεῦμα παρ'
ἐμοῦ ἐξελεύσεται, καὶ πνοὴν πᾶσαν ἐγὼ ἐποίησα.» Καί: «Ἰδοὺ ὁ παῖς

And again:

"A spirit is in mortals; she who teaches me is the breath of the Almighty" (Job 32:8).[279]

And again:

"As the Lord lives, who has judged me in this way, and the Almighty, who has made my soul bitter, the divine breath that remains in my nostrils" (Job 27:2–3).[280]

Zechariah:

"I am in you, and my spirit stands in your midst" (Hag 2:4b–5a).[281]

Solomon:

"The spirit of the Lord has filled the world" (Wis 1:7).[282]

Isaiah:

"They provoked the holy spirit, and it turned to enmity against them" (Isa 63:10).[283]

"The house of Jacob provoked the spirit of the Lord" (Mic 2:7).[284]

Joel:

"And it will happen in the last days that I will pour out from my spirit upon all flesh"—[all flesh] that believes, of course—"and upon your sons, and upon your daughters" *et cetera* (Joel 2:28; cf. Acts 2:17).[285]

Isaiah:

"The spirit of the Lord is upon me, because he has anointed me" (Isa 61:1)[286]

And:

"Seven spirits will come to rest upon him" (see Isa 11:2–3).[287]

And:

"The spirit of the Lord descended, and he led them" (Isa 62:14).[288]

And:

"The spirit of knowledge filled Bezalel, the builder of the tent" (Exod 31:3–11).[289]

The spirit was stirred up, and the spirit was raising up Elijah in a chariot, and it was asked by Elisha for a double amount [of Elijah's spirit] (4 Kgdms 2:9–11).[290]

And:

"The spirit will go out from me, and I made every breath" (Isa 57:16).[291]

And:

μου ὁ ἐκλεκτός, ὁ ἀγαπητός μου, εἰς ὃν εὐδόκησεν ἡ ψυχή μου, θήσω τὸ Πνεῦμά μου ἐπ' αὐτόν.» Καί: «Οὐαί, τέκνα ἀποστάται, τάδε λέγει Κύριος· Ἐποιήσατε βουλὴν οὐ δι' ἐμοῦ, καὶ συνθήκην οὐ διὰ τοῦ Πνεύματός μου.» Καί: «Ἐκεῖ συνήντησαν ἔλαφοι, καὶ εἶδον τὰ πρόσωπα ἀλλήλων· ἀριθμῷ παρῆλθον, καὶ μία αὐτῶν οὐχ ὑπελείφθη, διότι Κύριος ἐνετείλατο αὐταῖς, καὶ τὸ Πνεῦμα αὐτοῦ συνήγαγεν αὐτάς.» Καὶ ὅτι ἡ ἀνάστασις διὰ τοῦ Πνεύματος ἐνεργεῖται, Δαβὶδ λέγει· «Ἀντανελεῖς τὸ πνεῦμα αὐτῶν, καὶ ἐκλείψουσι, καὶ εἰς τὸν χοῦν αὐτῶν ἐπιστρέψουσιν. Ἐξαποστελεῖς τὸ Πνεῦμά σου, καὶ κτισθήσονται, καὶ ἀνακαινιεῖς τὸ πρόσωπον τῆς γῆς.»

"Behold my chosen servant, my beloved, with whom my soul is well pleased; I will place my spirit upon him" (Isa 42:1; cf. Matt 12:18).[292]

And:

"'Woe, rebellious children,'" thus says the Lord, 'You made a plan not through me, and an agreement not through my spirit'" (Isa 30:1).[293]

And:

"There deer met, and they saw one another's faces. They passed by in number, and not one of them was left behind, because the Lord commanded them, and his spirit gathered them" (Isa 34:15b–16).[294]

And because the resurrection is effected through the spirit, David says:

"You will take away their spirit, and they will die, and they will return into their dust. You will send out your spirit, and they will be created, and you will renew the face of the earth" (Ps 103:29–30).[295]

NOTES

1. All chapter headings (except for this first, untitled, chapter) translate Ps.-Gregory's Greek; all subheadings are my own additions.

2. LXX Ps 32:6. Ps.-Gregory omits (with A'; Lucianic MSS) τοῦ before κυρίου.

3. LXX Ps 147:7.

4. LXX Ps 106:20.

5. LXX Ps 103:30.

6. LXX Jer 23:18. Ps.-Gregory reads ὑποστηρίγματι for the LXX's ὑποστήματι.

7. The source of this apparent quotation is unclear; see the Commentary.

8. 1 Cor 1:24. Ps.-Gregory adds δέ after Χριστός.

9. Ps.-Gregory quotes only Prov 8:27a, and an edited version of v. 30. He reads ἔχαιρε for the LXX's προσέχαιρε; ηὐφραινόμην for εὐφραινόμην; and omits ἐν before τῷ προσώπῳ αὐτοῦ.

10. Ps.-Gregory follows Paul's LXX-deviant quotation of Isa 40:13 in Rom 11:34 by adding γάρ before ἔγνω (cf. 1 Cor 2:16) and reading ἤ for καί.

11. LXX Gen 1:2. Ps.-Gregory reads (with Justin *1 Apol.* 59.3 and 64.3) τῶν ὑδάτων for the LXX's τοῦ ὕδατος.

12. Ps.-Gregory quotes an edited version of Gen 1:26–27, omitting most of v. 26 and the last phrase of v. 27c. The quoted text follows the LXX.

13. LXX Gen 3:22.

14. Ps.-Gregory summarizes Gen 1:6, just as he does below with Gen 1:14–16.

15. Ps.-Gregory shows several deviations from LXX Gen 18:1–3.
    v. 1: Same.
    v. 2: Ps.-Gregory omits αὐτοῦ after ὀφθαλμοῖς; reads παρειστήκεισαν for the LXX's εἰστήκεισαν; ἰδοὺ προσέδραμεν for ἰδὼν προσέδραμεν; συνάντησιν αὐτῶν for συνάντησιν αὐτοῖς; omits ἀπὸ τῆς θύρας τῆς σκηνῆς αὐτοῦ after συνάντησιν αὐτῶν.
    v. 3: Ps.-Greogry omits ἄρα before εὗρον.

16. LXX Gen 18:9–10. Ps.-Gregory (with the MT) omits ἀποκριθείς before the second εἶπεν.

17. The Migne text reads ὁμοουσίας for Zacagni's ὁμοουσίου.

18. LXX Gen 11:7. Ps.-Gregory (with the MT) omits καί before καταβάντες and ἐκεῖ after συγχέωμεν; trans. (with the MT) αὐτῶν / τὴν γλῶσσαν.

19. LXX Ps 109:3. Ps.-Gregory reads (with A'; Lucianic MSS) ἐγέννησα for the LXX's ἐξεγέννησα.

20. Conflation of Ps 71:17b and Ps 71:5; see the Commentary.

21. LXX Ps 2:7–8.

22. LXX 2 Kgdms 7:14; cf. the parallel in 1 Chr 17:13.

23. LXX Gen 19:24. Ps.-Gregory omits the opening καί; trans. (with Irenaeus *Haer.* 3.6.1 and other Christian authors) κύριος / ἔβρεξεν; omits ἐπὶ Σόδομα καὶ Γόμορρα after ἔβρεξεν; trans. (with Irenaeus *Haer.* 3.6.1; Tertullian *Prax.* 16.2) θεῖον καὶ πῦρ.

24. According to Zacagni, one of the Vatican codices (he doesn't indicate which one) has καὶ τό before the quotation of Gen 9:6; he omits the phrase since it is lacking in the Sifanus version. The 1562 edition of Sifanus, however, does read *etiam illud* before the quotation.

25. The Migne text reads ἐκχυθήσεται for Zacagni's ἐκχυθήσηται.

26. LXX Gen 9:6. Ps.-Gregory adds Καὶ πᾶς to the beginning of the quotation; omits ἀνθρώπου after αἷμα.

27. LXX Exod 34:4–6.
   v. 4: Ps.-Gregory omits τὸ πρωί before ἀνέβη; omits μεθ' ἑαυτοῦ after ἔλαβεν Μωυσῆς; omits δύο before πλάκας.
   v. 5: Ps.-Gregory omits αὐτῷ after παρέστη; reads (with Cyril of Alexandria *Jul.* 9 [PG 76:952]; Eusebius *Dem. ev.* 5.17) ἐλάλησε for the LXX's ἐκάλεσεν.
   v. 6: Ps.-Gregory reads (with Cyril of Alexandria *Jul.* 9 [PG 76:952]) ἀπὸ προσώπου Κυρίου for the LXX's πρὸ προσώπου αὐτοῦ.

28. Codex 451 reads πρὸς Ἀβραάμ; Sifanus also reads *ad Abrahamum*.

29. LXX Gen 31:13. Ps.-Gregory omits the LXX's ὁ θεός.

30. Ps.-Gregory follows the reading of Deut 32:43 in Heb 1:6, omitting the initial καί.

31. LXX Exod 9:5. Ps.-Gregory reads Κύριος for the LXX's ὁ θεός; adds ἡμέρα after αὔριον.

32. Ps.-Gregory quotes a severely edited LXX Hag 2:4–5. See the Commentary.

33. LXX Exod 19:10–11.
   v. 10: Ps.-Gregory adds (with many patristic witnesses, including Cyprian *Test.* 2.25) αὐτῶν after τὰ ἱμάτια.
   v. 11: Ps.-Gregory omits τῇ before τρίτῃ.

34. Ps.-Gregory follows the non-LXX text of Joel 2:28 [3:1] in Acts 2:17 (except reading Κύριος for θεός and reading ἐνύπνια for ἐνυπνίοις). He deviates from both Acts and the LXX in making αἱ θυγατέρες ὑμῶν the subject of ἐνυπνιασθήσονται.

35. LXX Joel 2:31. Ps.-Gregory adds (with Chrysostom) τήν before ἡμέραν.

36. LXX Joel 2:32a. Ps.-Gregory omits (with Chrysostom) πᾶς after ἔσται.

37. LXX Ps 101:20b–22a. Ps.-Gregory reads (with R) ἐκ τοῦ οὐρανοῦ for the LXX's ἐξ οὐρανοῦ; reads τοῦ ἰδεῖν for the LXX's τοῦ ἀκοῦσαι. Codex 451 follows the LXX.

38. LXX Ps 2:4.

39. LXX Ps 29:9.

40. LXX Amos 4:11.

41. After the Amos quotation, Sifanus adds "*Et Isaias*" in parentheses, noting that it was lacking in his MSS and he added it as a conjecture. Sifanus notes John 12 in the margin, indicating that the phrase ὅτε εἶδε τὴν δόξαν αὐτοῦ is drawn from John 12:41, which reads ταῦτα εἶπεν Ἠσαΐας ὅτι εἶδεν τὴν δόξαν αὐτοῦ (D reads ὅτε). The phrase makes no sense in its current context, however. The text here is clearly corrupt, either through scribal omission or displacement.

42. LXX Isa 53:1.

43. LXX Bar 3:36–38. Ps.-Gregory omits ὑπό after ἠγαπημένῳ; he reads (with numerous patristic witnesses) ταῦτα for τοῦτο.

44. LXX Ps 49:2–3.

45. LXX Ps 83:8.

46. LXX Ps 117:27.

47. LXX Mal 3:1b. Ps.-Gregory adds (with B and Lucianic MSS) ἑαυτοῦ after ναός.

NOTES   65

48. LXX Zech 9:9. Ps.-Gregory omits (with Matt 21:5) δίκαιος καὶ σῴ-
ζων αὐτός before πραΰς; reads (with Justin *Dial.* 53.3; cf. John 12:15 and
Irenaeus *Haer.* 3.19.2 and 4.33.1) ὄνου for the LXX's νέον.

49. LXX Zech 2:10–11. Ps.-Gregory omits ἰδού before ἐγώ.

50. Ps.-Gregory follows exactly the wording of Matt 11:10 (cf. Mark
1:2; Luke 7:27), which is itself a composite quotation of Mal 3:1 and
Exod 23:20.

51. Codex 1907 begins here.

52. LXX Zech 14:4.

53. LXX Zech 3:1–2a. Ps.-Gregory adds (with Eusebius, Cyprian) κύριος; adds τόν before Ἰησοῦν. Codex 451 reads ἔδειξέ με τὸν Ἰησοῦν.

54. Codex 1907 (with LXX) reads ἐάν ἐν ταῖς ὁδοῖς. Codex 451 reads δέ
before διακρινεῖς.

55. LXX Zech 3:6–7.
    3:6: Ps.-Gregory adds τόν before Ἰησοῦν.
    3:7: Ps.-Gregory omits ἐν before ταῖς ὁδοῖς; reads (with Lucianic
         MSS and Theodoret) πορεύσῃ for the LXX's πορεύῃ; and
         (with B, Catanae texts) φυλάξῃ for φυλάξῃς.

56. LXX Zech 3:8. Ps.-Gregory reads (with B) Ἰησοῦς for the LXX's
Ἰησοῦ.

57. LXX Isa 65:1a. Ps.-Gregory adds καί between the clauses.

58. Zacagni plausibly suggests that the quotation is from Isa 33:17:
βασιλέα μετὰ δόξης ὄψεσθε. The quotation and comment are lacking in
Codex 451 and the Sifanus translation, and are thus placed in parentheses.

59. LXX Zeph 2:11. Ps.-Gregory omits τῆς γῆς at the end of the
phrase (with V; Chrysostom).

60. LXX Isa 65:1b. Ps.-Gregory reads πάρειμι for the LXX's εἰμί;
reads (with Catenae MSS; Eusebius *Ecl. proph.*; Cyril of Alexandria)
ἐπεκαλέσαντο for ἐκάλεσαν.

61. LXX of Ps 79:2c–3. Ps.-Gregory omits v. 3a: ἐναντίον Ἐφραιμ καὶ
Βενιαμιν καὶ Μανασση.

62. LXX Ps 71:6a.

63. LXX Mic 5:2. Ps.-Gregory follows the non-LXX reading of Mic
5:2 in Matt 2:6 with only minor variations (trans. σοῦ / γάρ, adds μοι before ἡγούμενος, and reads ὅς for ὅστις). Unlike Matthew, however, Ps.-

Gregory does include the last phrase from LXX Mic 5:2, with some slight deviations (Ps.-Gregory omits αἱ before ἔξοδοι [retained by Codex 1907]; reads ἀφ' ἡμερῶν αἰῶνος for the LXX's ἐξ ἡμερῶν αἰῶνος). Codex 451 reads ἕως αἰῶνος; Sifanus also reads *usque in seculum*.

64. Ps.-Gregory essentially follows the composite quotation in Acts 3:22–23 (itself composed of elements from Deut 18:15, 16, 19, and Lev 23:29); reads ὁ θεὸς ἡμῶν for Acts ὁ θεὸς ὑμῶν (ℵ* reads ἡμῶν); λαλήσει for λαλήσῃ; the last phrase reads καὶ ἔσται, ὃς ἂν μὴ ἀκούσῃ for Acts's ἔσται δὲ πᾶσα ψυχὴ ἥτις ἐὰν μὴ ἀκούσῃ; reads ἐξολοθρευθήσεται for ἐξολεθρευθήσεται.

65. Codex 451 reads τὴν περὶ αὐτοῦ; Sifanus also reads *de illo*.

66. LXX Deut 18:17–18. Ps.-Gregory omits (with Cyril of Alexandria *Comm. Jonah* Proem. [PG 71:600]) ὅσα before ἐλάλησαν; trans. (with Cyril of Alexandria *Comm. Jonah* Proem. [PG 71:600]) αὐτοῖς / ἀναστήσω; adds μέσου before τῶν ἀδελφῶν.

67. Codex 451 and Sifanus omit Νεανίσκε.

68. Ps.-Gregory follows the NT quotations precisely.

69. Codex 1907 reads τοῖς τοῦ κυρίου for the LXX's τοῖς Χριστοῦ.

70. Codex 1907 reads ὑπερέχον for ὑπέροχον.

71. Codex 451 reads Σοφονίας for Ἡσαΐας. Sifanus lacks any attribution.

72. Sifanus reads *vester* (ὑμῶν) for ἡμῶν.

73. LXX Isa 40:9b–10. Ps.-Gregory reads κυρίας (with some LXX MSS) for κυριείας.

74. LXX Ps 131:11. Ps.-Gregory reads (with L) ἐπὶ τοῦ θρόνου for the LXX's ἐπὶ τὸν θρόνον. Codex 451 reads (with Irenaeus *Haer.* 3.9.2) αὐτον for αὐτήν; Sifanus also reads *eum*.

75. LXX Ps 88:4–5.

76. Codex 1907 reads ἕως εἰς τοὺς αἰῶνας for εἰς τὸν αἰῶνα.

77. LXX 1 Chr 17:11–14.
    v. 11: Ps.-Gregory reads (with Eusebius) αἱ before ἡμέραι.
    v. 12: Ps.-Gregory reads τὴν βασιλείαν for τὸν θρόνον; reads εἰς τὸν αἰῶνα for ἑώς αἰῶνος.
    v. 13: Ps.-Gregory reads καθώς for ὡς; omits (with Eusebius) ὄντων.
    v. 14: Ps.-Gregory adds ἡ before βασιλεία; ἡ βασιλεία αὐτοῦ for ἐν βασιλείᾳ αὐτοῦ; adds (with Eusebius) ὁ before θρόνος.

NOTES

78. The Migne text reads Σολομών for Zacagni's Σάλωμων.

79. The Migne editor cites the quotation as LXX 2 Chr 6:17–18, but Ps.-Gregory follows almost exactly the wording of the parallel passage in 3 Kgdms 8:26–27. Ps.-Gregory lacks ὅτι before εἰ ἀληθῶς.

80. LXX Jer 17:9.

81. LXX Amos 4:12b–13. Codex 451 reads ἐπικαλεῖσθαι; Sifanus reads *ut invocet*. Ps.-Gregory reads Ἐπικαλεῖστο τὸν θεόν σου· ἑτοιμάζου, Ἱερουσαλήμ, ὅτι for the LXX's ἑτοιμάζου τοῦ ἐπικαλεῖσθαι τὸν θεόν σου, Ἰσραηλ· διότι ἰδού; reads ἀποστέλλων for ἀπαγγέλλων; reads χριστὸν μου for χριστὸν αὐτοῦ; reads ὑψηλά for ὕψη.

82. LXX Mic 1:2–3. Ps.-Gregory adds πάντες after λαοί; reads λόγον for the LXX's λόγους; adds (with many patristic witnesses) κατοικοῦντες after πάντες οἱ; reads ἐκ ναοῦ ἁγίου αὐτοῦ for ἐξ οἴκου ἁγίου αὐτοῦ; omits (with B*, Eusebius *Dem. ev.*) καὶ ἐπιβήσεται after καταβήσεται; reads ὑψηλά for ὕψη. The Migne text omits Zacagni's καί before καταβήσεται.

83. LXX Gen 49:10. Ps.-Gregory reads (with *Dial. AZ* 47) ἕως οὗ ἔλθῃ for the LXX's ἕως ἂν ἔλθῃ; reads ᾧ ἀπόκειται for the LXX's τὰ ἀποκείμενα αὐτῷ. Codex 451 read ὃ ἀπόκειται; Sifanus also reads *quod reconditum & repositum est*. See the Commentary for a discussion of the ᾧ ἀπόκειται variant.

84. LXX Num 24:17–18a. Ps.-Gregory omits (with Justin *Dial.* 106.4; Cyril of Alexandria *Jul.* 8 [PG 76:900; Athanasius *Inc.* 33.4]) ἀναστήσεται before ἄνθρωπος; reads τοὺς for πάντας; adds ἐθνῶν after κληρονομία. Codex 451 reads τοὺς υἱοὺς Σούρ for τοὺς υἱοὺς Σήθ; Sifanus reads *filios Sur*.

85. Codex 451 read περὶ τούτων οὐ παρεγένετο for τούτων οὐ περιεγένετο; Sifanus reads *Dauid autem de his rebus non aduenit*.

86. Codex 451 read ταπεινῶν; Sifanus also reads *humilium*.

87. Codex 451 reads ἀσεβεῖς for ἀσεβῆ; Sifanus also reads *impios*.

88. LXX of Isa 10:33–34; 11:1–5.
    10:33: Ps.-Gregory omits γάρ; trans. (with A´) οἱ ὑψηλοί / ταπεινωθήσονται; reads (with S; Eusebius *Ecl. proph.*; Cyril of Alexandria; Tertullian) συνταράξει for συνταράσσει.
    10:34: Ps.-Gregory omits οἱ ὑψηλοι before μαχαίρᾳ.
    11:2: Ps.-Gregory omits (with Justin) τοῦ before θεοῦ.
    11:4: Ps.-Gregory reads (with S; Lucianic and Catenae MSS; Theodoret and Irenaeus [Latin]) τοὺς ἐνδόξους for τοὺς ταπεινούς.

11:5: Ps.-Gregory adds (= MT) αὐτοῦ after ὀσφύν (Zacagni reads ὀσφήν for ὀσφύν); reads ἀλήθειαν ἠλειμμένος for ἀληθείᾳ εἰλημένος; adds (with Eusebius; Theodoret; = MT) αὐτοῦ after πλευράς.

89. LXX Isa 11:10.

90. LXX Ps 44:7–8. Ps.-Gregory reads περί for the LXX's παρά. Sifanus lacks the phrase "with the oil of joy among your companions."

91. LXX Ps 101:26–28. Ps.-Gregory omits an initial κατ' ἀρχάς (read in both the LXX and Heb 1:10); reads (with Heb 1:12; B'; L'; A') ἑλίξεις for the LXX's ἀλλάξεις; follows LXX in reading καὶ ἀλλαγήσονται (Heb 1:12 adds ὡς ἱμάτιον).

92. The Migne editor adds a second μ to Ἐμμανουήλ, lacking in Zacagni.

93. LXX Isa 7:14. Ps.-Gregory reads (with Matt 1:23) καλέσουσι for the LXX's καλέσεις.

94. LXX Isa 8:4. Ps.-Gregory reads Καὶ πρὶν ἐπιγνῶναι πατέρα ἢ μητέρα for the LXX's διότι πρὶν ἢ γνῶναι τὸ παιδίον καλεῖν πατέρα ἢ μητέρα; adds ἔδεται at the end of the quotation; omits ἔναντι βασιλέως Ἀσσυρίων.

95. Codex 1907 reads πῶς ἤμην for παῖς ἤμην.

96. LXX Wis 8:19–20. Ps.-Gregory omits δέ after παῖς.

97. The phrase in parentheses is lacking in Codex 1907.

98. The Migne text misprints ἄρχον for Zacagni's ἄρχων.

99. LXX Isa 9:5b–6. Ps.-Gregory omits ἐγενήθη after ἡ ἀρχή (with Justin, Basil, Cyprian and many patristic witnesses). Ps.-Gregory adds a series of titles, based on the MT, but lacking in the LXX. They are partially witnessed by the LXX recensions (α' σ' θ'). Eusebius (*Dem. ev.* 7.1 [336]), Athanasius, and Chrysostom (with A'; Lucianic MSS) parallel Ps.-Gregory final phrase: θαυμαστὸς Σύμβουλος, Θεὸς ἰσχυρός, ἐξουσιαστής, Ἄρχων εἰρήνης, Πατὴρ τοῦ μέλλοντος αἰῶνος. *Dial. TA* 5.6 parallels Ps.-Gregory's titles exactly. Codex 451 reads καὶ καλεῖται τῆς μεγάλης βουλῆς ἄγγελος, θεὸς ἰσχυρός; Sifanus also reads *et vocatur, magni consilii nuntius, Deus validus*.

100. This quotation possibly derives from the lost *Apocryphon of Ezekiel*. See the Commentary. Sifanus reads *Ecce virtus peperit & non peperit*, perhaps reading δύναμις for δάμαλις.

101. LXX Isa 7:15.

102. Codex 451 reads καταβήσονται for διαβήσονται; Sifanus also reads *descendent*.

103. LXX Isa 45:14–15. Ps.-Gregory reads (with Lucianic MSS; Eusebius; Cyprian; Theodoret, Cyril of Alexandria) Σαβαείμ for the LXX's Σεβωιν; adds (with Lucianic MSS; Catenae MSS; Eusebius *Ecl. proph.*; Theodoret) a redundant διαβήσοντα καὶ πρὸς σέ after χειροπέδαις; omits ἐροῦσιν before οὐκ ἔστι θεός; omits ὁ before the final θεός. Codex 451 adds καὶ θεὸς τοῦ Ισραηλ and Σωτήρ, Sifanus also adds "&."

104. The Migne text and Zacagni read ἐπέτρεψε, I have emended it to the LXX's ἐπέστρεψε. Sifanus also notes that his exemplar had ἐπέτρεψε, but he reads ἐπέστρεψε.

105. Ezek 44:1–2.

    44:1: Ps.-Gregory adds Κύριος before κατὰ τὴν ὁδόν; omits the LXX's τῶν ἁγίων τῆς ἐξωτέρας after πύλης.

    44:2: Ps.-Gregory adds (with V) Υἱὲ ἀνθρώπου before Ἡ πύλη αὕτη; omits (with A and Origen) οὐκ ἀνοιχθήσεται after κεκλεισμένη ἔσται; adds (with Lucianic MSS) οὐ before μή; omits τοῦ before Ἰσραήλ; adds καὶ ἐξελεύσεται after εἰσελεύσεται.

106. LXX Isa 49:1–2. After quoting an adapted version of Isa 49:1b, Ps.-Gregory adds the phrase μάχαιραν ὀξεῖαν from Isa 49:2. Ps.-Gregory omits μου after μητρός; reads (with Eusebius *Ecl. proph.*) ἐκάλεσα for the LXX's ἐκάλεσε; reads τὸ ὄνομα αὐτοῦ for τὸ ὄνομά μου.

107. Dan 2:34–35 (Theodotion).

    v. 34: Ps.-Gregory reads ἰδού, for Theodotion's ἐθεώρεις; omits ἕως οὗ; reads ἐτμήθη for ἀπεσχίσθη (with o', Justin and other patristic witnesses); omits ἐξ ὄρους (with MT and many patristic witnesses); reads τὸν ἀνδριάντα for τὴν εἰκόνα. Ps.-Gregory omits vv. 34b and 35a, adding a phrase from v. 35b.

    v. 35b: Ps.-Gregory reads καὶ ἐγένετο εἰς ὄρος μέγα for Theodotion's ἐγενήθη ὄρος μέγα.

108. The Migne text prints ἐνωτίζου for Zacagni's ἐνωτίσου.

109. LXX Isa 1:2–3. Ps.-Gregory adds ἡ before γῆ; reads οὐδὲ ὁ λαός for the LXX's καὶ ὁ λαός.

110. LXX Isa 8:1–3.

    v. 1: Ps.-Gregory omits σεαυτῷ after λαβέ; reads (with 88 and 538) καινοῦ χάρτου μεγάλου for the LXX's καινοῦ μεγάλου; reads ἐν αὐτῷ for εἰς αὐτόν; omits πάρεστιν γάρ and all of v. 2.

    v. 3: Ps.-Gregory trans. (with Lucianic MSS; Basil; Chrysostom; Theodoret) κύριος / μοι.

111. The Migne text prints διανοῖγον for Zacagni's διανοίγει.

112. Ps.-Gregory follows the text of Luke 2:23. See the Commentary.

113. Codex 451 reads ἅγιος μόνος, omitting καὶ ἄμωμος; Sifanus also reads *sanctus sit solus*.

114. LXX Ps 86:5. Ps.-Gregory reads ἐγεννήθη for the LXX's ἐγενήθη. Sifanus reads *ipse altissimus fundamenta eius iecit*.

115. LXX Isa 49:6–9 with influence from Isa 42:6b–7. See the Commentary.
    49:9: Ps.-Gregory reads λέγων for the LXX's λέγοντα; reads ἐξέλθετε for ἐξέλθατε; reads ἀνακαλύφθητε for ἀνακαλυφθῆναι.

Codex 451 and Sifanus omit ἐρήμου after κληρονομίαν.

116. LXX Bar 3:36.

117. LXX Isa 35:3– 4.

118. LXX Isa 40:9b–10a.

119. LXX Isa 35:5–6. Codex 1907 reads μογιλάλου.

120. LXX Isa 61:1. Ps.-Gregory omits (with Luke 4:18) ἰάσασθαι τοὺς συντετριμμένους τῇ καρδίᾳ.

121. LXX Ps 40:10.

122. Codex 1907 omits αὐτοῦ after τὸν λαόν.

123. LXX Isa 3:12b–14. Ps.-Gregory reads ἐκταράσσουσιν for the LXX's ταράσσουσι (with Catenae MSS); trans. (with Tertullian) εἰς κρίσιν / κύριος; trans. εἰς κρίσιν / τὸν λαὸν αὐτοῦ; reads (with Chrysostom) ἀρχόντων αὐτῶν for ἀρχόντων αὐτοῦ.

124. LXX Ps 2:1–2.

125. LXX Lam 4:20. Ps.-Gregory reads θεὸς κύριος for the LXX's χριστὸς κυρίου; reads εἴπομεν for εἴπαμεν.
    Codex 451 reads omits θεός before Κύριος; Sifanus reads *nostrae Dominus dominus comphrensus est*; also reads *umbra ipsius*.

126. Codex 451 reads παρέδωκεν ἑαυτόν; Sifanus also reads *tradidit seipsum*.

127. LXX Isa 53:4–9.
    v. 4: Ps.-Gregory reads αὐτός for the LXX's οὗτος; ἀνομίας for ἁμαρτίας; omits εἶναι.
    v. 5: Ps.-Gregory trans. (with Hexaplaric MSS; Catenae MSS: Cyril of Alexandria; Eusebius) ἀνομίας / ἁμαρτίας.

NOTES

v. 6: Ps.-Gregory reads ἕκαστος τὴν ὁδόν for the LXX's ἄνθρωπος τῇ ὁδῷ; reads (with 958) διὰ τὰς ἁμαρτίας for ταῖς ἁμαρτίαις.

v. 7: Ps.-Gregory reads (with A'; *Barn.* 5.2; Theodoret) κείραντος for κείροντος.

v. 8: Ps.-Gregory adds (with Lucianic MSS; Justin; Athanasius) αὐτοῦ after ταπεινώσει; omits ἡ κρίσις αὐτοῦ ἤρθη· τὴν γενεὰν αὐτοῦ τίς διηγήσεται; reads ἁμαρτιῶν for the LXX's ἀνομιῶν. Sifanus retains ἡ κρίσις αὐτοῦ ἤρθη (*iudicium eius sublatum est*).

v. 9: Ps.-Gregory omits τῆς before ταφῆς.

128. LXX 53:12. Ps.-Gregory adds the phrase ὅτι ἀνομίαν οὐκ ἐποίησε (from Isa 53:9).

129. Codex 1907 reads ἐκ τούτου for ἐκ τούτων.

130. LXX Isa 50:6. Ps.-Gregory reads (with Hexaplaric MSS; Catenae MSS; Eusebius *Ecl. proph.*; Athanasius); ἔδωκα for the LXX's δέδωκα.

131. LXX Isa 53:2b–3. Ps.-Gregory reads (with Hexaplaric MSS; Lucianic MSS; Justin *Dial.* 13.4; Eusebius; Theodoret) τοὺς υἱοὺς τῶν ἀνθρώπων for the LXX's πάντας ἀνθρώπους.

132. LXX Isa 53:8. Ps.-Gregory adds (with Eusebius, Cyril of Alexandria, and Cyprian) δέ after τήν.

133. LXX Ps 21:17–19.

v. 17: Ps.-Gregory adds (with L'; A'; Cyprian *Test.* 2.20; = MT) μου after πόδας.

v. 18: Ps.-Gregory reads ἐξηρίθμησαν for the LXX's ἐξηρίθμησα.

134. LXX Jer 11:19a.

135. LXX Jer 11:19b. Ps.-Gregory reads ἀπὸ τῶν ζώντων for the LXX's ἀπὸ γῆς ζώντων.

136. LXX Zech 11:12–13; Jer 32:6–9; see Matt 27:9–10. See the Commentary.

137. LXX Deut 28:66–67. Ps.-Gregory reads a heavily adapted LXX text:

v. 66: Ps.-Gregory reads Ὄψεσθε τὴν ζωὴν ὑμῶν κρεμαμένην for καὶ ἔσται ἡ ζωή σου κρεμαμένη; reads ὀφθαλμῶν ὑμῶν for ὀφθαλμῶν σου (with *Dial. AZ* 36; Melito *Pasc.* 94); omits καὶ φοβηθήσῃ ἡμέρας καὶ νυκτός (Melito *Pasc.* 94 omits καὶ φοβηθήσῃ); reads καὶ οὐ μὴ πιστεύσητε for καὶ οὐ πιστεύσεις τῇ ζωῇ σου; adds ἐάν τις ἐκδιηγεῖται ὑμῖν before v. 67.

v. 67: Ps.-Gregory reads Πῶς ἐγένετο ἑσπέρα; for Πῶς ἂν γένοιτο ἑσπέρα;.

138. LXX Amos 8:9. Ps.-Gregory trans. (with Tertullian *Adv. Jud.* 10.17; = MT) ἐκείνῃ / τῇ ἡμέρᾳ; adds ὁ θεός after κύριος; omits (with many patristic witnesses) καί before δύσεται; omits (with Cyril of Alexandria and Cyprian *Test.* 2.23) ἐπὶ τῆς γῆς.

139. LXX Jer 15:9.

140. LXX Isa 65:2. Ps.-Gregory reads (with Hexaplaric MSS; Eusebius *Ecl. proph.*) διεπέτασα for the LXX's ἐξεπέτασα; trans. (with Rom 10:21) ὅλην τὴν ἡμέραν to the beginning of the verse; trans. ἀπειθοῦντα / ἀντιλέγοντα.

141. LXX Isa 62:10. Ps.-Gregory reads (with Eusebius *Ecl. proph.*) ἄρατε for ἐξάρατε.

142. Uncertain quotation. Codex 451 reads only ὅτι ἐκ ξύλων αἷμα στάξει, omitting "when the tree of trees is bent, and rises." Sifanus also reads only *quia de lignis sanguis destillabit*. See the Commentary.

143. LXX Zech 14:6–7. Codex 1907 reads καὶ οὐχὶ νύξ.
v. 6: Ps.-Gregory adds καὶ ἔσται before quotation (with Eusebius *Dem. ev.*; = MT); trans. ἐκείνῃ / τῇ ἡμέρᾳ.
vv. 6–7: Ps.-Gregory omits καὶ ψύχη καὶ πάγος· ἔσται μίαν ἡμέραν.
v. 7: Ps.-Gregory reads τὸ πρὸς ἑσπέραν for the LXX's καὶ πρὸς ἑσπέραν. Codex 1907 reads καὶ οὐχὶ νύξ.

144. Ps 68:21–22. Codex 451 omits καί before ἔδωκαν. Ps.-Gregory reads (with B') παρακαλοῦντα for the LXX's παρακαλοῦντας (Codex 451 reads with the LXX).

145. LXX Ps 87:7.

146. LXX Zech 13:7. Ps.-Gregory reads ἐπὶ τὸν ποιμένα for ἐπὶ τοὺς ποιμένας (with Justin; Eusebius *Ecl. proph.*; = MT); omits μου after τοὺς ποιμένας (with Lucianic MSS; Gregory Naz.; Theodoret.); reads ἐπ' ἄνδρα τοῦ λαοῦ for the LXX's ἐπ' ἄνδρα πολίτην (with σ'; Justin); reads μου for αὐτοῦ (with B-S*; σ'; Justin = MT); omits λέγει κύριος παντοκράτωρ before πατάξατε; reads πάταξον for πατάξατε (with Justin; Eusebius *Ecl. proph.*); reads τὸν ποιμένα for τοὺς ποιμένας (with *Barn.* 5.12; Justin; Eusebius *Ecl. proph.*= Matt 26:31; Mark 14:27); adds μου after ποιμένα; reads διασκορπισθήσονται τὰ πρόβατα for ἐκσπάσατε τὰ πρόβατα (with A'; Justin; Cyril of Alexandria; Theodoret; = Matt 26:31, Mark 14:27); adds τῆς ποίμνης after τὰ πρόβατα (with A'; *Barn.* 5.12; = Matt 26:31).

147. LXX Zech 14:20. Ps.-Gregory adds καί at the beginning of the quotation; omits παντοκράτορι after κυρίῳ.
Codex 451 reads ἐπὶ τῶν χαλινῶν; Sifanus also reads *in frenis*.

148. LXX Ps 43:24.

NOTES

149. LXX Ps 3:8.

150. LXX Ps 43:27.

151. LXX Ps 81:8. Ps.-Gregory reads Κύριε for the LXX's ὁ θεός.

152. Codex 451 and Sifanus omit νῦν ὄψεσθε.

153. LXX Isa 33:10–11a. Ps.-Gregory reads νῦν σωθήσεσθε for the LXX's νῦν αἰσθηθήσεσθε.

154. Sifanus reads *in afflictione sua*. The LXX punctuates differently, taking ἐν θλίψει as the beginning of the new sentence.

155. Codex 451 reads ὅτι αὐτὸς πέπαικε, καὶ ἰάσατο; Sifanus also reads *quoniam ipse percussit & sanavit*.

156. The Migne text prints (with LXX Hos 6:2) ἀναστησόμεθα for Zacagni's ἀναστησώμεθα.

157. LXX Hos 5:15b; 6:1–3a.
   5:15: Ps.-Gregory reads ζητήσουσιν for the LXX's ἐπιζητήσουσι (Tertullian reads *quaerant*).
   6:1: Ps.-Gregory adds καί before ὀρθριοῦσι.
   6:2: Ps.-Gregory omits καὶ ζησόμεθα.
   6:3: Ps.-Gregory reads διώξωμεν for διώξομεν (with Lucianic MSS). Codex 451 and Sifanus omit καὶ γνωσόμεθα after ἐνώπιον αὐτοῦ. Codex 1907 adds καί before εὑρήσομεν.

158. LXX Ps 15:10.

159. LXX Ps 87:5. Ps.-Gregory reads ὡσεί for ὡς (with S; L'; A').

160. The quotation follows closely the form of Isa 28:16 witnessed in 1 Pet 2:6. See the Commentary for details.

161. Codex 451 reads οἰκονομίας; Sifanus reads *dispositionis*. Codex 1907 adds καί after ἥτις.

162. LXX Ps 46:6.

163. Migne corrects Zacagni's ἐθέτησαν to ἐτέθησαν.

164. Dan 7:9 (Theodotion). Ps.-Gregory omits ἕως ὅτου after ἐθεώρουν; adds καὶ ἰδού before θρόνοι. Sifanus reads *ascendens* for ἐρχόμενος.

165. Dan 7:13–14 (Theodotion).
   v. 13: Ps.-Gregory omits αὐτῷ after προσήχθε.
   v. 14: Ps.-Gregory omits καί before αὐτῷ ἐδόθη; trans. (with Cyril of Jerusalem) ἡ ἀρχή / ἡ τιμή; adds (with B; Hippol.[P]; = MT) καί before γλῶσσαι; reads παρελεύσει for the LXX's παρελεύσεται.

166. LXX Ps 109:1.

167. LXX Ps 44:10b.

168. Codex 451 reads γοῦν for οὖν.

169. Codex 1907 reads ἐν τῷ οἴκῳ for τῷ οἴκῳ.

170. Codex 451 and Sifanus read ὑμῶν (*vestris*) for αὐτῶν.

171. Codex 1907 reads ἐπιλαβόμενος τῆς χειρός.

172. LXX Jer 38:31–32.

173. LXX Jer 9:26. The first phrase of the quotation follows the LXX; the second varies considerably. See the Commentary.

174. This is not a direct quotation from an extant scriptural passage. It shares vocabulary with Jer 4:4 and Deut 10:16. See the Commentary.

175. Codex 451 adds Ἰερεμίου.

176. LXX Jer 4:3; Deut 10:16. Ps.-Gregory reads σπείρετε for the LXX's σπείρητε in Jer 4:3b (with S; Lucianic MSS; Justin; Origen; other Greek patristic witnesses). The second half of Ps.-Gregory's quotation shares some vocabulary with Jer 4:4, but is closer in wording to Deut 10:16: καὶ περιτεμεῖσθε τὴν σκληροκαρδίαν ὑμῶν. Codex 451 reads ἐπ' ἀκάνθας. See the Commentary.

177. Codex 451 omits Ἰερεμίας.

178. LXX Jer 4:4a. Ps.-Gregory adds καί before περιτέμνεσθε; reads περιτέμνεσθε for περιτμήθητε; omits ὑμῶν after θεῷ (with Origen; Cyril of Jerusalem; Cyril of Alexandria; Theodoret; Tertullian; = MT); omits καὶ περιέλεσθε before τὴν ἀκροβυστίαν. See the Commentary.

179. Codex 451 reads ἐδούλευσεν; Sifanus also reads *servivit*.

180. Codex 451 omits οὖν after Ἵνα; reads ἐδεήθη for ἐδέησε; reads διαχωρίζῃ for χωρίζῃ.

181. LXX Jer 7:22. See the Commentary for detailed analysis of this and the following quotation.

182. Codex 1907 reads προσενέγκαι for προσενεγκεῖν.

183. Codex 1907 reads ὁλοκαυτώματα for ὁλοκαυτωμάτων.

184. Codex 451 reads μάταιόν μοι βδέλυγμα ἐστί; Sifanus also reads *vana mihi abominatio est*.

185. LXX Isa 1:11–14.

NOTES 75

v. 13: Ps.-Gregory adds μοι before σεμίδαλιν (with A'; Lucianic MSS; Basil; Chrysostom; Tertullian; *Barn.* 2.5 [Latin]); reads νεομηνίας for νουμηνίας (with Lucianic MSS); adds ὑμῶν after σάββατα (with Origen; Basil).

v. 14: Ps.-Gregory omits (with S; Hexaplaric MSS; Lucianic MSS; Origen; Basil; Chrysostom; Theodoret; Cyril of Alexandria; Tertullian) καὶ τὰς νουμηνίας ὑμῶν after ἀργίαν.

186. Codex 1907 reads καὶ μετ' ὀλίγα.

187. LXX Isa 1:16. Ps.-Gregory adds (with 1 *Clem.* 8.4; Origen [Latin]) καί after λούσασθε; reads γίνεσθε for γένεσθε.

188. LXX Ps 49:13. Ps.-Gregory reads οὐ for the LXX's μή.

189. LXX Ps 49:9.

190. LXX Ps 49:14a. Codex 451 reads δικαιοσύνης for αἰνέσεως; Sifanus also reads *iustitiae* (cf. Ps 4:6).

191. The words in parentheses are lacking in Codex 451 and Sifanus, according to Zacagni. In the 1562 edition of Sifanus, however, the words "*& non olfaciam in conventionibus vestris*" are read after the phrase "I will not look on the outward appearance of their peace-offerings" in the same quotation.

192. Codex 451 reads σωτηρίους ἐπιφανείας αὐτῶν; Sifanus also reads *salutares apparitiones eorum*.

193. LXX Amos 5:21–23.
v. 21: Ps.-Gregory adds τάς before ἑορτάς (with Lucianic MSS; Justin; Origen; Chrysostom; Cyril of Alexandria; Theodoret).
v. 22: Ps.-Gregory adds καί after διότι (with A'; Cyril of Alexandria); adds (with Justin) αὐτά after προσδέξομαι.
v. 23: Ps.-Gregory omits σου after ὀργάνων.

194. LXX Mal 1:10–11. The entire quotation is lacking in Sifanus (1562).
v. 10: Ps.-Gregory reads μου for the LXX's μοι (with Eusebius *Dem. ev.* and *Ecl. proph.*).
v. 11: Ps.-Gregory reads (with Justin; Eusebius; Cyril of Alexandria; Theodoret) προσφέρεται for the LXX's προσάγεται.

195. Codex 1907 reads παῦσαι for καταπαῦσαι.

196. Codex 1907 reads πενομένου ἐκ γῆς Αἰγύπτου.

197. LXX Exod 20:9–10; cf. Deut 5:13–14. Ps.-Gregory paraphrases the commandment in these parallel passages.

198. The Migne text omits the phrase καὶ ἡ παιδίσκη σου, read in Zacagni after ὁ παῖς σου. Sifanus also reads *& puer tuus & ancilla tua*.

199. Codex 1907 adds πρῶτος after Δαβίδ.

200. LXX Ps 4:7b.

201. LXX Ps 85:17. Sifanus (1562) lacks the phrase, "because you, O Lord, helped me and comforted me."

202. LXX Ps 59:6.

203. LXX Ezek 9:4. Ps.-Gregory adds Υἱὲ ἀνθρώπου before the quotation; reads μέσον for the LXX's μέσην; reads ἀνθρώπων for ἀνδρῶν; reads (with Chrysostom) στεναζόντων for καταστεναζόντων; reads κατωδυνωμένων for κατοδυνωμένων; reads ταῖς ἀδικίαις for πάσαις ταῖς ἀνομίαις. Codex 451 reads ἐπὶ τὸ μέτωπον; Sifanus also reads *in frontem* and adds *urbem* before *Hierusalem*.

204. Codex 451 reads καὶ ἕκαστος πέλυξ ἐστὶ τῇ χειρὶ αὐτοῦ. Sifanus reads *unicuique*.

205. Codex 1907 reads καὶ παρθένους for παρθένον. Codex 451 and Sifanus add καί (&) before ἀποκτείνατε.

206. LXX Ezek 9:2, 5–6.

9:2: Ps.-Gregory reads ἀπὸ τῆς πύλης βλεπούσης πρὸς βορρᾶν for the LXX's ἀπὸ τῆς ὁδοῦ τῆς πύλης τῆς ὑψηλῆς τῆς βλεπούσης πρὸς βορρᾶν (Cyril of Alexandria also omits τῆς ὑψηλῆς).

9:5: Ps.-Gregory reads ἀκούοντες for the LXX's καὶ τούτοις εἶπεν ἀκούοντός μου; omits ὀπίσω αὐτοῦ after πορεύεσθε; reads φείσασθε for φείδεσθε.

9:6: Ps.-Gregory adds μου after σημεῖον.

207. LXX Ps 67:12.

208. Ps.-Gregory follows the non-LXX reading in Rom 10:15. He reads exactly a variant reading of Rom 10:15 (witnessed in ℵ^c and D; cf. also Nah 1:15), reading εἰρήνην for [τὰ] ἀγαθά. This latter reading is also witnessed in Marcion (according to Tertullian) and Chrysostom.

209. Codex 451 reads ἤνοιξας; Sifanus also reads *aperuisti*.

210. LXX Isa 48:8. Ps.-Gregory reads ἠπίστασο for the LXX's ἠπίστω; reads ᾔδειν for ἔγνων; reads ἀπειθῶν ἀπειθήσεις for ἀθετῶν ἀθετήσεις.

211. Codex 451 reads ἐπὶ τοῖς ἔθνεσιν. Codex 1907 omits τόπῳ.

NOTES 77

212. LXX Mal 1:11. See the Commentary on chapter 12 for a comparison of Ps.-Gregory's various quotations of this passage.

213. Codex 1907 reads σπείσουσι.

214. LXX Mic 4:1–2.
    v. 1: Ps.-Gregory omits (with Justin; Eusebius; Cyril of Alexandria; Theodoret) τοῦ before κυρίου.
    v. 2: Ps.-Gregory reads φωτιοῦσιν ἡμᾶς ταῖς ὁδοῖς αὐτοῦ for δείξουσιν ἡμῖν τὴν ὁδὸν αὐτου. Justin also reads φωτιοῦσιν ἡμᾶς.

215. LXX Jer 1:9b–10.
    v. 9: Ps-Gregory reads ἐν τῷ στόματί σου for the LXX's εἰς τὸ στόμα σου.
    v. 10: Ps-Gregory reads κατέστησα for κατέστακα (with Ps.-Chrysostom); omits (with B; S; Hexaplaric MSS; Lucianic MSS and many patristic authors) ἐπί before βασιλείας; reads (with A; Origen [Latin]; Theodoret) βασιλεῖς for βασιλείας; reads κατακόπτειν for κατασκάπτειν.

216. The Migne text reads ἐξερρίζωσεν for Zacagni's ἐξερίζωσεν.

217. Codex 451 reads δομημάτων. Sifanus reads *stolonibus malleolisque*.

218. Codex 1907 reads μέ.

219. LXX Ps 17:44–46.
    v. 44: Ps.-Gregory reads ῥῦσαι (with B'' and La[R]) for the LXX's ῥύσῃ; reads (with R and L') ἀντιλογίας for ἀντιλογιῶν.
    v. 45: Ps.-Gregory reads μου for μοι (with R and A).

220. LXX Gen 12:3. Ps.-Gregory reads πάντα τὰ πέρατα for the LXX's πᾶσαι αἱ φυλαί.

221. LXX Deut 32:20–21.

222. LXX Isa 53:9. Ps.-Gregory reads δώσει for the LXX's δώσω.

223. LXX Isa 65:1.

224. Codex 1907 reads ἔθνου.

225. Isa 65:1b. This passage is lacking in Codex 451 but is found in Sifanus. Ps.-Gregory reads πάρειμι for the LXX's εἰμί; omits τῷ before ἔθνει; reads ἐπεκαλέσαντο (with Eusebius *Ecl.proph.*; Cyril of Alexandria) for ἐκάλεσαν.

226. LXX Ps 68:9.

227. LXX Ps 21:23. Ps.-Gregory reads Ἀπαγγελῶ for the LXX's διηγήσομαι.

228. LXX Isa 52:5b. Ps.-Gregory trans. διὰ παντός / τὸ ὄνομά μου; trans. διὰ παντὸς τὸ ὄνομά μου / βλασφημεῖται.

229. LXX Mal 1:10b. Ps.-Gregory reads μου (with Justin; Theodoret; Tertullian) for the LXX's μοι.

230. The passage in parentheses is lacking in Codex 451 and in Sifanus.

231. LXX Mal 1:11.
Mal 1:11a: Ps.-Gregory reads Ὅτι for the LXX's διότι; reads μέχρι δυσμῶν for ἕως δυσμῶν; adds λέγει Κύριος παντοκράτωρ at the end of the quotation.
Mal 1:11b: Ps.-Gregory omits καὶ θυσία καθαρά; reads καί for the LXX's διότι.

232. Zacagni does not indicate a reason for the parentheses here; the passage is lacking in Sifanus.

233. LXX Mal 1:12a.

234. LXX Ps 2:8.

235. This seems not to be a direct quotation from any extant biblical MSS; its sense is close to Exod 32:10 and Deut 9:14. See the Commentary.

236. Codex 451 and Sifanus add καί (&) after Σοδόμον.

237. LXX Isa 1:10. Ps.-Gregory reads ἀκούετε for the LXX's ἀκούσατε; reads υἱοὶ Σοδόμων for ἄρχοντες Σοδόμων.

238. This quotation is an extensively edited version of Isa 1:13b–16. See the Commentary.

239. LXX Ps 64:2.

240. LXX Zeph 2:11b. Ps.-Gregory reads ὅτι for the LXX's καί; reads τῷ κυρίῳ for αὐτῷ; trans. ἕκαστος / ἐκ τοῦ τόπου αὐτοῦ. Codex 1907 omits ἕκαστος.

241. LXX Mal 1:11. The two basic phrases of the passage are inverted and edited; see the Commentary on chapter 12 for details.

242. LXX Isa 65:15–16.
v. 15: Ps.-Gregory reads δουλεύουσί μοι for the LXX's δουλεύουσιν αὐτῷ.
v. 16: Ps.-Gregory adds πάσης before the LXX's τῆς γῆς.

243. LXX Ps 21:32. Ps.-Gregory reads (with some MSS) ὅν for the LXX's ὅτι.

NOTES 79

244. Sifanus reads, "*Atqui postquam dixisset David.*"

245. LXX Ps 67:7a.

246. LXX Isa 11:9b. Ps.-Gregory reads Πληρωθήσεται for the LXX's ἐνεπλήσθη; reads πᾶσα ἡ γῆ for ἡ σύμπασα (Lucianic MSS; Catena MSS; Eusebius *Ecl. proph.;* Athanasius; Chrysostom; Thedoret all add γῆ); reads θάλασσαν for θαλάσσας (with Cyril of Alexandria; = MT). Codex 451 reads καλύψαι.

247. LXX Ps 21:28–29.

248. Codex 451 reads τοὺς Ἰουδαίους, τίς ὁ κρατῶν ἐστιν ἄρα; Sifanus reads, "*Quid igitur obtinet.*" Sifanus adds *nunc* before *igitur*, according to Zacagni (*nunc* is lacking in 1562 edition).

249. Sifanus reads, "*quae nunc negligitur.*"

250. Zacagni rightly notes that the passage in brackets should follow the phrase "since the Temple no longer exists, nor its place."

251. Sifanus lacks "of God."

252. Matt 21:43. Ps.-Gregory reads ἀπὸ τῶν Ἰουδαίων for Matthew's ἀφ' ὑμῶν.

253. LXX Ps 110:3.

254. LXX Ps 109:1.

255. LXX Isa 45:1. Ps.-Gregory adds ὁ before Κύριος; omits (with *Barn.* 12.11; Tertullian; = MT) ὁ θεός. Sifanus reads, "*Dicit Dominus Christo meo Cyro.*"

256. Codex 451 and Sifanus add τῆς χειρός (*manus*).

257. LXX Isa 45:1–3.
  v. 1: Ps.-Gregory omits οὗ before ἐκράτησα; adds (with Hexaplaric MSS) σου after τῆς δεξιᾶς; reads ἐπακούσουσιν for ἐπακοῦσαι; reads (with Lucianic MSS) πύλας for θύρας.
  v. 2: Ps.-Gregory omits Ἐγώ before ἔμπροσθέν σου; reads (with Lucianic MSS; Origen; Epiphanius; Eusebius *Dem. ev.*; Theodoret; Cyril of Alexandria) συνθλάσω for συγκλάσω.

258. Codex 451 and Sifanus lack the phrase καὶ εἰς ἀσκὸν ἐκδαρέντι.

259. Sifanus reads, "*ad educendum oculos compenditorum.*"

260. LXX Isa 42:6–7.
  v. 6: Ps.-Gregory reads (with Catena MSS) ὁ καλέσας for the LXX's ἐκάλεσα; omits καί after δικαιοσύνῃ; reads ἐκράτησα for

κρατήσω; reads (with Justin *Dial.* 26.2, 122.3) ἰσχύσω for ἐνισχύσω; reads δώσω for ἔδωκα; adds (with *Barn.*14.7; Justin; Cyprian; = MT) καί before δώσω.

v. 7: Ps.-Gregory adds καί before ἐξαγαγεῖν; reads (with *Barn.*14.7; Justin *Dial.* 26.2, 122.3) πεπεδημένους for δεδεμένους.

261. LXX Isa 49:6. Ps.-Gregory reads μέγα σοι τοῦτο, κληθῆναι for the LXX's μέγα σοί ἐστι τοῦ κληθῆναι (Origen; Hilary; Tyconius read τοῦτο); omits σε after κληθῆναι (with Lucianic and Catenae MSS); reads καὶ στῆσαι for τοῦ στῆσαι; reads (with Justin; Theodoret) τοῦ before Ιακωβ; reads στρέψαι for ἐπιστρέψαι; reads καὶ τέθεικα for ἰδοὺ τέθεικα; adds (from Isa 42:7; with S; Lucianic MSS; Catenae MSS; Eusebius *Dem. ev.* and *Ecl. proph.*; Theodoret; Tyconius; Hilary) εἰς διαθήκην γένους after τέθεικά σε.

262. Codex 451 and Sifanus read τὸν προφήτην (*prophetam*) for τὸν Θεσβίτην.

263. LXX Mal 4:4–5 [3:23–24].
v. 4: Ps.-Gregory adds τὴν before ἡμέραν (with V; Lucianic MSS; Hippolytus; Cyril of Alexandria; Theodore Mopsuestia; Theodoret).
v. 5: Ps.-Gregory reads καρδίας πατρῶν πρὸ υἱούς for καρδίαν πατρὸς πρὸς υἱόν; reads ἐλθών for ἔλθω; omits καί before πατάξω.

264. LXX Isa 62:2. Ps.-Gregory trans. δικαιοσύνην / δόξαν; adds (with Hexaplaric MSS; Eusebius; Hilary = MT) πάντες οἱ before βασιλεῖς; omits (with Hexaplaric MSS; Lucianic MSS; Eusebius; = MT) σου after τὸ ὄνομα.

265. LXX Isa 65:15b–16a.
v. 15: Ps.-Gregory reads μοι for αὐτῷ (with S; Hexaplaric MSS; Lucianic MSS; Eusebius *Dem. ev.*; Tertullian; Cyprian).

266. This quotation is not found in Hosea. See the Commentary.

267. Ps.-Gregory's last four chapters (19–22) are lacking in Codex 451 and Sifanus. See the Commentary.

268. LXX Jer 4:9. Ps.-Gregory trans. (with Hexaplaric MSS) ἐκείνη / τῇ ἡμέρᾳ.

269. LXX Ezek 47:8–9. The Migne text reads ἰαθήσεται for Zacagni's ἰαθήσηται.
v. 8: Ps.-Gregory adds Κύριος after εἶπε; omits the LXX's passage between Γαλιλαίαν and ὑγιάσει τὰ ὕδατα; reads (with Theodoret) ἁγιάσει for ὑγιάσει.

NOTES 81

v. 9: Ps.-Gregory reads καὶ ἔσται πάσῃ ψυχῇ, ἐφ' ἢν ἂν ἐπέλθῃ τὸ ὕδωρ τοῦτο, ζήσεται καὶ ἰαθήσεται for the LXX's καὶ ἔσται πᾶσα ψυχὴ τῶν ζῴων τῶν ἐκζεόντων ἐπὶ πάντα, ἐφ' ἃ ἂν ἐπέλθῃ ἐκεῖ ὁ ποταμός, ζήσεται, καὶ ἔσται ἐκεῖ ἰχθὺς πολὺς σφόδρα.

270. LXX Jer 29:20. Ps.-Gregory reads (with Hexaplaric MSS; Lucianic MSS; Chrysostom; Ps.-Epiphanius *Test.* 28) ὡς for ὥσπερ.

271. LXX Isa 19:1. Ps.-Gregory adds πάντα before τὰ χειροποίητα.

272. LXX Isa 19:21. Ps.-Gregory reads Γνωσθήσεται for the LXX's γνωστὸς ἔσται; reads Φοβηθήσονται Κύριον for γνώσονται οἱ Αἰγύπτιοι τὸν κύριον (Φοβηθήσονται also read by 538; Sa; and Ps.-Epiphanius *Test.* 25.2).

273. LXX Isa 48:16. Ps.-Gregory reads ἐξαπέσταλκε for the LXX's απέσταλκε.

274. The Migne text omits Zacagni's κύριος after εἶπε (LXX also reads κύριος).

275. LXX Num 11:16–17. Ps.-Gregory reads Ἀνάγαγέ μοι for the LXX's Συνάγαγέ μοι; reads (with Didymus) πρεσβυτέρους for the LXX's ἄνδρας ἀπὸ τῶν πρεσβυτέρων Ἰσραήλ; omits the remainder of v. 16 and the first phrase of v. 17; reads καὶ λήψομαι ἀπὸ τοῦ ἐπὶ σὲ Πνεύματος. καὶ ἐκχεῶ ἐπ' αὐτούς for the LXX's καὶ ἀφελῶ ἀπὸ τοῦ πνεύματος τοῦ ἐπὶ σοὶ καὶ ἐπιθήσω ἐπ' αὐτούς; reads καὶ ἀντιλήψομαί σε for the LXX's καὶ συναντιλήμψονται μετὰ σοῦ.

276. LXX Ps 50:12–14.
v. 13: Ps.-Gregory omits v. 13a: μὴ ἀπορρίψῃς με ἀπὸ τοῦ προσώπου σου; trans. (with Lucianic MSS) τὸ ἅγιον / σου.
v. 14: Ps.-Gregory omits v. 14a: ἀπόδος μοι τὴν ἀγαλλίασιν τοῦ σωτηρίου σου; reads (with Lucianic MSS) στήριξον for στήρισον.

277. LXX Ps 138:7a.

278. LXX Job 33:4.

279. LXX Job 32:8. Ps.-Gregory (with Lucianic MSS; Ps.-Basil *Eunom.* 192 [PG 29:761]) adds με after διδάσκουσα.

280. LXX Job 27:2–3. Ps.-Gregory omits 27:3a: ἦ μὴν ἔτι τῆς πνοῆς μου ἐνούσης.

281. LXX Hag 2:4b–5a. Ps.-Gregory reads ἐγώ εἰμι for the LXX's διότι μεθ' ὑμῶν ἐγώ εἰμι; omits λέγει κύριος παντοκράτωρ; adds ἐν ὑμῖν after ἐγώ εἰμι.

282. LXX Wis 1:7.

283. LXX Isa 63:10. Ps.-Gregory omits (with A'; Tychonius) αὐτοῦ after τὸ πνεῦμα τὸ ἅγιον.

284. LXX Mic 2:7a. Ps.-Gregory adds ὁ before οἶκος; adds τοῦ before Ἰακώβ; reads παρώξυναν for the LXX's παρώργισεν.

285. LXX Joel 2:28. Ps.-Gregory reads καὶ ἔσται ἐν ταῖς ἐσχάταις ἡμέραις for the LXX's καὶ ἔσται μετὰ ταῦτα (following Acts 2:17). The second part of Ps.-Gregory's quotation is a loose paraphrase of Joel 2:28.

286. LXX Isa 61:1.

287. Ps.-Gregory alludes to a tradition locating seven works of God's spirit in Isa 11:2–3. See the Commentary.

288. LXX Isa 63:14. Ps.-Gregory omits παρά (= MT).

289. LXX Exod 31:3–11; cf. Exod 35:30–35. Ps.-Gregory summarizes the passage where God fills Bezalel with his spirit.

290. LXX 4 Kgdms 2:9–11. Ps.-Gregory summarizes this passage, focusing on the role of the spirit.

291. Isa 57:16. Ps.-Gregory omits γάρ after πνεῦμα.

292. Matt 12:18. Ps.-Gregory follows Matthew's version of Isa 42:1, except for reading ὁ ἐκλεκτός for Matthew's ὃν ᾑρέτισα.

293. LXX Isa 30:1. Ps.-Gregory reads συνθήκην for συνθήκας.

294. LXX Isa 34:15b–16.
- v. 15: Ps.-Gregory trans. (with Hexaplaric MSS; Eusebius; Theodoret; = MT) ἔλαφοι / συνήντησαν.
- v. 16: Ps.-Gregory reads οὐκ ὑπελείφθη for οὐκ ἀπώλετο; omits ἑτέρα τὴν ἑτέραν οὐκ ἐζήτησαν after οὐκ ἀπώλετο; reads διότι κύριος for ὅτι κύριος.

295. LXX Ps 103:29–30.

Commentary

FROM THE OLD TESTAMENT: Ἡ παλαιά (with διαθήκη understood) refers to the Old Testament (see, e.g., Eusebius *Hist. eccl.* 5.17.3; Origen *Comm. Jo.* 1.3 [17]).

CHAPTER 1: PROOFS OF THE TRINITY

1.1. Introduction: A paradigmatic reference to the Trinity

Ps 32:6: Ps.-Gregory begins his collection with Ps 32:6, a well-known *testimonium* for the Trinity in early Christian literature. This classic proof-text and his exegetical comments serve as a sort of introduction to the following proofs of the Trinity. Psalm 32:6 is often employed, in combination with the Johannine prologue, to demonstrate that God created the world through his Word and through his Spirit. Irenaeus cites this text (in connection with John 1:3) in his exposition of the "rule of truth" that the one God created all things through his word (*Haer.* 1.22.1; cf. *Haer.* 3.8.3; 3.24.2; *Epid.* 5). Theophilus uses it to refer to God's Word and Spirit in creation (*Autol.* 1.7.3). It is preserved in the later general TCs: Cyprian *Test.* 2.3 (under the heading, "That the same Christ is the Word of God"; this TC also includes John 1:1–5 and Ps 106:20) and Ps.-Epiphanius *Test.* 3.2 (under the heading "That he was the joint-creator" [συνκτίστης]).

Theophilus (*Autol.* 1.7.3) and Irenaeus (*Epid.* 5; *Haer.* 3.24.2) identify God's wisdom (σοφία) with God's Spirit. In contrast, Ps.-Gregory identifies Christ with God's Wisdom (see also *Dial. AZ* 7; Tertullian *Prax.* 7.3). In either case, this early Christian teaching is a development of Jewish reflection on the role of God's Wisdom in creation (e.g., Prov 8; Sir 24).

This evidence suggests, then, that Ps 32:6 was a central text in early Christian teaching on Wisdom's role in creation.

Ps.-Gregory's further *testimonia* and comments, however, show a connection with the Trinitarian controversies of the third and fourth centuries. Several writers used Ps 32:6 and related texts to refute the "Sabellian" position that, in orthodox eyes, failed to distinguish adequately between Father, Son, and Spirit in the Godhead.

Tertullian attacked the "Sabellianism" of a certain Praxeas; Eusebius of Caesaria opposed the similar views of Marcellus of Ancyra (d. ca. 374). Marcellus, according to Eusebius, used the analogy of human speech to clarify the relationship between the Father and the Logos in the Godhead: he described the Logos as "remaining immanent when the Father was silent, but being active in creating the universe, just as our logos is quiet when we are silent, but active when we speak" (*Marc.* 1.1.4, my translation).

Apparently reacting to this "Sabellian" position, Ps.-Gregory insists that the word is not a human word, but rather a "subsistent" (ἐνυπόστατος) word. Ps.-Gregory's comments mirror other Christian authors:

Ps.-Gregory *Test.* 1	Tertullian *Prax.* 7.3–6	Eusebius *Dem. ev.* 5.5 (Exposition of Psalm 32)
Ps. 32:6 (interpreted with John 1:1 and 15:26) Ps 147:7 Ps 106:20 "Now 'Word' is not a meaningful impression of the air brought forth by speech-producing organs."	Ps 32:6 with John 1:3 "For you will say, what is a word, but a voice and sound of the mouth, and (as the grammarians teach) air when struck against, intelligible to the ear, but for the rest a sort of void, empty, and incorporeal thing."	Ps 32:6 (interpreted with John 1:1–3) Ps 106:20 Ps 147:7 Eusebius explains that the Logos is not like a spoken (προφορικός) human word, produced by the tongue and organs of the throat and mouth.

See also the combination of Ps 32:6 and Ps 106:20 in Eusebius's quotation of Marcellus (*Marc.* 2.2.9). In another TC, Eusebius uses Ps. 32:6 to demonstrate that the Logos is secondary to God, paralleling other texts used by Ps.-Gregory in his opening collection: Prov 8:22–31, Ps 106:20, Gen 1:26, Gen 19:24, Ps 109:3, and John 1:1–4 (*Praep. ev.* 7.12).

Most strikingly, Ps.-Gregory's exegetical comments on Ps 32:6 parallel those of Basil of Caesarea *On the Holy Spirit* almost word for word.

| Ps.-Gregory *Test.* 1.1 | Basil *Spirit* 38 |
Quotation of Ps 32:6	Quotation of Ps 32:6
Οὐ Λόγος οὖν ὑπάρχει ἀέρος, τύπωσις σημαντικὴ διὰ Φωνητικῶν ὀργάνων ἐκφερομένη· οὔτε Πνεῦμα στόματος ἀτμός, ἐκ τῶν ἀναπνευστικῶν μερῶν ἐξωθούμενος· ἀλλὰ Λόγος μὲν ὁ πρὸς Θεὸν ἐν ἀρχῇ, καὶ Θεὸς ὤν. Πνεῦμα δὲ στόματος Θεοῦ, τὸ Πνεῦμα τῆς ἀληθείας, ὃ παρὰ τοῦ Πατρὸς ἐκπορεύεται. Τρία τοίνυν νόει, τὸν προστάττοντα Κύριον, τὸν δημιουργοῦντα Λόγον, τὸν στερεοῦντά τουτέστι τὸ Πνεῦμα.	Οὔτε οὖν λόγος ἀέρος, τύπωσις σημαντική, διὰ Φωνητικῶν ὀργάνων ἐκφερομένη· οὔτε πνεῦμα, στόματος ἀτμός, ἐκ τῶν ἀναπνευστικῶν μερῶν ἐξωθούμενος· ἀλλὰ Λόγος μὲν ὁ πρὸς Θεὸν ὢν ἐν ἀρχῇ, καὶ Θεὸς ὤν. Πνεῦμα δὲ στόματος Θεοῦ, τὸ Πνεῦμα τῆς ἀληθείας, ὃ παρὰ τοῦ Πατρὸς ἐκπορεύεται. Τρία τοίνυν νοεῖς, τὸν προστάσσοντα Κύριον, τὸν δημιουργοῦντα Λόγον, τὸ στερεοῦν τὸ Πνεῦμα.

Note: In this comparison and elsewhere, single underlining signifies exact parallels between texts; double underlining indicates a close, but not exact, parallel.

Despite the almost verbatim nature of these comments, it is unlikely that one author is the source for the other. The contexts in which these comments occur are quite different. Basil's chapter 38 is an extended discussion on the role of the Spirit in the creation, and he refers to none of the other texts adduced by Ps.-Gregory. Since a direct literary relationship between the two authors is unlikely, the most probable explanation is that both authors are relying on an exegesis of Ps 32:6 drawn from a common, written catechetical source.

See also *Dial. AZ* 11, with its similar exegetical comment on Ps 32:6, ὅτι δὲ οὔτε λόγος διὰ Φωνητηρίων ὀργάνων ἀναπεμπόμενος, οὔτε πνεῦμα διὰ τῶν ἀναπνευστικῶν δῆλον ὅτι ἐκ τοῦ ἀσώματον εἶναι τὸν θεόν.

1.2. *God sends out the Word and the Spirit*

Ps.-Gregory distinguishes between a "spoken" or "uttered" (προφορικός) word and a subsistent (ἐνυπόστατος) one. He does not have in mind the Stoic distinction between the logos immanent in one's mind (ἐνδιάθετος) and a spoken logos (προφορικός), but rather the distinction, discussed above, between a "human" word and the divine Word that exists as a distinct entity within the Godhead. The point is expressed similarly in other Christian works. Anathema 8 of the First Sirmian Creed (351), for example, reads, "If anyone says that the Son is the immanent (ἐνδιάθετος) or proceeding (προφορικός) Logos of God, let him be anathema" (text of creed *apud* Athanasius *Syn.* 27). See also Cyril of Jerusalem *Cat.* 11.10, Ἡμεῖς δὲ οἴδαμεν τὸν Χριστὸν γεννηθέντα λόγον οὐ προφορικόν, ἀλλὰ λόγον ἐνυπόστατον καὶ ζῶντα.

In this TC, Ps.-Gregory's quotations of Ps 147:7, Ps 106:20, and Ps 103:30 are all linked by the catch-word ἀποστέλλω (ἐξαποστέλλω in Ps 103). In a similar fashion, Ps.-Epiphanius groups Ps 106:20 with three other texts under the heading "that he was sent out" (ὅτι ἀπεστάλη; *Test.* 4). Epiphanius also combines Ps 103:30 and Ps 147:7 (*Pan.* 74.5.2). See also *Alt. Sim.* 10–11 (quoting Ps 106:20, Ps 32:6, Ps 147:4, and the Johannine prologue in a discussion on Christ as the Word of God).

Epiphanius's exegesis of Ps 147:7 parallels that of Ps.-Gregory: he argues (against Paul of Samosata) that the Logos is not a human word, but rather is ἐνυπόστατος (*Pan.* 65.5). Cyprian quotes Ps 106:20, with (*inter alia*) Ps 32:6 and the Johannine prologue, to prove "that the same Christ is the Word of God" (*Test.* 2.3).

1.3. Proof of the subsistence of the Word

The interpretation of Jer 23:18 was important in the fourth-century Trinitarian debates (see R. P. C. Hanson, *The Search for the Christian Doctrine of God: The Arian Controversy 318–381* [Edinburgh: T & T Clark, 1988], 545). In his quotation of the passage, Marius Victorinus reads ὑποστάσει for ὑποστήματι (*Against Arius* 2.5).

Hippolytus closely parallels Ps.-Gregory here. After combining John 1:1–3 and Ps 32:6 (*Noet.* 12.3–4), Hippolytus quotes Jer 23:18 and comments, Λόγος δὲ θεοῦ μόνος ὁρατός, ἀνθρώπου δὲ ἀκουστός (13.2). He then identifies this Λόγος as the one who is sent (ἀπεστάλθη) (13.2–3). Hippolytus of course does not yet use the technical language of the fourth-century debates.

1.4. Wisdom's role in creation

You complete the years, O God, by your power: Alfred Resch lists this as "Logion 23," and compares it with Ps 102:28: τὰ ἔτη σου οὐκ ἐκλείψουσιν (*Agrapha: Aussercanonische Schriftfragmente* [TU 30, 3/4; n.f. 15, 3/4; Leipzig: Hinrichs, 1906], 309). After this quotation, Ps.-Gregory quotes 1 Cor 1:24 ("But Christ is the power of God and the wisdom of God") as an introduction to his proofs on Christ's role in creation.

[Speaking] in the person of Wisdom: Ps.-Gregory here uses πρώοσοπον as a technical term to distinguish the "person" speaking in a particular scriptural passage. Πρώοσοπον, in addition to meaning face, mask, or presence, referred in classical Greek to a character in drama or literature. In the patristic writers, this literary sense takes on theological implications, being used to distinguish between the words of the Father, the Son, and the Spirit in scripture.

In reference to the Word, Justin says, "sometimes He speaks as from the person (ἀπὸ προσώπου) of God the Lord and Father of all; sometimes as from the person of Christ; sometimes as from the person of the people answering the Lord or His Father, just as you can see even in your own writers, one man being the writer of the whole, but introducing the persons who converse" (*1 Apol*. 36.2).

Tertullian comments on his collection of scriptural *testimonia*, "In these few quotations the distinction (of persons in) the Trinity is clearly set forth. For there is the Spirit himself who speaks, and the Father to whom he speaks, and the Son of whom he speaks. In the same manner, the other passages also establish each one of several persons (*persona*) in his special character" (*Prax*. 11.9–10).

On this "prosopological exegesis," see Michael Slusser, "The Exegetical Roots of Trinitarian Theology," *TS* 49 (1988): 461–76.

Ps.-Gregory's use of the term πρώοσοπον is especially appropriate in this context, as it echoes the phrase τῷ προσώπῳ αὐτοῦ from the quotation of Prov 8:30.

Prov 8:27–30: Proverbs 8 was central to Christian speculation on the role of God's Wisdom in creation.

Tertullian introduces his quotation of Prov 8:22–30 in the same fashion as Ps.-Gregory, "Listen therefore to Wisdom herself, constituted in the character of a Second Person" (*Prax*. 6.1). In the same document, Tertullian quotes or alludes to Prov 8:27, Isa 40:13, 1 Cor 1:24, Ps 32:6, and the Johannine prologue in his discussion of Christ as God's pre-existent Word and Wisdom (*Prax*. 19.2–3; cf. *Prax*. 7). Theophilus, after citing an edited version of Prov 8:27–29 in his discussion of God's pre-existent Word and Wisdom, continues (as does Ps.-Gregory) with a discussion of Genesis 1 (*Autol*. 2.10.6–10). Irenaeus also cites an edited version of Prov 8:22–31 in his discussion of God's pre-existent Word and Wisdom (*Haer*. 4.20.3); Irenaeus's reading of Genesis 1:1 (*Epid*. 43: "God established a Son in the beginning") seems to be influenced by Prov 8:22 (see Oskar Skarsaune, *The Proof from Prophecy: A Study in Justin Martyr's Proof-Text Tradition. Text-Type, Provenance, Theological Profile* [NovTSup 56; Leiden: Brill, 1987], 387). Justin quotes Prov 8:22–36 in his discussion of Wisdom and creation (*Dial*. 61–62). See also *Dial. AZ*. 13.

Cyprian quotes Prov 8:22–31 under the heading, "That Christ is the first-born, and that he is the wisdom of God, by whom all things were made" (*Test.* 2.1; Cyprian's TC includes 1 Cor 1:24); cf. Prov 8 in Ps.-Epiphanius *Test.* 1.2 and especially *Test.* 3 ("That he was the joint-creator," including quotations of Prov 8:27–30 and Ps 32:6).

Isa 40:13: Irenaeus connects "the advisor" with God's Word (*Haer.* 5.1.1); Tertullian combines the text with Prov 8:27 in denying that God received help from any lower powers in creating the universe (*Prax.* 19.2). Tertullian goes on to quote 1 Cor 1:24 in this same chapter.

1.5. Trinitarian references in the Genesis creation account

Ps.-Gregory's reflection on a "wisdom Christology" moves now to an explicit consideration of the creation texts in Genesis.

the proof of the holy Trinity: The term "proof" (ἀπόδειξις) is used by Eusebius for the title of his extensive collection of TCs: *Proof of the Gospel* (ἀπόδειξις τοῦ εὐαγγελίου).

Gen 1:26–27: Ps.-Gregory follows a long-standing Trinitarian interpretation of the plural "Let us make." Already Justin (interpreting Gen 1:26 with Gen 3:22, Ps.-Gregory's next quotation) had argued that God did not speak to himself in the passage but rather "conversed with some one who was numerically distinct from Himself, and also a rational being" (*Dial.* 62.3).

Justin offers a christological reading, connecting Gen 1:26–27 with Prov 8 to show that God is speaking with Christ (*Dial.* 62), an interpretation followed by Ps.-Epiphanius (*Test.* 2–3; these chapters on the creation include Gen 1:26, Prov 8:27–30, and Ps 32:6). Irenaeus and Theophilus give it a Trinitarian interpretation. Irenaeus: "For with Him were always present the Word and Wisdom, the Son and the Spirit, by whom and in whom, freely and spontaneously, he made all things, to whom also he speaks, saying, 'Let us make man after our image and likeness'" (*Haer.* 4.20.1). Theophilus: "But to no one else than to his own word and wisdom did he say, 'Let us make'" (*Autol.* 2.18.2).

Ps.-Gregory again seems to be opposing positions such as that of Marcellus, who interpreted "Let us make humans in our own image" as analogous to a human's internal deliberations, as if a sculptor should say, "Come, let us make a statue," after having designed the statue in his mind (Eusebius *Marc.* 2.2.41). This position was condemned by Anathema 14 of the First Sirmian Creed, "Anyone who says that in the passage 'Let us make man,' the Father was not talking to the Son, but God was talking to himself, let him be anathema" (*apud* Athanasius *Syn*. 27). Novatian includes the passage (with Gen 19:24, Ps 2:7–8, Ps 109:1, and Isa 45:1) in his TC demonstrating the distinctiveness of the Father and the Son against a Sabellian interpretation (*Trin*. 26.3–7).

See also *Dial. AZ* 3–12, where the author uses many of the same supporting texts and exegesis found in Ps.-Gregory, and Ps.-Epiphanius Test. 2. For a discussion of this passage in Jewish and early Christian literature until the time of Justin, see R. McL. Wilson, "The Early History of the Exegesis of Gen. 1.26," *StPatr* 1 (1957): 420–37.

For we have been formed spiritually: I have translated the term νοητῶς as "spiritually" in order to emphasize the implicit contrast with the creation of the physical aspect of humans. The term, however, may also be rendered as "intellectually"—indicating the creation of the noetic function in humans.

Ps.-Gregory's detailed connections with Cyril of Alexandria *Against Julian* 28–29 should be noted. Both quote the same edited version of Gen 1:26–27, and both use the phrase "formed spiritually" (μεμορφώμεθα νοητῶς) in reference to humans becoming conformed to the image of the Son. Cyril uses the same verb ζωογονέω to refer to the Spirit's activity in creation, and the same phrase to describe the Trinity, ἡ ἁγία τε καὶ ὁμοούσιος Τριάς. *Barnabas* also connects the renewal of the believer and Gen 1:26 (6.11–12).

Gen 3:22: As noted above, Justin also connects Gen 1:26–27 and Gen 3:22 (*Dial*. 62.1–3); as does *Dial. AZ* 12. Ps.-Basil employs Gen 1:26, Gen 3:22, Gen 11:7, and Gen 19:24 to prove that God is speaking not to himself, but to the Son and the Spirit (*Eunom*. 183).

God created all things through the Word: Cyril of Alexandria parallels Ps.-Gregory's comment that the phrase "and God said, 'Let there be'" proves that creation is through the Word (*Julian* 1.28). Ps.-Gregory distinguishes between the God who commands (the Father) and the God who carries out the commands (the Son).

1.6. Theophany of the Trinity: Appearance to Abraham at Mamre

Ps.-Gregory discusses here a classic *testimonium* on the appearance of the Trinity to Abraham at Mamre.

Justin's discussion of OT theophanies as appearances of Christ (*Dial*. 56–60) begins with this theophany:

56–57: Theophany to Abraham at Mamre (Gen 18) and the two Lords (Gen 19:24). Interpreted with Ps 109:1 and Ps 44:7–8.
58:     Theophanies to Jacob
59–60: Theophany to Moses at the burning bush.

For a detailed analysis of Justin's discussion of the theophanies and their witness to a "second God," see Skarsaune, *Proof from Prophecy*, 409–24.

Irenaeus also knows this sequence: the theophany at Mamre interpreted with Gen 19:24 is followed by the theophanies to Jacob and Moses (*Epid.* 44–46). Novatian too follows the traditional sequence: after a discussion of Gen 1:26–27, theophanies to Abraham (Mamre theophany interpreted with Gen 19:24) and to Jacob are presented (*Trin.* 17–19).

Eusebius shows the same general cluster of texts and interpretations (*Dem. ev.* 5):

5.5:   Creation texts (Ps 32:6 interpreted with John 1:1 and Psalms)
5.6:   "Two Lords" (Isa 48:12–16)
5.7:   Christological interpretation of Gen 1:26–27
5.8:   Interpretation of Gen 19:24 as "Two Lords"
5.9:   "Second Lord" in the Abraham texts, including theophany at Mamre
5.10–12: Theophanies to Jacob
5.13–18: Theophanies and "Second Lord" texts in Exodus and Numbers

Justin, Irenaeus, and writers as late as Eusebius interpret this text christologically (i.e., one of the three was Christ); Ps.-Gregory follows a later Christian exegesis that understands this passage in a Trinitarian manner. For a fuller discussion, see L. Thunberg, "Early Christian Interpretations of the Three Angels in Gen. 18," *StPatr* 7 (1966): 560–70.

Notice: it says that God appeared to him, yet there were three men who were seen: The comments of Ps.-Gregory and Cyril of Alexandria clearly follow the same written exegetical tradition; again, a direct literary relationship between the two seems to be ruled out by minor variations and the different contexts within which the passage is quoted within the two works.

Ps.-Gregory *Test.* 1	Cyril *Julian* 26
Quotation of Gen 18:1–3; the words καὶ μεθ' ἕτερα; quotation of Gen 18:9–10.	Quotation of Gen 18:1–3; the words καὶ μεθ' ἕτερα; quotation of Gen 18:9–10. Cyril's quotation follows the LXX where Ps.-Gregory deviates.
Ἰδοὺ δὴ φησὶν ὀφθῆναι μὲν αὐτῷ τὸν θεόν, εἶναί γε μὴν τρεῖς ἄνδρας τοὺς ἑωραμένους· αὐτὸν δὲ πάλιν οὐχ ὡς τρισὶν εἰπεῖν· Κύριοι, εἰ εὕρηκα χάριν ἐναντίον ὑμῶν, μὴ παρέλθητε τὸν παῖδα ὑμῶν. Κύριον δὲ μοναδικῶς τοὺς τρεῖς ὀναμάζοντα, καὶ ὡς ἕνα καταίρειν ἀξιοῦν, καὶ ὡς εἷς φωνεῖ· Ἥξω	Ἰδοὺ δὴ μάλα σαφῶς ὦφθαι μὲν αὐτῷ φησι τὸν θεόν, εἶναί γε μὴν τοὺς ἑωραμένους ἄνδρας τρεῖς, προσθέοντα δὲ τὸν θεσπέσιον Ἀβραὰμ οὐχ ὡς τρισὶν εἰπεῖν· Κύριοι, εἰ εὗρον χάριν ἐναντίον ὑμῶν, μὴ παρέλθητε τὸν παῖδα ὑμῶν, Κύριον δὲ μοναδικῶς ὀναμάζοντα τοὺς τρεῖς, ὡς ἕνα παρ' ἑαυτῷ καταίρειν ἀξιοῦν, ἐπεὶ καὶ ὡς εἷς ὄντες οἱ τρεῖς ἔφασκον ὡς ἐκ προσώπου πάλιν ἑνός· Ποῦ Σάρρα ἡ γυνή σου; καὶ τὸ ἐπαναστρέφων ἥξω κατὰ τὸν καιρὸν τοῦτον εἰς ὥρας.
Ὅρα οὖν τοὺς ὀφθέντας τρεῖς μὲν ὄντας, καὶ ὑφεστῶτας ἰδιοσυστάτως ἕκαστον· τῷ γε μὴν τῆς ὁμοουσίας λόγῳ συνειλημμένους εἰς ἕνα, καὶ τὰς διαλέξεις ποιησαμένους.	Ἄθρει δὴ οὖν, ἄθρει τοὺς ὀφθέντας αὐτῷ τρεῖς μὲν ὄντας καὶ ἰδιοσυστάτως ἕκαστον ὑφεστηκότας, τῷ γε μὴν λόγῳ τῆς ὁμοουσιότητος εἰς ἕνα συνειλημμένους καὶ τὰς διαλέξεις οὕτω ποιεῖσθαι σπουδάσαντας.

1.7. Conversations between Father and Son; including Father "begetting" the Son

In the *testimonia* literature, the OT theophanies of Christ are closely connected with passages in which the Father is understood as speaking to the Son.

Gen 11:7: As noted, Ps.-Basil employs Gen 1:26, 3:22, 11:7, and 19:24 (*Eunom.* 183). Novatian combines Gen 11:7 with Gen 1:16–27 (*Trin.* 17).

Tertullian articulates the hermeneutical principle behind the exegesis of the theophanies. The Son not only made things at the time of creation, "but also that which has been done by God since that time" (*Prax.* 16.1). "It is the Son, therefore, who has judged from the beginning, destroying the proud tower, confusing the languages, punishing the whole world by the violence of the waters, raining upon Sodom and Gomorrah fire and brimstone, God from God" (*Prax.* 16.2). The governing principle seems to be that the eternal, unchanging God cannot be the direct cause of change within the mutable creation.

Ps 109:3 with Ps 71:17: Ps.-Gregory reads a conflated version of Ps 71:17 and Ps 71:5:

Ps.-Gregory Test. 1: πρὸ τοῦ ἡλίου τὸ ὄνομα αὐτοῦ, καὶ πρὸ τῆς σελήνης.

Ps 71:17b: πρὸ τοῦ ἡλίου διαμενεῖ τὸ ὄνομα αὐτοῦ.

Ps 71:5: καὶ συμπαραμενεῖ τῷ ἡλίῳ, καὶ πρὸ τῆς σελήνης γενεὰς γενεῶν.

This combination of Ps 109:3 and this adapted version of Ps 71:17 is known in the earlier *testimonia* tradition. Skarsaune notes the following parallels to Ps.-Gregory (*Proof from Prophecy*, 235):

Ps.-Gregory Test. 1	Justin *Dial.* 45.4	Justin *Dial.* 76.7	Irenaeus *Epid.* 43
Ἐκ γαστρὸς πρὸ ἑωσφόρου ἐγέννησά σε· (Ps 109:3) καὶ πρὸ τοῦ ἡλίου τὸ ὄνομα αὐτοῦ, καὶ πρὸ τῆς σελήνης (Ps 72:17 and 5)	ὃς καὶ πρὸ ἑωσφόρου καὶ σελήνης ἦν (Ps 109:3 / Ps 71:5)	πρὸ ἡλίου καὶ σελήνης (Ps 71:17 and 5) ἐκ γαστρὸς γεννηθήσεσθαι αὐτόν (Ps 109:3)	Before the daystar I begot you (Ps 109:3), your name is before the sun (Ps 71:17)

Irenaeus falsely attributes this quotation to "Jeremiah," a possible indication that he drew the quotation from a TC on the pre-existence of Christ. For detailed arguments on this point, see Joseph P. Smith., trans., *Proof of the Apostolic Preaching* (ACW 16; Westminster, Md.: Newman; London: Longmans, Green, 1952), 181–82 n. 206.

J. Rendel Harris, noting similar passages in Lactantius and Cyprian, saw evidence for the common use of the "Testimony Book" for proofs of Christ's pre-existence (*Testimonies* [2 vols.; Cambridge: Cambridge University Press, 1916–20], 1:71–74). See also the detailed discussion by Alessandro Falcetta, "Testimonies: The Theory of James Rendel Harris in the Light of Subsequent Research" (Ph.D. diss., University of Birmingham, 2001), 124–30.

See also Tertullian's discussion of Pss 109 and 71 (*Marc.* 5.9) and Ps.-Epiphanius *Test.* 1, where, under the heading, "That before the ages the Son was begotten," Ps 109:3, Prov 8:23–25, and Ps 71:5 are quoted.

Ps.-Gregory's series of texts at this point are all linked by the concept of the Father "begetting" the Son: Ps 109:3 with Ps 71:17, Ps 2:7–8, and 2 Kgdms 7:14.

Ps 2:7–8: Tertullian quotes a combination of Ps 2:7 and Ps 109:3 in the context of his discussion on creation (*Prax.* 7.2; he also refers to Prov 8, the Johannine prologue, and Ps 32:6 in this chapter). See also the combination of Ps 2:7, Ps 109:3, and Prov 8:22 in *Prax.* 11.3.

2 Kgdms 7:14: Both Ps 2:7–8 and 2 Kgdms 7:14 (along with its wider context of Nathan's prophecy of eternal rule for David's descendant [2 Kgdms 7:12–16]) are widely influential *testimonia* (see, e.g., Ps 2:7–8 in Acts 13:33, the Gospel accounts of Jesus' baptism, Irenaeus *Epid.* 49, 1 *Clem.* 36.4, and Justin *Dial.* 88.8, 122.6; see 2 Kgdms 7 in 2 Cor 6:18, Rev 21:7, Justin *Dial.* 118.2, Irenaeus *Epid.* 36. and *Alt. Sim.* 9).

Of special interest are combinations of these texts: in Heb 1:5 they form part of a larger TC designed to prove that the Son is greater than the angels; Tertullian quotes Ps 2:7–8 and then alludes to Nathan's prophecy in arguing that these passages apply to Jesus and not to another descendant of David (*Adv. Jud.* 14.12–13; cf. *Marc.* 3.20.9). The Jewish eschatological background to these texts is evident in 4QMidrash on Eschatology (=4QFlorilegium and 4QCatena^a), which quotes 2 Sam 7:14 along with Ps 2:1–2 in its reflection on events of the last days.

1.8. References to plurality within the Godhead: Gen 19:24

1.8.1. Paradigmatic reference to two Lords

Ps.-Gregory begins this section with a reference to Gen 19:24, a central proof in the *testimonia* literature for the existence of "two Lords." Skarsaune has shown that in his combination of Gen 19:24 with Ps 109:1 and Ps 44:7–8 Justin (*Dial.* 56.12–15) likely draws on a TC designed to prove the existence of two Lords (Gen 19:24 and Ps 109:1) or two "Gods" (Ps 44:7–8) (*Proof from Prophecy*, 209, cf. further lit. there). See also a similar collection of "two Lords" and "two Gods" texts in Irenaeus *Haer.* 3.6.1 (including Ps 109:1, Gen 19:24, Ps 44:7–8). In his interpretation of OT theophanies as the appearance of Christ (*Dial.* 56–60), Justin's key text is Gen 19:24: he uses it as proof that one of the three visitors to Abraham at Mamre was Christ (see

Skarsaune, *Proof from Prophecy*, 208–9, 410–13). Irenaeus also combines a discussion of the theophany at Mamre with a quotation of Gen 19:24 (*Epid.* 44).

Cyril of Jerusalem combines Gen 19:24 with Gen 1:26–27 as proofs of Christ's pre-existence (*Cat.* 10.6). Tertullian's discussion of Christ's role in creation is followed by allusions to Gen 11:7 and to Gen 19:24 (*Prax.* 16.2); Novatian employs the text (with Gen 1:26, Ps 2:7–8, Ps 109:1, and Isa 45:1) in a TC demonstrating the distinctiveness of the Father and the Son (*Trin.* 26) against a Sabellian interpretation.

Anathema 17 of the First Sirmian Creed addresses this passage in the context of the Trinitarian debates: "If anyone does not understand 'The Lord rained down fire from the Lord' as applying to the Father and the Son, but rather means that he rained down from himself, let him be anathema. For the Son the Lord rained down from the Father the Lord" (*apud* Athanasius *Syn.* 27).

The form used by Ps.-Gregory parallels the non-LXX form evidenced in TCs found in Irenaeus and Tertullian:

trans.   κύριος / ἔβρεξεν (with Irenaeus *Haer.* 3.6.1);
trans.   θεῖον καὶ πῦρ (with Irenaeus *Haer.* 3.6.1; Tertullian *Prax.* 16.2).

1.8.2. Passages in which God the Father speaks, referring to a God or Lord different from himself

What about the following passage [spoken] in the person of God: Ps.-Gregory presents a series of seven texts in which God the Father speaks, yet seems to refer to a God or Lord different from himself:

Gen 9:6:	God refers to "image of God" in the third person
Exod 34:4–6:	The Lord speaks "in the name of the Lord"
Gen 31:13:	The Lord speaks, but refers to "another" God in the third person
Deut 32:43	(cf. Heb 1:6): The Lord speaks in the first person in Deut 32:37–42, but the narrative shifts without warning into a third person description of God in 32:43.
Hag 2:4–5:	God refers to his Word and Spirit
Exod 19:10–11:	The Lord refers to "the Lord" (third person)
Joel 2:28–31:	The Lord refers to the "day of the Lord" not "my day"

Do you see that God created humankind in the image of "God": Ps.-Gregory understands "image of God" to refer to the image of Christ.

Exod 34:4–6: Eusebius provides the same interpretation for this text (*Dem. ev.* 5.17).

Gen 31:13: Already Philo discusses the concept of "two Gods" in regard to this passage (*Somn.* 1.227–230). Justin (*Dial.* 58.5) includes this passage in his larger discussion of OT theophanies (*Dial.* 56–60).

Deut 32:43 (cf. Heb 1:6): The Migne editor attributes the quotation to Ps 96:7, but it more likely derives from Deut 32:43. See Harold W. Attridge, *The Epistle to the Hebrews* (Hermeneia; Philadelphia: Fortress, 1989), 57. The passage is taken from Deut 32:1–43 ("The Song of Moses"), a popular source of early Christian *testimonia* (see F. F. Bruce, *The Epistle to the Hebrews* [rev. ed.; NICNT; Grand Rapids: Eerdmans, 1990], 264). See also Justin *Dial.* 130.1 and *Alt. Sim.* 7.

Hag 2:4–5: Ps.-Gregory presents a drastically edited text, and adds the phrase "my good word" (ὁ λόγος ὁ ἀγαθός) apparently based on the Hebrew הדבר in Hag 2:5 (also witnessed in several Greek versions). See also the use of this passage in Ps.-Gregory *Test.* 22.

Ps.-Gregory *Test.* 1	LXX Hag 2:4–5
<u>Ἴσχυε</u>, Ζοροβάβελ διότι ἐγώ μεθ' ὑμῶν εἰμι, καὶ ὁ Λόγος μου ὁ ἀγαθός, <u>καὶ τὸ Πνεῦμά μου ἐν μέσῳ ὑμῶν</u>.	4 καὶ νῦν <u>κατίσχυε</u> Ζοροβαβελ λέγει κύριος καὶ κατίσχυε Ἰησοῦ ὁ τοῦ Ιωσεδεκ ὁ ἱερεὺς ὁ μέγας καὶ κατισχυέτω πᾶς ὁ λαὸς τῆς γῆς λέγει κύριος καὶ ποιεῖτε· διότι μεθ' ὑμῶν ἐγώ εἰμι λέγει κύριος παντοκράτωρ 5 <u>καὶ τὸ πνεῦμά μου ἐφέστηκεν ἐν μέσῳ ὑμῶν</u>·

Epiphanius (*Pan.* 76.38.4), Cyril of Jerusalem (*Cat.* 16.29), and Ps.-Basil (*Eunom.* 161) all use this text (in LXX form) to refer to the Spirit. See also its application to the coming of Christ in Ps.-Epiphanius *Test.* 5.17.

Exod 19:10–11: Cyprian quotes this passage under the heading, "That Christ should rise again from the dead on the third day" (*Test.* 2.25).

Joel 2:28–31: The passage in Joel 2:28–32 is paradigmatic for the eschatological outpouring of the Spirit (Acts 2:17–21); similar uses are found elsewhere in the *testimonia* literature (e.g., Novatian *Trin.* 29.2). Regarding textual form, cf. Justin *Dial.* 87.6 (text mixes the

Acts 2:17 version with LXX Joel 2:28–29; see Skarsaune, *Proof from Prophecy*, 122–23).

1.8.3. *Further references to "two powers in heaven" passages*

Ps 101:20–22: Since this is a narrative passage, Ps.-Gregory argues that David would have used the personal pronoun "his" if he had been referring to the Lord's name. Since the word "Lord" is repeated, this indicates a reference to "another Lord."

Ps 2:4 and Ps 29:9: Ps.-Gregory finds a reference to two heavenly figures by an overly literal reading of the poetic parallelism.

Amos 4:11: Novatian echoes this same interpretation, combining Amos 4:11 and Gen 19:24 to demonstrate the distinction between God and the other "Lord" who destroyed Sodom and Gomorrah (*Trin.* 18.5).

Isa 53:1: The passage is quoted already in John 12:38 and Rom 10:16 (Isa 53:1a) as a proof against non-believers in the message of Jesus Christ; Justin employs it in the same manner (e.g., *Dial.* 42.2, 114.2, 118.4). Tertullian parallels Ps.-Gregory, using it as a "two Lords" proof-text (*Prax.* 13.3), as does Cyprian (*Test.* 2.4, "That Christ is the hand and arm of God").

CHAPTER 2: OTHER [PROOFS] BY THE SAME [AUTHOR], CONCERNING THE *PAROUSIA* OF THE INCARNATE LORD

This long TC on the Incarnation includes general passages on the revelation of the divine in the world as well as passages understood as prophecies of specific events in Jesus' life. This section may be compared with Ps.-Epiphanius *Test.* 5 ("That he would come"; composed of 53 passages, many of which parallel Ps.-Gregory's collection).

Concerning the *parousia*: The term παρουσία took on a technical meaning in early Christianity to describe the "coming" of Christ. In the *testimonia* literature, a distinction is often made between Christ's humble παρουσία as a human being and his future παρουσία in glory (e.g., Irenaeus *Haer.* 4.33.11–12; Tertullian *Marc.* 3.7).

2.1. Various references to manifestations of the divine

Bar 3:36–38: The text is used as a proof of the incarnation in much of the *testimonia* literature: Irenaeus *Epid.* 97 (cf. the allusion in *Haer.* 4.20.4); Ps.-Epiphanius quotes Bar 3:36–37 and Bar 3:38 separately in his TC, "That he appeared, and being God became man" (*Test.* 6.1, 6.3). Cyprian quotes Bar 3:36–38 under the heading "That Christ is God" (*Test.* 2.6). Hippolytus relates that Noetus used this text as a proof that Christ is the same as the Father (*Noet.* 2.5, 5.1). The first three authors attribute the passage to Jeremiah, a common ancient practice in referencing Baruch. For the later *testimonia* tradition, see Cyril of Jerusalem *Cat.* 11.15; Lactantius *Inst.* 4.13.8; Commodian *Carm.* 371–372.

Ps 49:2–3: Irenaeus quotes the text as part of a lengthy TC proving the full divinity of Christ (*Haer.* 3.6.1). Cyprian quotes Ps 49:1–6 under the heading, "That Jesus Christ shall come as judge" (*Test.* 2.28); Cyril of Jerusalem also applies it to the second *parousia* (*Cat.* 15.21). Eusebius notes that it may apply to Christ's first or second appearance (*Dem. ev.* 6.3).

2.2. References to Jesus' entry into Jerusalem (and the Temple)

Moving from general references to manifestations of the divine presence in the world, Ps.-Gregory gives a series of texts referring specifically to Jesus' entry into Jerusalem. This entry is closely connected with Jesus' appearance in the Temple—the classic locus for the manifestation of the divine presence. The "two *parousias*" texts in the *testimonia* literature reflect this same combination of general references to epiphanies of the divine and specific events in the earthly life of Jesus.

Cyril of Jerusalem's proofs of the incarnation (*Cat.* 12.8–11) share several texts with Ps.-Gregory in this section: Mal 3:1; Zech 2:10–11; Ps 71:6, Zech 9:9, 14:4. Eusebius also shows a partial overlap with this section: Zech 2:10–11, 3:1; Mal 3:1–2 (*Dem. ev.* 5.26–28).

Mal 3:1b: Ps.-Epiphanius applies this text (together with Zech 9:9 and Gen 49:11) to Jesus' entry into Jerusalem (*Test.* 37.3). Eusebius refers it to the second *parousia* (*Dem. ev.* 5.28).

Zech 9:9: Skarsaune locates this text within Justin's kerygma source ("The Coming of the Messiah"; see *Proof from Prophecy*, 260; detailed discussion, pp. 74–76). This *testimonium* was applied specifically to Jesus' coming into Jerusalem (Matt 21:5, John 12:15, Irenaeus *Epid.* 65), but also more generally to Jesus' *parousia* as a humble human (Irenaeus *Haer.* 4.33.1, 12; Ps.-Epiphanius *Test.* 5.18; Cyril of Jerusalem *Cat.* 12.10; cf. Justin's use in his discussion of the two *parousias* [*Dial.* 52]). Cyprian includes it under the heading, "That he will reign as a king forever" (*Test.* 2.29).

Mal 3:1 / Exod 23:20; cf. Matt 11:10: In the Synoptic Gospels (cf. Mark 1:2; Luke 7:27), the text is applied to John the Baptist as a precursor of Jesus. Ps.-Epiphanius includes the text in his TC on Jesus' "coming" (*Test*. 5.21b).

Zech 14:4: Tertullian understands this as a prediction that Jesus would use the Mount of Olives as a resting place after teaching in Jerusalem (*Marc*. 4.39.19; cf., e.g., Luke 21:37).

2.3. Reference to the two parousias of Christ

Zech 3:1–5: I translate ὁ διάβολος as "the devil"; alternatively it could be translated as "the accuser." Ps.-Gregory doubtless understood it in the former sense.

Zechariah 3:1–5 serves two basic functions in the *testimonia* literature: (1) Since the LXX translates יהושע ("Joshua") with the name Ἰησοῦς (Jesus), both the high priest mentioned here and Moses' successor were understood to foreshadow Jesus Christ (see, e.g., Justin *Dial*. 113 and 115.4; Tertullian *Adv. Jud*. 9.21); (2) The filthy clothes of the high priest symbolize Jesus' first, humble *parousia*; his splendid clothes represent the *parousia* in glory (see *Barn*. 7.9; Tertullian *Marc*. 3.7.6; *Adv. Jud*. 14.7; Skarsaune, *Proof from Prophecy*, 309–10). Oddly, Ps.-Gregory omits the references to the change of clothes in his quotation of Zech 3:1–5.

Justin also sees the text as a reference to Jesus' role as the eschatological high priest (*Dial*. 116).

2.4. Further references to manifestations of the divine

Isa 65:1a: The quotation is used as a proof that God is turning to the Gentiles (cf. Rom 10:20; Justin *Dial*. 119.4; Cyprian *Test*. 1.21) and as a proof of the incarnation (Irenaeus *Epid*. 92; *Haer*. 3.6.1; Hippolytus *Noet*. 12).

Isa 33:17: I follow Zacagni's suggestion that the quotation is from Isa 33:17: βασιλέα μετὰ δόξης ὄψεσθε; cf. the use of Isa 33:17 in Ps.-Epiphanius *Test*. 5.24. Cyprian includes Isa 33:14–17 in his TC, "That [Christ] will reign as a king forever" (*Test*. 2.29).

Ps 79:2c–3. Irenaeus also understands Ps 79:2c as a manifestation of the Word, identifying Christ as the one seated on the cherubim (*Haer*. 3.11.8).

Ps 71:6a. Tertullian argues that this passage applies to the incarnation of Christ, and not to Solomon (*Marc*. 5.9.10). See similar arguments in Eusebius *Dem. ev*. 7.3 (354–355); Lactantius *Inst*.

4.16.14; Cyril of Jerusalem *Cat.* 12.9; and *Alt. Sim.* 44–46. The whole of Ps 71 saw heavy use as a *testimonium*; e.g., Justin (also arguing that the Psalm does not apply to Solomon) quotes the entire Psalm (*Dial.* 34:3–6). Cyril also understands the passage as applying to the silent and unknown nature of Christ's birth (*Cat.* 12.9); cf. Chrysostom, *Demonstration against Jews and Greeks that Christ is God* (PG 48:816); Lactantius *Inst.* 4.16.14.

2.5. References to the Davidic Messiah and a "prophet like Moses"

This section begins a series of references to the Messiah, with many specific references to his Davidic origin. Included among these passages is a reference to the expected "prophet" predicted by Moses.

Mic 5:2: This passage is quoted already as a non-LXX *testimonium* to Jesus' birth in Bethlehem in Matt 2:6 (see Raymond E. Brown, *The Birth of the Messiah: A Commentary on the Infancy Narratives in the Gospels of Matthew and Luke* [updated ed.; ABRL; New York: Doubleday, 1993], 184–87). See also Cyprian *Test.* 2.12 ("That Christ should be born in Bethlehem"); Cyril of Jerusalem *Cat.* 12.20; and Eusebius *Dem. ev.* 7.2 (341). These authors use the passage in extended discussions of the incarnation. Justin (*1 Apol.* 34.1 and *Dial.* 78.1), Irenaeus (*Epid.* 63), and Tertullian (*Adv. Jud.* 13.2) parallel Ps.-Gregory in quoting the Matthean form of the passage.

Deut 18:15–19 / Lev 23:29; cf. Acts 3:22–23: For a similar composite quotation, see Ps.-Clement *Hom.* 3.55.3. Deuteronomy 18:15–19 was widely understood by both Jews and Christians as a reference to an eschatological "prophet like Moses" (4Q*Testimonia* 5–7; the Samaritan Pentateuch conflates Deut 18:18–19 with Deut 5:28–29; Luke quotes the same LXX-deviant text of Deut 18:15 in Acts 7:37 [Stephen's speech]; allusions to this passage are found in Mark 9:7 par. and John 6:14). See also Tertullian *Marc.* 4.22.10 and Cyril of Jerusalem *Cat.* 12.17.

2.6. Excursus on Jesus' divine authority

Ps.-Gregory cites several NT accounts of Jesus' miracles to demonstrate Jesus' divine power and authority. This is an apparent proof of the claim that Jesus is the "prophet like Moses."

Isa 40:10: This is included in Cyprian's collection, "That Christ is the Hand and Arm of God" (*Test.* 2.4). In Ps.-Gregory's context, it continues the references to Christ as the manifestation of God's authority and power. See also Cyril of Jerusalem *Cat.* 12.8.

2.7. Davidic descent of the Messiah

Ps.-Gregory presents a series of promises to David that a descendant of his would always occupy the throne. The promises were of course understood messianically in Judaism and early Christianity.

Ps 131:11: The text is often applied as a *testimonium* to Jesus' birth: Tertullian *Marc.* 3.20.6; Irenaeus *Epid.* 64; *Haer.* 3.9.2; cf. *Epid.* 36; Cyprian *Test.* 2.11. The quotation in Acts 2:30 combines elements of Ps 131:11 and 2 Sam 7:12–13. See also Cyril of Jerusalem *Cat.* 12.23 and Eusebius *Dem. ev.* 4.16 (187); 7.3 (351).

3 Kgdms 8:26–27: 3 Kingdoms 8:27 is quoted in Ps.-Epiphanius *Test.* 5.54 ("That he would come"). See also Eusebius *Dem. ev.* 6.12.

2.8. Miscellaneous Texts on the Incarnation

Jer 17:9: The passage is included in "two parousias" TCs: Tertullian *Adv. Jud.* 14.6; *Marc.* 3.7.6; Irenaeus *Haer.* 4.33.11. In general, it functions as a traditional proof for the incarnation: Irenaeus *Haer.* 3.18.3; 3.19.2; Cyprian *Test.* 2.10 ("That Christ is both man and God"); Ps.-Epiphanius *Test.* 6.2 ("That he appeared, and being God became a human"); Lactantius *Inst.* 4.13.10.

Amos 4:12b–13: Although Ps.-Gregory correctly attributes this passage to Amos, other early Christian authors give false attributions, a possible signal that they quote from a TC and not a biblical MS. Clement attributes the quotation to Isaiah (*Strom.* 5.14) and to Hosea (*Protr.* 79.2), and Tertullian to Joel (*Marc.* 3.6.6; but cf. *Herm.* 28.9 where the quotation is correctly attributed; see also *Prax.* 28.9).

2.9. A messianic cluster: Gen 49:10–11, Num 24:17, and Isa 11:1–10

The texts Gen 49:10–11, Num 24:17, and Isa 11:1, 10 often are grouped together as messianic proof-texts: Justin *1 Apol.* 32 (see Skarsaune, *Proof from Prophecy*, 140–44, 260, 269–73; the texts form part of Justin's "kerygma source" on the coming of the Messiah); Irenaeus *Epid.* 57–59; Ps.-Epiphanius *Test.* 5 (under the heading ὅτι ἥξει); Eusebius *Dem. ev.* 3.2. (95–96). Already in pre-Christian Jewish texts (Qumran; targumic traditions; portions of the testament literature) these texts are interpreted messianically, and often grouped together (see John J. Collins, *The Scepter and the Star: The Messiahs of the Dead Sea Scrolls and other Ancient Literature* [ABRL; New York/London: Doubleday, 1995], 56–68; other messianic texts in this literature are 2 Sam 7:14, Jer 23:5 and 33:15, and Amos 9:11). Several NT passages allude to this messianic grouping: Rev 5:5 and

22:16, Heb 7:14, and Luke 1:78. For detailed discussion, see Pierre Prigent, "Quelques *testimonia* messianiques: leur histoire littéraire de Qoumrân aux Pères de l'église," *TZ* 15 (1959): 419–30; Albl, *Early Christian Testimonia*, 208–16; Falcetta, "Theory of James Rendel Harris," 119–124.

Of particular interest is Justin's conflation of Num 24:17, Isa 11:1, 10 (with Isa 51:5) (*1 Apol.* 32.12); another reading of Num 24:17 seems influenced by Gen 49:10 (*Dial.* 106.4). See Skarsaune, *Proof from Prophecy*, 50–52.

Gen 49:10: The non-LXX reading ᾧ ἀπόκειται (which allows a messianic interpretation) is widely attested: Justin *1 Apol.* 32.1 (see Skarsaune, *Proof from Prophecy*, 25–29, for a detailed discussion); Irenaeus *Epid.* 57 and *Haer.* 4.10.2; Novatian *Trin.* 9; Eusebius *Dem. ev.* 3.2 (95); 7.1 (332). The variant is also followed in the Syriac tradition; see Robert Murray, *Symbols of Church and Kingdom: A Study in Early Syriac Tradition* (Cambridge: Cambridge University Press, 1975), 282–84. Alessandro Falcetta notes (together with a survey of other evidence) the variant's use in the Slavonic version of Josephus' *Jewish War* ("The Logion of Matthew 11:5–6 Par. from Qumran to Agbar," *RB* 110 [2003]: 239–43). The LXX of Gen 49:10 is found in a TC of Athanasius (*Inc.* 40.3); see also Eusebius *Dem. ev.* 1.3 (6). For further references and discussion, see Albl, *Early Christian Testimonia*, 214.

Num 24:17: The text was seen as a proof of Christ's divinity and humanity. The "star" reference indicated divinity, the "man" or "leader" his humanity: Irenaeus *Epid.* 58; Cyprian *Test.* 2.10 ("That Christ is both man and God"); Lactantius *Inst.* 4.13.10. Athanasius includes the same non-LXX reading as Ps.-Gregory (Athanasius omits the last phrase) in his TC on Jesus' birth (*Inc.* 33.4).

Isa 11:1–10: Verses from this passage are found in various TCs: Isa 11:1 and 11:10 in Novatian *Test.* 9 (an overview of Christ's life, including Gen 49:10); Isa 11:1–3 in Cyprian *Test.* 2.11 (on the birth of Christ).

Isa 10:33: "Lebanon will fall with the exalted ones." Eusebius claims that "Lebanon" refers to Jerusalem—more generally the passage refers to the "falling away" of the Jewish people after the appearance of Christ (*Dem. ev.* 2.3 [74]). One sees here how the *testimonia* tradition used not only specific messianic proof-texts, but also applied the larger context of these passages.

2.10. Further references to "two powers in heaven" passages

In the last two quotations in this section, Ps.-Gregory parallels Heb 1:8–12, where Ps 44:6–7 and Ps 101:26–28 are also quoted; Ps.-Gregory also alludes to Heb 3:1 in his exegetical comment on Ps 44:6–7, "he became high priest, and apostle of our confession." However, Ps.-Gregory does diverge from the Hebrews quotation in both instances, reading closer to the LXX (see textual notes).

I have argued elsewhere that in this section (Heb 1:8–13), the author of Hebrews collects "two powers" quotations (passages that refer to two "Gods" or two "Lords") and applies them to the "Son" (Albl, *Early Christian Testimonia*, 205–6). T. F. Glasson argues that the wider context of Ps 101:26–27 shows that its quotation is part of such "two powers" speculation ("'Plurality of Divine Persons' and the Quotations in Hebrews I.6ff.," *NTS* 12 [1965–66]: 271); see also the classic "two powers" discussion in Alan F. Segal, *Two Powers in Heaven: Early Rabbinic Reports about Christianity and Gnosticism* (SJLA 25; Leiden: Brill, 1977). One can argue, then, that Ps.-Gregory does not rely directly on Hebrews here, but on a "two powers" *testimonia* tradition that was also a source for the Hebrews catena.

Ps 44:6–7: Justin makes frequent use of this passage as a proof of Christ's divinity, likely drawing on a "two heavenly powers" TC and not directly on Hebrews (see Skarsaune, *Proof from Prophecy*, 126, 209); cf. the similar use in Irenaeus *Epid.* 47–49 (grouping of "two powers texts," including Ps 109:1; Isa 45:1; Ps 2:7–8) and *Haer.* 3.6.1 (with Ps 109:1; Gen 19:24); Tertullian *Prax.* 13.1 (with Isa 45:14–15; John 1:1, Ps 109:1; Isa 53:1; Gen 19:24). In the later tradition: Cyprian *Test.* 2.6 ("That Christ is God"); Lactantius *Inst.* 4.13.9.

You see that God is anointed by "God": Tertullian mirrors Ps.-Gregory's comment, "Now since he here speaks to God, and affirms that God is anointed by God" (*unctum Deum a Deo*) (*Prax.* 13.2).

CHAPTER 3: CONCERNING HIS BIRTH FROM A VIRGIN

The *testimonia* literature features a common core of texts used to prove the virgin birth. Following are some select parallels:

Ps.-Gregory Test. 3	Ps.-Epiphanius Test. 8–14	Acts Pet. 24	Irenaeus Epid. 53–57	Tertullian Adv. Jud. 9	Justin Dialogue 76–77
Isa 7:14/Matt 1:23, Isa 8:4, Wis 8:19–20, Isa 9:5–6, Apocr. Ezek. Frag. 3, Isa 7:15, Isa 45:14–15, Ezek 44:1–2, Isa 49:1–2, Dan 2:34–35, Isa 1:2–3, Isa 8:1–3, Luke 2:23, Ps 86:5	Isa 7:14/Matt 1:23, Ezek 44:2; 46:12, Isa 66:7, Isa 61:1, Dan 2:34, Isa 28:16, Isa 9:5, Isa 8:4	Isa 53:8, Apocr. Ezek. Frag. 3, Isa 7:13–14, Dan 2:34, Isa 28:16, Dan 7:13	Isa 7:14–16, Isa 61:1, Isa 66:7, Isa 9:5, Gen 49:11	Isa 7:13–14/Matt 1:23, Isa 7:15, Isa 8:4, Isa 11:1	Dan 7:13, Dan 2:34, Isa 53:8, Gen 49:11, Isa 9:5, Isa 8:4

Ps.-Gregory shows awareness both of apocryphal gospel traditions relating to Jesus' infancy (see notes on Isa 7:15 and Isa 1:2–3) and of canonical gospel traditions (he draws directly on Matt 1:23 and Luke 2:23 for two of his quotations). He has a marked interest in the virginity of Mary (using *Apocr. Ezek.* Frag. 3; Isa 8:1–3), including an argument for her continued virginity after the birth of Jesus (using Ezek 44:1–2). He understands the virgin birth as a proof of Jesus' supernatural nature (using Wis 8:19–20; Dan 2:34–35; Luke 2:23).

On TCs as a source for both apocryphal and canonical gospel narratives of Jesus' infancy, see Enrico Norelli, "Avant le canonique et l'apocryphe: Aux origines des récits de la naissance de Jésus,"

RTP 126 (1994): 305–24. Norelli makes a persuasive case that references to Jesus' birth in *Acts Pet.* 24 and *Ascen. Isa.* 11.12–14 are independent of accounts in Matthew and Luke, and instead evidence the use of a first-century *testimonia* source. See also Falcetta, "Theory of James Rendel Harris," 190–93.

Isa 7:14: Ps.-Gregory reproduces the comment of Matt 1:23: ὅ ἐστιν μεθερμηνευόμενον μεθ' ἡμῶν ὁ θεός (although he reads ἑρμηνεύεται for Matthew's ἐστιν μεθερμηνευόμενον). The text is widely used: Ps.-Epiphanius *Test.* 8 (under the heading, "That [he was born] from a virgin"); Novatian *Trin.* 9.6 (in a TC surveying Jesus' life); Cyprian *Test.* 2.8 (using Isa 7:10–15 in a TC on the virgin birth); Lactantius *Inst.* 4.12.4.

Isa 8:4: The combination of Isa 7:14 and Isa 8:4 is found already in Justin (Isa 7:10–17 and Isa 8:4 are conflated in *Dial.* 43.5–6 and 66.2–3). Skarsaune argues that Justin relies on a *testimonia* source that proved the virgin birth, using Isa 8:4 to argue for the superhuman nature of Christ (*Proof from Prophecy*, 199–203). See also the combination of Isa 7:13–14 (together with the comment from Matt 1:23), Isa 7:15, and Isa 8:4 in Tertullian *Adv. Jud.* 9.1; cf. *Marc.* 3.12–13; see also the basic combination in Commodian *Carm.* 405–410, *Alt. Sim.* 15–16, and Athanasius's use of both texts in his TC on the Incarnation (*Inc.* 33.3–4).

Isa 9:5b–6: Ps.-Gregory's quotation begins with Isa 9:5b, an obscure reference that differs markedly from the Hebrew. Irenaeus sees an allegorical reference here to those who have not believed in Christ: at the judgment, they will wish that they would have been burned with fire before the Son of God was born, rather than facing punishment for their unbelief after his *parousia* (*Epid.* 56).

Ps.-Gregory adds a series of titles, based on the MT, but lacking in the LXX. They are partially witnessed by the LXX recensions (α'; σ'; θ'). Eusebius (*Dem.* 7.1 [336]), Athanasius, and Chrysostom (with A'; Lucianic MSS) parallel most of Ps.-Gregory's names: θαυμαστὸς Σύμβουλος, Θεὸς ἰσχυρός, ἐξουσιαστής, Ἀρχῶν εἰρήνης, Πατὴρ τοῦ μέλλοντος αἰῶνος. Eusebius discusses the variant translations of this passage (*Dem. ev.* 7.1 [336–37]). The *Dialogue of Timothy and Aquila* 5.6 matches Ps.-Gregory's titles precisely.

The application of the passage's messianic titles to Jesus occurs regularly in the *testimonia* literature; see Justin *1 Apol.* 35.2 and Irenaeus *Epid.* 55–56. In Skarsaune's view, Isa 9:6a MT (LXX 9:5a) proved the "hiddenness of the Messiah" (i.e., that the Messiah would be hidden until he grew to manhood) in Justin's kerygma source

(*Proof from Prophecy*, 146, 266; see *1 Apol.* 35.2). Irenaeus quotes an LXX-deviant version of Isa 9:5 (*Epid.* 55) that shows connections with Ps.-Gregory's text ("wonderful counselor, mighty God"); Irenaeus then immediately quotes a LXX version of Isa 9:5 (*Epid.* 56).

Ps.-Epiphanius combines Isa 9:5 and Isa 8:4 under the heading, "That he was a child" (*Test.* 14).

The text also did double duty as a passion *testimonium*: Cyprian uses Isa 9:5 under the heading, "That in the passion and the sign of the cross is all virtue and power" (*Test.* 2.21); the reference to the "rulership" on his shoulder was understood as an allusion to the cross (see also Justin *1 Apol.* 35.2; Irenaeus *Epid.* 56; and *Alt. Sim.* 44).

Behold the heifer has given birth, and has not given birth: This phrase possibly is taken from the lost *Apocryphon of Ezekiel*. It was transmitted in the *testimonia* tradition in a "short form" (e.g, "she has given birth and has not given birth" in *Acts Pet.* 24) and a "long form" as witnessed in Ps.-Gregory. As in Ps.-Gregory, the passage is used as a proof of Jesus' virgin birth (*Acts Pet.* 24; Clement of Alexandria *Strom.* 7.94; Tertullian *Carn. Chr.* 23 [with Isa 7:14]; Epiphanius *Pan.* 30.30.3 [with Isa 7:14]). See the discussion in James R. Mueller, *The Five Fragments of the Apocryphon of Ezekiel: A Critical Study* (JSPSup 5; Sheffield: Sheffield Academic Press, 1994), 120–38; Albl, *Early Christian Testimonia*, 124; Resch, *Agrapha*, 306 (Logion 18d; Resch finds the original source in Job 21:10).

Isa 7:15: Tertullian quotes this same phrase in his discussion of Isa 7:13–14 (with the interpretive phrase from Matt 1:23) and Isa 8:4 (*Adv. Jud.* 9.1; cf. *Marc.* 3.13.3). Irenaeus sees it as a proof of Jesus' humanity (*Haer.* 3.21.4); Ps.-Gregory applies it to Mary's feeding of the infant Jesus. See also Gregory of Nyssa, *In illud: Tunc et ipse Filius* 8.

Isa 45:14–15: The *testimonia* literature takes the phrases "they will offer prayers to you" and "God is in your midst" as direct address to Christ, proving his equality with God. Ps.-Epiphanius understands it as a general testimonium to Christ's appearance in the world (*Test.* 5.28; 6.9).

Elsewhere, the passage is used not as a proof of the virgin birth, but in general to demonstrate Christ's equality with God. Tertullian understands the passage as addressed to the "person of Christ" (*Prax.* 13.2) and combines it with other "two powers" passages (Ps 44:6–7; John 1:1; Ps 109:1; Isa 53:1; Gen 19:24). Cyprian includes it under the heading "That Christ is God" (*Test.* 2.6); Hippolytus, admitting that Noetus uses it to establish the identity of Christ and God, argues for a distinction between the two (*Noet.* 2–4); see also *Dial. AZ* 93–97; Cyril of Jerusalem *Cat.* 11.16; Eusebius *Dem. ev.* 5.4; Lactantius *Inst.* 4.13.7.

Ezek 44:1–2: The "closed" gate was widely understood as a reference to the continued virginity of Mary after the birth of Jesus. See Rufinus *Symb.* 9; Jerome *Comm. in Ezech.* 13 (PL 25.430). Ps.-Epiphanius also reflects this interpretation, including Ezek 44:12 under the heading, "That after his birth, he would protect the virgin who bore him" (*Test.* 9; his next quotation from Job 3:10–11 proves "that the womb is a gate" [*Test.* 10]); see also *Dial. TA* 19.26–20.6. For further references, see J. N. D. Kelly's note (*A Commentary on the Apostles' Creed* [ACW 20; Westminster, Md., Newman Press, 1955], 113 n. 60).

Isa 49:1: Cyril of Jerusalem connects this passage with Matt 1:20–21, arguing that God gave Jesus his name before his birth (*Cat.* 10.12). Eusebius makes the same connection (*Ecl. Proph.* 4.24).

Dan 2:34–35: Texts with "stone" references were widely applied to Christ and his followers in early Christianity (see Albl, *Early Christian Testimonia*, 265–85; Falcetta, "Theory of James Rendel Harris, 133–40). Already Justin applies the title "stone" (λίθος) to Christ without further justification (*Dial.* 34.2; 86.2–3; 100.4; 126.1); Cyprian devotes a TC to proving that "Christ is also called a stone" (*Test.* 2.16). Ps.-Gregory's particular identification of the "stone cut without hands" in Dan 2:34 with the virgin birth of Jesus is widespread: Justin *Dial.* 76.1; Irenaeus *Haer.* 3.21.7; *Acts Pet.* 24; Ps.-Epiphanius quotes it under the heading "that without a father on earth or intercourse [Christ was born]" (*Test.* 13a). See also the comment in *Dial. AZ* 113–114 that Mary is the mountain from which the "stone" Christ was cut.

Isa 1:2–3: The passage is used elsewhere in the *testimonia* literature as a proof for Israel's rejection of Christ (e.g., Cyprian *Test.* 1.3). By including it in a TC on the virgin birth, however, Ps.-Gregory seems more interested in its reference to the "ox and donkey" (Isa 1:3), a passage which influenced later portrayals of Jesus' birth (see Brown, *Birth of the Messiah*, 399). Ps.-Gregory presupposes knowledge of some apocryphal gospel account which includes details about the ox and the donkey at Jesus' birth (e.g., *Prot. Jas.* 22.2; *Gospel of Ps.-Matthew* 14).

Isa 8:1–3: Irenaeus conflates Isa 8:3 and Isa 9:6 in his discussion of the virgin birth (*Haer.* 4.33.11). See also the combination with Isa

8:4 in *Haer.* 3.16 and the extensive discussion of these texts in Eusebius *Dem. ev.* 7.1. Novatian also sees Isa 8:3 as a reference to Mary (*Trin.* 28).

Luke 2:23: The passage is not a direct quotation, but alludes to the commandment in Exod 13:2, 12, 15. Tertullian quotes Luke's version and parallels Ps.-Gregory's comments, "For who is really holy but the Son of God? Who properly opened the womb but he who opened a closed one?" (*Carn. Chr.* 23). On the gnostic interpretation of this passage, see Irenaeus *Haer.* 1.3.4.

Ps 86:5: Tertullian (*Prax.* 27.5, 10; cf. *Marc.* 4.13.6) and Ps.-Epiphanius (*Test.* 6.5) apply the passage to the incarnation of Christ.

CHAPTER 4: CONCERNING THE MIRACLES WHICH
THE LORD WAS DESTINED TO PERFORM
WHEN HE BECAME INCARNATE

Isa 49:6–9: Ps.-Gregory falsely attributes the passage to Jeremiah, apparently because he connects it closely with the following quotation of Bar 3:36. Quotations from Baruch were routinely attributed to Jeremiah in ancient times.

The text is a reworking of Isa 49:6b, 8b–9a, with influence from Isa 42:6b–7.

Ps.-Gregory *Test.* 4	LXX Isa 42:6b–7	LXX Isa 49:6, 8b–9
Ἰδοὺ τέθεικά σε εἰς διαθήκην γένους, καὶ εἰς φῶς ἐθνῶν, τοῦ καταστῆσαι τὴν γῆν, καὶ κληρονομίαν ἐρήμου, λέγων τοῖς ἐν δεσμοῖς, Ἐξέλθετε· καὶ τοῖς ἐν τῷ σκότει, Ἀνακαλύφθητε.	ἔδωκά σε εἰς διαθήκην γένους, εἰς φῶς ἐθνῶν, 7 ἀνοῖξαι ὀφθαλμοὺς τυφλῶν, ἐξαγαγεῖν ἐκ δεσμῶν δεδεμένους καὶ ἐξ οἴκου φυλακῆς καθημένους ἐν σκότει.	6 ἰδοὺ τέθεικά σε εἰς φῶς ἐθνῶν 8 ἔδωκά σε εἰς διαθήκην ἐθνῶν τοῦ καταστῆσαι τὴν γῆν καὶ κληρονομῆσαι κληρονομίαν ἐρήμου 9 λέγοντα τοῖς ἐν δεσμοῖς ἐξέλθατε καὶ τοῖς ἐν τῷ σκότει ἀνακαλυφθῆναι

Isaiah 42:6 and 49:6 are regularly combined in the *testimonia* literature. Justin (*Dial.* 121.4–123.2) and *Barnabas* (14.7–8) include these passages in their extensive TCs regarding the Gentiles (see Skarsaune, *Proof from Prophecy*, 62, 348–49).

See also Ps.-Gregory's similar combination later in his work (*Test.* 16) and commentary there.

Bar 3:36: Ps.-Gregory quotes Bar 3:36–38 at the beginning of his long TC on the Incarnation (2.1 above). This repetition demonstrates again the nature of Ps.-Gregory's work as a meta-collection of earlier TCs with little attention to his work's overall cohesiveness.

Isa 35:3–6: This passage is a central *testimonium* for Jesus' healing activity. Skarsaune has shown how Isa 35:5–6 formed part of the "kerygma source" employed by Justin (*Proof from Prophecy*, 58–59, 148–50; see *1 Apol.* 48.1–3; *Dial.* 69.5); cf. the same use of Isa 35:3–6 in Irenaeus *Epid.* 67 and its use in the "two *parousias*" TC in Irenaeus *Haer.* 4.33.11. See also Isa 35:4–6 in Tertullian *Adv. Jud.* 9.30.

Cyprian quotes Isa 35:3–6 under the heading, "That Christ our God should come, the Enlightener and Savior of the human race" (*Test.* 2.7). Novatian employs Isa 35:5–6 in his TC of Christ's life (*Trin.* 9; see also his use of Isa 35:3–6 in *Trin.* 12.4). Ps.-Epiphanius closely parallels Ps.-Gregory's order in his TC, "That he would heal many" (*Test.* 33), quoting Isa 35:3–4a, followed by καὶ πάλιν and a quotation of Isa 35:4b–6. See also Eusebius *Dem. ev.* 6.21.

See also Falcetta's study of this passage in the *testimonia* tradition ("The Logion of Matthew").

Isa 61:1: Luke has Jesus quote Isa 61:1–2 (with Isa 58:6) as paradigmatic for his mission (Luke 4:18–19). Ps.-Epiphanius uses portions of the text three times for various purposes (*Test.* 4.3; 12.2; 87); it is often used in the *testimonia* literature as a proof for the "anointing" of Jesus at his baptism (Irenaeus *Haer.* 3.9.3; *Epid.* 53; Ps.-Epiphanius *Test.* 12.2; Novatian *Trin.* 29.13). Cyprian uses it as a proof that Christ is both man and God (*Test.* 2.10).

Barnabas closely parallels Ps.-Gregory's use of these three passages, quoting Isa 42:6–7, 49:6–7, and 61:1–2 (14.7–9); see also Tertullian *Prax.* 11.5–6 (Isa 42:1, 49:6, 61:1; Tertullian uses the passages to prove a distinction between Father and Son). Justin also draws on a similar grouping of texts, quoting Isa 49:6, 42:6–7, and 49:8 (*Dial.* 121.4–122.6); see Skarsaune for further references and his conclusion that Justin draws on a *testimonia* source (*Proof from Prophecy*, 62, 348–49). Justin employs these passages as proof of Christ's mission to the Gentiles; see already the use of Isa 49:6 for this purpose in Acts 13:47. On the combination of Isa 35:5–6 and Isa 61:1 at Qumran and in Matthew and Justin, see Falcetta, "The Logion of Matthew," 224–35.

The source behind this group of quotations, then, may originally have focused on Christ's mission to the Gentiles. Falcetta's study shows, however, that Isa 35:5–6 and Isa 61:1 belonged at one point to TCs witnessing to the miracles associated with the coming of the Messiah ("The Logion of Matthew"). Ps.-Gregory follows in this latter tradition.

CHAPTER 5: CONCERNING [HIS] BETRAYAL

Psalm 40:10 is used already in John 13:18 (though in a markedly different version) as a proof of Judas's betrayal. See also its use in Tertullian *Marc.* 4.40; Ps.-Epiphanius *Test.* 43.2; and Rufinus *Symb.* 20.

CHAPTER 6: CONCERNING [HIS] PASSION

6.1. Concerning Jesus' Trial before Jewish and Roman Authorities
The first three texts (Isa 3:12–14; Ps 2:1; Lam 4:20) in this chapter are understood as *testimonia* to Jesus' trial before the Jewish and Roman authorities.

Already in Acts 4:25–28, Ps 2:1 is applied to the opposition of Herod and Pontius Pilate against Jesus. The same application is found in Justin *1 Apol.* 40; Irenaeus *Epid.* 74; Melito *Pasc.* 62; Tertullian *Marc.* 4.42.2 (with Isa 3:13–14); Tertullian *Res.* 20 (with Isa 3:13); Ps.-Epiphanius *Test.* 41.1. John Dominic Crossan shows how the influence of Ps 2:1 can be traced to the earliest passion narratives (*The Cross that Spoke: The Origins of the Passion Narrative* [San Francisco: Harper & Row, 1988], 61–75). See also the use of Isa 3:14 in Cyril of Jerusalem *Cat.* 13.12.

Ps.-Epiphanius connects Lam 4:20 with Ps 2:1–2 in his TC to demonstrate "That they would come together against him" (*Test.* 41). The phrase συνελήμφθη ἐν ταῖς διαφθοραῖς αὐτῶν was apparently taken as a reference to Jesus' arrest (see the same interpretation in Cyril of Jerusalem *Cat.* 13.7 and Rufinus *Symb.* 19).

Lamentations 4:20 has a much wider interpretive range in the *testimonia* literature; for a comprehensive overview, see Jean Daniélou, "Nous vivrons a son ombre [Lam., 4, 20]," in idem, *Études d'exégèse judéo-chrétienne (Les Testimonia)* (ThH 5; Paris: Beauschesne, 1966), 76–95. The passage is applied to Christ's passion in general, often in creative ways. Justin's version reads πνεῦμα πρὸ προσώπου ἡμῶν χριστὸς κύριος; he finds here a reference to Christ as the breath in our nose, identifying the nose as a symbol of the cross! (*1 Apol.* 55.5). Irenaeus takes "shadow" as an indication of the sufferings of Christ's body (*Epid.* 71). Rufinus also applies the passage to the passion (*Symb.* 19). The passage is often found in combination with Deut 30:15 in the passion *testimonia*.

Elsewhere, the passage proves that Christ is the Spirit of God (e.g., Irenaeus *Haer.* 3.10.2; Tertullian *Marc.* 3.6.7; *Prax.* 14.10).

6.2. References to the Suffering Servant

Ps.-Gregory continues his presentation on the passion with a series of texts from the so-called "Servant Songs" of Isaiah. These texts have long been recognized as an influence on the earliest passion narratives. Ps.-Gregory's texts parallel closely those employed in Justin's *testimonia* source.

Isaiah 53: This chapter is an especially rich source for early Christian *testimonia* on the passion of Jesus. Quotations appear already in the NT: Luke 22:37; Acts 8:32–33; 1 Pet 2:22. Skarsaune finds Isa 53 used in Justin's "kerygma source" to prove the sufferings of the Messiah (*Proof from Prophecy*, 139, 151; see, e.g., *1 Apol.* 50–51). Other important early uses in passion *testimonia* are Irenaeus *Epid.* 68–70; *Barn.* 5.2; Melito *Pasc.* 64; Tertullian *Adv. Jud.* 10.15–16; and Cyprian *Test.* 2.15 ("That Christ is called a sheep and a lamb who was to be slain, and concerning the mystery [sacramentum] of the passion"). Ps.-Epiphanius applies various verses to different aspects of the passion (*Test.* 51.2, 55.3, 63, 71.2). Within the "two *parousias*" pattern (i.e., Christ's humble and glorious *parousias*), passages from Isa 53 were favorite examples of Christ's humble *parousia*: Justin *1 Apol.* 52.3; Tertullian *Marc.* 3.7; cf. *Adv. Jud.* 14; Irenaeus *Haer* 4.33.12; Cyprian *Test.* 2.13. See also Lactantius *Inst.* 4.18.16 and 4.18.24.

Isa 53:12: Skarsaune concludes that Justin drew on a *testimonia* source for his non-LXX version of this passage (*Proof from Prophecy*, 62–63; see *1 Apol.* 50.2). See also its use in Luke 22:37 and Tertullian's application of the prophecy to Jesus' crucifixion between two robbers (*Marc.* 4.42.4). For the influence of this passage on the account in the earliest passion narrative, see Crossan, *Cross that Spoke*, 164–65.

Isa 50:6: For other combinations of Isa 50:6 ("I gave my back to lashes") and Isa 53 in the passion *testimonia*, see Justin *Dial.* 89.3 (allusion); *Barn.* 5.14; Irenaeus *Epid.* 68; *Haer.* 4.33.12; Tertullian *Res.* 20; Cyprian *Test.* 2.13; Ps.-Epiphanius *Test.* 48.3; Cyril of Jerusalem *Cat.* 13.13; Rufinus *Symb.* 21–22. For the possible influence of Isa 50:6 on the passion narrative, see Crossan, *Cross that Spoke*, 142–43.

Isa 53:2–3: On the central position of Isa 53:2–3 in Justin's discussion of Christ's humble *parousia*, see Skarsaune, *Proof from Prophecy*, 154–55.

Isa 53:8: Ps.-Gregory omits this phrase in his long quotation of Isa 53:4–9 earlier in this chapter. The passage is singled out elsewhere in the *testimonia* tradition as a proof of Christ's supernatural origin: Justin *1 Apol.* 51.1; Irenaeus *Epid.* 70; *Acts Pet.* 24; Justin *Dial.* 63.1–3; 76.1–2; see Skarsaune, *Proof from Prophecy*, 199–203. The passage is also included in TCs on Christ's glorious *parousia*: Irenaeus *Haer.* 4.33.11; Tertullian *Adv. Jud.* 14.6 (cf. *Marc.* 3.7.6).

6.3. Further references to the passion

Ps 21:17–19: The influence of Psalm 21 on the canonical Gospel passion narratives is well established: the Gospels both quote and allude to the Psalm (e.g., quotation of Ps 21:1 in Matt 27:46 and Mark 15:34; allusions to the "casting of lots" in the Synoptics and the actual quotation of Ps 21:19 in John 19:24).

Ps.-Gregory's connection of the Suffering Servant passages and Psalm 21 references is standard in the *testimonia* literature.

Barnabas, Justin, and Irenaeus exhibit the following parallels:

Barn. 5.2–14	Justin *1 Apol.* 38.1–6 (cf. *1 Apol.* 35.3–5; *Dial.* 97.1–3)	Irenaeus *Epid.* 79–80
Isa 53:5, 7, Zech 13:7, Composite psalm (incl. Ps 21:21; Ps 118:120; Ps 22:17), Isa 50:6–7	Isa 65:2, Isa 50:6–8, Ps 21:19, 17; Ps 3:6; Ps 21:8	Isa 65:2, Ps 21:17, Ps 21:15, Composite psalm (inc. Ps 21:21; Ps 118:120; Ps 22:17), Deut 28:66, Ps 21:19

For arguments that a common *testimonia* source is used by these three writers, see Smith, *Proof of the Apostolic Preaching*, 207 n. 324; Skarsaune, *Proof from Prophecy*, 80–82; Albl, *Early Christian Testimonia*, 109 nn. 57–58.

Other close parallels abound. See Tertullian *Adv. Jud.* 10.4 (cf. *Marc.* 4.42.4); Cyprian's TC on the crucifixion, including Ps 21:17–23 (*Test.* 2.20); Novatian's TC, including Isa 53:7; Isa 65:2; Ps 68:22; Ps 21:19; Ps 21:17 (*Trin.* 28); Ps.-Epiphanius *Test.* 51.5 and 62; and a combination of Ps 21:17 and Ps 118:120 in Commodian *Carm.* 269.

Jer 11:19: Justin alleges that "the Jews" have deleted this passage from their copies of scripture, although it "is still written in some copies in the synagogues of the Jews (for it is only a short time since they were cut out)" (*Dial.* 72.2). For evidence that a TC lies behind Justin's list of "deleted" texts (*Dial.* 72–73) see Enrico Norelli, "Il Martirio di Isaia come *testimonium* antigiudaico?" *Henoch* 2 (1980): 37–57.

Tertullian includes the passage in his TC on the cross (*Adv. Jud.* 10.12; cf. *Marc.* 3.19.3; 4.40.3), understanding "bread" to refer to the body of Christ, and "wood" to the cross.

Ps.-Epiphanius's TC on the crucifixion includes both parts of Jer 11:19; he follows this sequence: Jer 11:19a; Isa 53:7; Wis 2:20; Jer 11:19b; Ps 21:17 (*Test.* 51). Cyril of Jerusalem also splits up the quotation, citing Deut 28:66 afterwards (*Cat.* 13.19). Cyprian quotes this passage in two separate passion TCs (*Test.* 2.15 and 2.20). See also Commodian *Carm.* 270–276 (Ps 21:17; Wis 2:20; Jer 11:19; Deut 28:66); Lactantius *Inst.* 4.18.21–30 (Isa 53; Jer 11:19; Deut 28:66; Ps 21:17–19); *Alt. Sim.* 28 (Isa 65:2; Jer 11:19; Deut 28:66) and 32–33 (Isa 53:1–12; Isa 50:6–7; Jer 11:19); and Rufinus *Symb.* 23 (Jer 11:19 and Deut 28:66).

Jeremiah 11:19 is often part of TCs centered on vocabulary and images involving wood, a tree, or other images of the cross; these are understood as prophecies of Christ's crucifixion. *Barnabas* expresses the prophetic logic behind these collections: "for he had to suffer on a tree" (5:13). Wood/cross collections are found in Justin *Dial.* 86; Irenaeus *Epid.* 79; Tertullian *Marc.* 3.18–19 and Cyprian *Test.* 2.20–22. For further discussion, see Gerardus Q. Reijners, *The Terminology of the Holy Cross in Early Christian Literature as Based upon Old Testament Typology* (Graecitas Christianorum Primaeva Fascicle 2; Nijmegen: Dekker & Van de Vegt, 1965); Daniélou, "La vie suspendue au bois (Deut., 28, 66)," in idem, *Études d'exégèse*, 53–75; idem, *The Theology of Jewish Christianity* (The Development of Christian Doctrine before the Council of Nicaea 1; London: Darton, Longman & Todd; Chicago: Henry Regnery, 1964), 270–78; Pierre Prigent, *Justin et l'Ancien Testament: L'Argumentation scriptuaire du traité de Justin contre toutes les hérésies comme source principale du Dialogue avec Tryphon et de la premiére apologie* (Ebib; Paris: Gabalda, 1964), 174–202; Albl, *Early Christian Testimonia*, 155–57.

Zech 11:12–13; Jer 32:6–9; cf. Matt 27:9–10: Ps.-Gregory follows the quotation in Matt 27:9–10. Though attributed to Jeremiah, Matthew's text appears to be a conflation of Zech 11:12–13 and the account of Jeremiah's purchase of a field (Jer 32:6–9). Some MSS of

Matthew's Gospel (22; syr^hmg; arm^mss) agree with Ps.-Gregory's attribution to Zechariah.

Irenaeus (*Epid.* 81), Tertullian (*Marc.* 4.40.2; with reference to Matthew's Gospel), and Ps.-Epiphanius (*Test.* 45.2) all follow Matthew's quotation and attribute it to Jeremiah. In Ps.-Epiphanius's same TC, however, he also quotes Zech 11:12, "I will say to them, 'If it is good in your judgment, give me my price—thirty pieces of silver'" (*Test.* 45.1). See also Tertullian's use of Zech 11:12 (*Res.* 20); Cyril of Jerusalem *Cat.* 13.10; Rufinus *Symb.* 20, and the discussion in Falcetta, "Theory of James Rendel Harris," 130–33.

CHAPTER 7: CONCERNING THE CROSS
AND THE DARKNESS THAT OCCURRED

As Ps.-Gregory's own heading indicates, he here combines two originally separate TCs: one on the cross, and one on the darkness that occurred during Jesus' crucifixion. Oddly, Ps.-Gregory mixes the two categories together, and then adds some miscellaneous texts. The texts fall into the following categories:

Cross: Deut 28:66; Isa 65:2; Isa 62:10; Uncertain quotation
Darkness: Amos 8:9; Jer 15:9; Zech 14:6–7
Miscellaneous Passion Texts: Ps 68:21–22; Ps 87:7; Zech 13:7; Zech 14:20

Deut 28:66: This passage is read often in TCs on Jesus' crucifixion: Irenaeus *Epid.* 79; Melito *Pasc.* 61; Tertullian *Adv. Jud.* 11.9; Cyprian *Test.* 2.20; Novatian *Trin.* 9.5. Pierre Prigent (*Justin et l'Ancien Testament*, 189–94) and Jean Daniélou ("La vie suspendue," 59) argue convincingly that a lacuna in Justin *Dial.* 74 originally contained a discussion of Deut 28:66.

The phrase "upon the tree" (ἐπὶ ξύλου) is added to many quotations of Deut 28:66 (Ps.-Epiphanius *Test.* 57.1; Tertullian *Adv. Jud.* 11.9; Commodian *Carm.* 333–334, 518–519, 772 (allusions); Hilary, and as late as Augustine; see Daniélou, "La vie suspendue," 66–68). Irenaeus assumes a connection between this passage and the "tree" of the crucifixion, although he does not quote the addition (*Haer.* 4.10.2; 5.18.3). Deuteronomy 28:66 is thus often included in wood/cross TCs (see comments on Jer 11:19, sect. 6.3 above).

Amos 8:9: For the use of Amos 8:9–10 in connection with Christ's passion, see *Gos. Pet.* 15; Irenaeus *Haer.* 4.33.12; Tertullian *Adv. Jud.* 10.17; Cyprian *Test.* 2.23 ("That at mid-day in his passion there should be darkness"); Ps.-Epiphanius *Test.* 61 ("that the sun would set at midday"). See also the use of Amos 8:9 alone in Tertullian *Marc.* 4.42.5 and *Adv. Jud.* 13.14.

Crossan has suggested, plausibly, that Amos 8:9–10 lies behind the Gospel passion narrative accounts of darkness at Jesus crucifixion (*Cross that Spoke*, 198–200).

Compare the following combinations of Deut 28:66 and the darkness at midday:

Ps.-Gregory *Test.* 7	Cyprian *Test.*	*Dial. AZ.* 36
Testimonies on the cross and the darkness that occurred, Deut 28:66 (cross testimony), Amos 8:9, Jer 15:9 (darkness testimonies)	2:20: TC "That the Jews would fasten Christ to the cross" (including Deut 28:66)	Deut 28:66 as a proof of Jesus' crucifixion
	2.21: TC "That in the passion and the sign of the cross is all virtue and power"	Quotation of Matt 27:45 (darkness from sixth to ninth hour).
	2.22: TC on the cross as a sign	Application of Deut 28:66 to crufixion narrative
	2.23: Testimonies on midday darkness at Christ's passion: Amos 8:9–10, Jer 15:9, Matt 27:45 (darkness from sixth to ninth hour)	

See also Daniélou's discussion on precise parallels between Ps.-Gregory and a sermon on the Passover attributed to Peter II, bishop of Alexandria: both cite essentially the same form of Deut 28:66 (adding ἐάν τις ἐκδιηγεῖται ὑμῖν, influenced by Hab 1:5), and follow up with quotations from Zech 14:7 and Amos 8:9 ("La vie suspendue," 68–69). See the text of the sermon in Marcel Richard, "Quelques nouveaux fragments des pères antenicéens et nicéens," *Symbolae Osloenses* 38 (1963): 80–81.

Jer 15:9: Irenaeus (*Haer.* 4.33.12), Cyprian (*Test.* 2.23), and *Alt. Sim.* 39 parallel Ps.-Gregory in combining Amos 8:9 and Jer 15:9 as *testimonia* to the darkness at Jesus' crucifixion.

Isa 65:2: The text is used already by Paul in his reflections on Israel's relationship with God (Rom 10:21). Skarsaune concludes that Isa 65:2 and Ps 21:17, 19 were included in the passion section of Justin's kerygma source (*Proof from Prophecy*, 146–48, 158; see, e.g., *1 Apol.* 35.3); cf. the parallel use of these texts as proofs of Jesus' crucifixion in *Barn.* 12.4 (in a TC on figures of the cross); Irenaeus *Epid.* 79; *Haer.* 4.33.12; Tertullian *Adv. Jud.* 13.10; Cyprian *Test.* 2.20 ("That the Jews would fasten Christ to the cross"); Novatian *Trin.* 9.8; 28.10; *Alt. Sim.* 28. On outstretched arms as a sign of the cross in patristic literature, see Reijners, *Holy Cross*, 123–33.

"Raise a sign for the nations" (Isa 62:10): Justin quotes this passage within a long quotation of Isa 62:10–63:6 (*Dial.* 26.3). On the numerous patristic references to "sign" as a name for the cross, see Reijners, *Holy Cross*, 118–48; see also his discussion on the sign of the cross in ibid., 148–80). It should be noted that other Greek writers use σημεῖον in this context, and not σύσσημον as does Ps.-Gregory (following his Isaiah text).

Uncertain quotation: See the discussions in Jean Daniélou, "Un testimonium sur la vigne dans Barnabé XII, 1," *RSR* 50 (1962): 389–99; repr. in idem, *Études d'exégèse judéo-chrétienne*, 99–107; Robert A. Kraft, *The Apostolic Fathers: A New Translation and Commentary. Volume 3: Barnabas and Didache* (New York: Thomas Nelson, 1965), 118; and Reijners, *Holy Cross*, 27–28. The source of this quotation is unknown; a close parallel is *Barn.* 12.1: Καὶ πότε ταῦτα συντελεσθήσεται; λέγει κύριος· ὅταν ξύλον κλιθῇ καὶ ἀναστῇ, καὶ ὅταν ἐκ ξύλου αἷμα στάξῃ. *Barnabas* attributes the saying to "another prophet." Several other parallels should be noted: 4 Ezra 5:5: "blood shall drip from the wood"; *Ladder of Jacob* 7:2: "a tree cut with an ax will bleed"; Ps.-Jerome *Comm. in Mark* 15:33, *"Hic stillavit sanguis de lingo"* (PL 30:639). Several scholars (e.g., Kraft, Reijners) also refer the first part of the quotation, Καὶ τότε ταῦτα συντελεσθήσεται, to 4 Ezra 4:33: "How long and when will these things be," although this reference is unconvincing to me. The *Ladder of Jacob* understands the tree as a sign of Christ's appearance on earth, while Ps.-Gregory and *Barnabas* refer the sign to Christ's passion. Compare also 4QPseudo-Ezekiel (4Q385, frg. 2, line 10). For Harris's analysis of this passage, see Alessandro Falcetta, "The Testimony Research of James Rendel Harris," *NovT* 45 (2003): 282.

Zech 14:6–7: See Cyril of Jerusalem *Cat.* 13.24 and Rufinus *Symb.* 24. Along with the references to the darkness, Cyril, Eusebius (*Dem. ev.*

6.18 [292–293]), and Rufinus apply references to the cold in this passage to the Gospel detail of Peter warming himself by the fire (John 18:18). Ps.-Gregory omits this reference in his quotation.

Ps 68:21–22: The passage appears to underlie the narratives of Jesus on the cross: Matt 27:34, 48; Mark 15:23, 36; Luke 23:36; John 19:29, and is widespread in the passion *testimonia* literature.

Crossan notes that several early Christian works (*Barn.* 7.3, 5; Irenaeus *Epid.* 82; *Gos. Pet.* 5.16; and Tertullian *Adv. Jud.* 10.4) differ from the canonical Gospels in reporting that Jesus was given vinegar mixed with gall to drink. He concludes that these texts preserve a passion tradition independent from that of the canonical Gospels (Crossan, *Cross that Spoke*, 208–18). See also Novatian *Trin.* 28.11; Ps.-Epiphanius *Test.* 53.1 ("That they would give him vinegar and gall to drink"); Irenaeus *Haer.* 4.33.12; Cyril of Jerusalem *Cat.* 13.29; and Rufinus *Symb.* 26.

Zech 13:7: Ps.-Gregory parallels the LXX-deviant form of this passage witnessed in the Gospels (Mark 14:27, Matt 26:31) and in Justin (*Dial.* 53.6). According to Krister Stendahl, already in NT times the Gospel form of the phrase was "a testimony which had an independent existence" (*The School of St. Matthew and its Use of the Old Testament* [2d ed.; Philadelphia: Fortress, 1968; repr.; Ramsey, N.J.: Sigler, 1991], 83).

Ps.-Gregory's text shows connections with various early Christian non-LXX forms.

Ps.-Gregory Test. 7	LXX Zech 13:7	Matt 26:31	Mark 14:27	Justin *Dial.* 53.6
Ῥομφαία, ἐξεγέρθητι ἐπὶ τὸν ποιμένα, καὶ ἐπ' ἄνδρα τοῦ λαοῦ μου·	ῥομφαία, ἐξεγέρθητι ἐπὶ τοὺς ποιμένας μου καὶ ἐπ' ἄνδρα πολίτην αὐτοῦ, λέγει κύριος παντοκράτωρ			Ῥομφαία, ἐξεγέρθητι ἐπὶ τὸν ποιμένα μου καὶ ἐπ' ἄνδρα τοῦ λαοῦ μου, λέγει κύριος τῶν δυνάμεων·

COMMENTARY

πάταξον τὸν ποιμένα μου, καὶ διασκορπισθήσονται τὰ πρόβατα τῆς ποίμνης.	πατάξατε τοὺς ποιμένας καὶ ἐκσπάσατε τὰ πρόβατα, καὶ ἐπάξω τὴν χεῖρά μου ἐπὶ τοὺς ποιμένας·	πατάξω τὸν ποιμένα, καὶ διασκορπισθήσονται τὰ πρόβατα τῆς ποίμνης.	πατάξω τὸν ποιμένα, καὶ τὰ πρόβατα διασκορπισθήσονται	πάταξον τὸν ποιμένα, καὶ διασκορπισθήσονται τὰ πρόβατα αὐτοῦ

Other early TCs witness some of these same variant readings: Irenaeus *Epid.* 76; *Barn.* 5.12. See also Cyril of Jerusalem *Cat.* 13.24.

CHAPTER 8: CONCERNING THE RESURRECTION OF CHRIST

Ps 81:8: Cyprian includes this text in his TC, "That Jesus shall come as a judge" (*Test.* 2.28).

Isa 33:10–11: Cyprian includes this text in his TC, "That after he had risen again he should receive from his Father all power, and his power should be everlasting" (*Test.* 2.26).

Hos 5:15b; 6:1–3a: Novatian quotes Hos 6:3a as a proof that the resurrection would occur in the morning (*Trin.* 9.8). Cyprian uses Hos 6:2 as a proof of the resurrection on the third day (*Test.* 2.25); Ps.-Epiphanius quotes Hos 6:1–2 as a general proof for the resurrection of the dead (*Test.* 85.1). Tertullian applies Hos 5:15, 6:1–2 to Jesus' resurrection (*Marc.* 4.43.1); cf. his unusual form of Hos 6:1–2 (*Adv. Jud.* 13.23). See also Cyril of Jerusalem *Cat.* 14.14; Lactantius *Inst.* 4.19.9; and *Alt. Sim.* 38–39 (inc. Hos 6:2 and Isa 33:10–11).

Ps 15:10: The passage is an established *testimonium* for the resurrection already in the NT: Ps 15:8–10 is quoted in Acts 2:25–28; Ps 15:10b in Acts 13:25. See its use in Cyprian's TC, "That he was not to be overcome of death, nor should remain in Hades (*apud inferos*)" (*Test.* 2.24), and in Ps.-Epiphanius's TC, "That he would be raised up" (*Test.* 74.1); see also Lactantius *Inst.* 4.19.8; Cyril of Jerusalem *Cat.* 14.4.

Ps 87:5: Ps.-Epiphanius also applies this to the resurrection (*Test.* 74.6). The passage is quoted often by Cyril of Jerusalem (e.g., *Cat.* 13.34; 14.1; 14.8).

Isa 28:16 (cf. 1 Pet 2:6): Ps.-Gregory's quotation follows most closely the adapted version of Isa 28:16 found in 1 Pet 2:6.

Ps.-Gregory *Test.* 8	1 Pet 2:6	Isa 28:16
ἰδοὺ τίθημι ἐν Σιὼν λίθον ἀκρογωνιαῖον ἐκλεκτὸν ἔντιμον· καὶ ὁ πιστεύων εἰς αὐτὸν οὐ καταισχυνθήσεται.	ἰδοὺ τίθημι ἐν Σιὼν λίθον ἀκρογωνιαῖον ἐκλεκτὸν ἔντιμον καὶ ὁ πιστεύων ἐπ' αὐτῷ οὐ μὴ καταισχυνθῇ	ἰδοὺ ἐγὼ ἐμβαλῶ εἰς τὰ θεμέλια Σιων λίθον πολυτελῆ ἐκλεκτὸν ἀκρογωνιαῖον ἔντιμον εἰς τὰ θεμέλια αὐτῆς, καὶ ὁ πιστεύων ἐπ' αὐτῷ οὐ μὴ καταισχυνθῇ

Compare also Paul's quotation in Rom 9:33, which begins with the same non-LXX reading ἰδοὺ τίθημι ἐν Σιὼν λίθον. This common form indicates use of a very early written *testimonia* source (see Albl, *Early Christian Testimonia*, 271–75).

Ps.-Gregory's comments use phrases from Ps 117:22–23. This Psalm is also quoted in 1 Pet 2:7 as part of Peter's "stone" TC. On the widespread application of passages with vocabulary and imagery concerning "stones" to Christ and his church, see Albl, *Early Christian Testimonia*, 265–85, and Falcetta, "Theory of James Rendel Harris," 133–140. Ps.-Gregory's comments suggest a more general use of the stone imagery rather than a specific application to Christ's resurrection, although Cyril of Jerusalem does apply Isa 28:16 to Christ's tomb (*Cat.* 13.35).

CHAPTER 9: CONCERNING HIS ASCENSION

Ps 46:6: Justin quotes Ps 46:6–10 in the context of his discussion that Jesus was called "King of glory" at his ascension (*Dial.* 36–37). Ps.-Epiphanius includes it in his TC, "That he would be taken up into heaven" (*Test.* 86.1); see also Cyril of Jerusalem *Cat.* 14.24; *Alt. Sim.* 40; and Eusebius *Dem. ev.* 6.2.

Daniel 7 and Ps 110:1: Daniel 7:13 and Ps 109:1 are already combined in Jesus' reply to the high priest's question (Mark 14:62 par.). Both are used to prove Jesus' exaltation into heavenly glory. Ps.-Gregory applies the texts to Jesus' ascension, but their general character was easily adaptable to other events in Jesus' glorification (resurrection, second *parousia*, activity as ruler/judge). See the combination of Ps 109:1 and Dan 7:13 in Justin *Dial.* 31–32; Irenaeus *Haer.* 4.33.11;

COMMENTARY 119

Sib. Or. 2.241–245; *Apoc. Pet.* 6; Cyprian *Test.* 2.26 ("That after he had risen again he should receive from his Father all power, and his power should be everlasting"); and *Alt. Sim.* 42.

Compare the use of Ps 109:1 by Ps.-Epiphanius, "That he sat at the right hand of the father, not only after he ascended, but even before that" (*Test.* 89.3; cf. Irenaeus *Epid.* 85), and his use of Dan 7:13–14 to prove Jesus' *parousia* as a judge, "That he would judge the inhabited world, and the judgment would be given to him" (*Test.* 94.5). Cyril of Jerusalem applies Ps 109:1 to the phrase of the Jerusalem Creed, "and he ascended into heaven, and sits at the right hand of the Father" (*Cat.* 14.27–28).

CHAPTER 10: CONCERNING THE GLORY OF THE CHURCH

The royal Ps 44 is used often in the *testimonia* literature to prove the full divinity of Christ (esp. 44:7: "Your throne, O God, is eternal"); see sect. 2.10 above. Here Ps.-Gregory applies the exalted language about the queen to the church, an application already made by Clement of Alexandria (*Strom.* 6.92.1).

CHAPTER 11: ON CIRCUMCISION

Ps.-Gregory here draws on anti-cultic *testimonia* sources witnessed in Justin and *Barnabas*. He closely parallels a sequence in Justin's *Dial.* 10–29, even to the extent of adopting the dialogue form. On Justin's anti-cultic *testimonia* and their corresponding cultic typologies, along with parallels in *Barnabas* and the Ps.-Clementine *Recognitions*, see Skarsaune, *Proof from Prophecy*, 166–74, 295–313.

Ps.-Gregory *Test.* 11–13	Justin *Dial.* 10–15
11: Ps.-Gregory introduces an imaginary Jewish interlocutor, "If you worship the same God, why do you not become circumcised?" Ps.-Gregory quotes Jer 38:31–32 to show that circumcision will cease because of God's new covenant.	10: Christians censured for not keeping the Law, in particular circumcision and observing Sabbath.
	11: Justin agrees that Christians worship the same God as the Jews. But God has given a new Law and covenant (Isa 51:4–5; Jer 38:31–32)
Circumcision *testimonia*	12: Justin calls for a second circumcision and perpetual Sabbath

12: TC against sacrifices	13: Jewish ritual washings and sacrifices do not achieve forgiveness of sin, rather only the blood of Christ (Isa 52:10–54:6).
13: TC against keeping the Sabbath	14: Baptism, symbolic meaning of unleavened bread
14: TC on sealing with the sign of the cross	15: True fasting

Cyprian's *Testimonies* follow the same general outline:

1.8: "That the first circumcision of the flesh is made void, and the second circumcision of the spirit is promised instead" (including Jer 4:3–4)
1.9: "That the former law which was given by Moses was to cease"
1.10: "That a new law was to be given"
1.11: "That another dispensation and a new covenant was to be given" (quoting Jer 38:31–32)

Ps.-Gregory's specific *testimonia* on circumcision parallel texts in Justin and *Barnabas* (see Skarsaune, *Proof from Prophecy*, 70–72).

Ps.-Gregory Test. 11	Barn. 9.5	Justin Dial. 15.7–16.1	Justin Dial. 28.2
Jer 9:26b UQ (elements of Jer 4:4; 9:26b; Deut 10:16) Jer 4:3b; Deut 10:16 Jer 4:4a	Jer 4:3–4 Deut 10:16 Jer 9:26b	Jer 4:4 (allusion) Deut 10:16–17	Jer 4:3b–4a Jer 9:25–26

Jer 9:26:

Ps.-Gregory Test. 11	LXX Jer 9:26	Dial. AZ 123	Clement Alex. Paed. 1.79.1	Barn. 9.5
Πάντα τὰ ἔθνη ἀπερίτμητα σαρκί, ὁ δὲ λαὸς οὗτος τῇ καρδίᾳ	πάντα τὰ ἔθνη ἀπερίτμητα σαρκί καὶ πᾶς οἶκος Ισραηλ ἀπερίτμητοι καρδίας αὐτῶν	Πάντα τὰ ἔθνη ἀπερίτμητα σαρκί, ὁ δὲ λαὸς οὗτος τῇ καρδίᾳ	<u>ἀπερίτμητα πάντα τὰ ἔθνη</u>, ὁ δὲ λαὸς οὗτος ἀπερίτμητος καρδία.	πάντα τὰ ἔθνη ἀπερίτμητα ἀκροβυστία, <u>ὁ δὲ λαὸς οὗτος ἀπερίτμητος καρδία.</u>

COMMENTARY 121

See also Justin's non-LXX form of Jer 9:26b, attributed to "Isaiah" (*1 Apol.* 53.11).

Ps.-Gregory's exegetical comments mirror the comments in the *Dialogue of Athanasius and Zacchaeus*. In fact, the editor of the *Dialogue*, Frederick C. Conybeare, used Ps.-Gregory to restore the text of the *Dialogue* (see *The Dialogues of Athanasius and Zacchaeus and of Timothy and Aquila. Edited with Prolegomena and Facsimiles* (Anecdota Oxoniensia; Oxford: Clarendon, 1898), 61 n. 3.

Ps.-Gregory *Test.* 11	*Dial. AZ* 123
Ὅτι δὲ οὐδένα δικαιοῖ ἡ περιτομή, δῆλον ἐκ τούτων· Ἀβραὰμ ἀπερίτμητος εὐηρέστησε τῷ θεῷ· πρῶτον γὰρ ὤφθη εὐαρεστῶν, καὶ τότε αὐτῷ τὴν περιτομὴν δίδωσι. Καὶ οἱ ἐν τῇ ἐρήμῳ δὲ γεννηθέντες, ἐν τοῖς τεσσαράκοντα ἔτεσιν ἀπερίτμητοι ἦσαν·	Ὅτι δὲ οὐδένα δικαιοῖ ἡ περιτομή, ἐντεῦθεν ἐστὶ [δῆλον ἐκ τούτων· Ἀβραὰμ ἀπερίτμητος εὐηρέστησε τῷ θεῷ πρῶ]τον γὰρ αὐτῷ ὤφθη· καὶ τότε αὐτῷ τὴν ἐντολὴν τῆς περιτομῆς δίδωσι· Καὶ οἱ ἐν τῇ ἐρήμῳ δὲ γεννηθέντες, ἐν τοῖς τεσσαράκοντα ἔτεσιν ἀπερίτμητοι ἦσαν·

Uncertain quotation:

Ps.-Gregory *Test.* 11	LXX Jer 4:4a	LXX Deut 10:16
Περιτέμνεσθε τὴν καρδίαν ὑμῶν, καὶ μὴ τὴν σάρκα τῆς ἀκροβυστίας ὑμων.	περιτμήθητε τῷ θεῷ ὑμῶν καὶ περιέλεσθε τὴν ἀκροβυστίαν τῆς καρδίας ὑμῶν	καὶ περιτεμεῖσθε τὴν σκληροκαρδίαν ὑμῶν (αʹ = ἀκροβυστίαν καρδίας)

This quotation shares vocabulary with Jer 4:4 and Deut 10:16. "Circumcising the flesh of the foreskin" is a technical phrase for circumcision (see, e.g., LXX Gen 17:11–25). See also Resch, *Agrapha*, 316 (Logion 39a).

Jer 4:3 / Deut 10:16:

Ps.-Gregory *Test.* 11	LXX Jer 4:3b-4	LXX Deut 10:16
Νεώσατε ἑαυτοῖς νεώματα, καὶ μὴ σπείρετε ἐπ' ἀκάνθαις· ἀλλὰ περιτέμνεσθε τὸ σκληρὸν τῆς καρδίας ὑμῶν.	νεώσατε ἑαυτοῖς νεώματα καὶ μὴ σπείρητε ἐπ' ἀκάνθαις 4 περιτμήθητε τῷ θεῷ ὑμῶν καὶ περιέλεσθε τὴν ἀκροβυστίαν τῆς καρδίας ὑμῶν	καὶ περιτεμεῖσθε τὴν σκληροκαρδίαν

Quotation of Jer 4:4a:

Ps. Gregory Test. 11	LXX Jer 4:4a	Justin *Dial*. 28.2
περιτέμνεσθε τῷ θεῷ τὴν ἀκροβυστίαν τῆς καρδίας ὑμῶν	περιτμήθητε <u>τῷ θεῷ</u> ὑμῶν καὶ περιέλεσθε τὴν ἀκροβυστίαν τῆς καρδίας ὑμῶν	περιτέμνεσθε τῷ κυρίῳ, καὶ περιτέμνεσθε <u>τὴν</u> ἀκροβυστίαν τῆς καρδίας ὑμῶν.

See also Justin *Dial*. 15.7; Tertullian *Marc*. 1.20. Lactantius's quotation of Jer 4:3–4 is falsely attributed to Isaiah. See also Resch, *Agrapha*, 316 (Logion 39b).

And those from Adam until Abraham: Justin shares Ps.-Gregory's argument, showing how Adam, Abel, Enoch, Lot, Noah, and Melchizedek, though uncircumcised, still found favor in God's eyes before the time of Abraham (*Dial*. 19.3–4). See very similar lists in Irenaeus *Haer*. 4.16.2; Tertullian *Adv. Jud*. 2.12–14; Cyprian *Test*. 1.8; *Alt. Sim*. 25.

For circumcision was given on account of the mixing of the people with the nations: Ps.-Gregory claims that circumcision was a way of keeping the Jewish people "pure" from mixture with other peoples before the birth of the Messiah. Justin and Tertullian also interpret circumcision as a "sign" of the separation of the Jews from other nations, but further connect it with the exclusion of the Jewish people from Jerusalem under Hadrian's decree (*Dial*. 16.2; *Adv. Jud*. 3).

See an argument similar to that of Ps.-Gregory in *Dial*. AZ 125.

CHAPTER 12: CONCERNING SACRIFICES

This chapter shares many texts with other anti-cultic collections:

- Justin *Dial*. 13–23: Isa 1:13–16 (allusion); Isa 1:16; Amos 5:18–6:7; Jer 7:21–22; Ps 49; Mal 1:10–12.
- Irenaeus *Haer*. 4.17.1–6: Ps 49:9–15; Isa 1:11; Jer 7:21–25; Mal 1:10–11.
- Tertullian *Adv. Jud*. 5: Mal 1:10–11; Ps 49:14; Isa 1:11–14.
- Cyprian *Test*. 1.16 ("That the ancient sacrifice should be made void, and a new one should be celebrated"): Isa 1:11–12; Ps 49:13–15; Mal 1:10–11.

Skarsaune identifies a section of Justin's "kerygma source" with the title, "The new law and the new covenant" (underlying

Dial. 11–47; cf. *1 Apol.* 37). The argument here is that the Jewish law has been replaced by the "new law" of Christ; Christian practices of baptism and the Lord's Supper have replaced Jewish cultic practices (*Proof from Prophecy*, 166–82; summary conclusion: pp. 181–82). The Jewish practices are "types" (τύποι) of Christian practices (e.g., the offering of fine flour is a type of the Eucharist; *Dial.* 41.1). Ps.-Gregory also follows his anti-cultic *testimonia* (chaps. 11–13) with references to Christian cultic practice (chap. 14 on initiation rituals).

Jer 7:22: Ps.-Gregory quotes two distinct versions of LXX Jer 7:22, attributing the second to "Isaiah."

The first version follows the basic sense of the LXX, with some deviations and additions.

Ps.-Gregory *Test.* 12 Version 1	LXX Jer 7:22
Ζῶ ἐγώ, λέγει Κύριος, ὅτι περὶ θυσιῶν, καὶ ὁλοκαυτωμάτων οὐκ ἐνετειλάμην πρὸς τοὺς πατέρας ὑμῶν, ἀφ᾽ ἧς ἡμέρας ἀνήγαγον αὐτοὺς ἐκ γῆς Αἰγύπτου, καὶ ἕως τῆς ἡμέρας ταύτης.	ὅτι οὐκ ἐλάλησα πρὸς τοὺς πατέρας ὑμῶν καὶ οὐκ ἐνετειλάμην αὐτοῖς ἐν ἡμέρᾳ ᾗ ἀνήγαγον αὐτοὺς ἐκ γῆς Αἰγύπτου περὶ ὁλοκαυτωμάτων καὶ θυσίας·

The second, which Ps.-Gregory attributes to "Isaiah," parallels the LXX-deviant quotation in *Barnabas* precisely (Ps.-Gregory reads προσενεγκεῖν for προσενέγκαι; Codex 1907 reads with *Barnabas*). See Resch, *Agrapha*, 317 (Logion 41).

Ps.-Gregory *Test.* 12 Version 2	LXX Jer 7:22	*Barn.* 2.7
Μὴ ἐγὼ ἐνετειλάμην τοῖς πατράσιν ὑμῶν, ἐκπορευομένοις ἐκ γῆς Αἰγύπτου προσενεγκεῖν μοι ὁλοκαυτώματα καὶ θυσίαν;	ὅτι οὐκ ἐλάλησα πρὸς τοὺς πατέρας ὑμῶν καὶ οὐκ ἐνετειλάμην αὐτοῖς ἐν ἡμέρᾳ ᾗ ἀνήγαγον αὐτοὺς ἐκ γῆς Αἰγύπτου περὶ ὁλοκαυτωμάτων καὶ θυσίας	Μὴ ἐγὼ ἐνετειλάμην τοῖς πατράσιν ὑμῶν ἐκπορευομένοις ἐκ γῆς Αἰγύπτου, προσενέγκαι μοι ὁλοκαυτώματα καὶ θυσίας;

Justin also draws from a non-LXX *testimonia* source for his quotation of Jer 7:21–22 (*Dial.* 22.6; see Skarsaune, *Proof from Prophecy*, 111); Justin's quotation is influenced by Jer 38:32.

Isa 1:11–14: The combination of Jer 7:22 and portions of Isa 1:11–14 occurs in other anti-cultic TCs:

Barn. 2.5–8 (*Barnabas* conflates Jer 7:22–23 with Zech 8:17 / 7:10); Clement *Paed*. 3.89–91; Irenaeus *Haer*. 4.17.1–4 (see Robert A. Kraft, "The Epistle of Barnabas: Its Quotations and their Sources" [Ph.D. diss., Harvard University, 1961], 95–117; Albl, *Early Christian Testimonia*, 148–153). See also the use of Isa 1:16 in Ps.-Epiphanius *Test*. 92.1 and the use of Isa 1:13–16 in *Alt. Sim*. 49–51.

Ps 49:9–14: Ps.-Gregory cites three separate passages from the Psalm. Justin cites the entire Psalm in an anti-cultic TC (*Dial*. 22.7–10).

Ps 49:13: The *Dialogue of Timothy and Aquila* 12.9–12 combines Ps 49:13 and Isa 1:10–14.

Amos 5:21–23: Tertullian combines Isa 1:13–14 and Amos 5:21 (*Marc*. 5.4.6). The reference to God's "smelling" in the assemblies refers to the stock phrase that sacrifices are a "pleasing odor" to the Lord.

Mal 1:10–11: This passage is explicitly connected with the Christian Eucharist (Justin *Dial*. 41.2; Irenaeus *Haer*. 4.17.5). Tertullian includes the passage in his anti-cultic TC (*Adv. Jud*. 5.6). Ps.-Gregory quotes the passage here, and then three times in chapter 16. Each of the versions differs slightly:

LXX Mal 1:10b–11	Ps.-Gregory Test. 12	Ps.-Gregory Test. 16	Ps.-Gregory Test. 16	Ps.-Gregory Test. 16
10 οὐκ ἔστι μοι θέλημα ἐν ὑμῖν λέγει κύριος παντοκράτωρ, καὶ θυσίαν οὐ προσδέξομαι ἐκ τῶν χειρῶν ὑμῶν.	οὐκ ἔστι μου θέλημα ἐν ὑμῖν, λέγει κύριος παντοκράτωρ, καὶ θυσίαν οὐ προσδέξομαι ἐκ τῶν χειρῶν ὑμῶν,		οὐκ ἔστι μου θέλημα ἐν ὑμῖν, λέγει κύριος παντοκράτωρ,	[Attributed to ὁ προφήτης.]

COMMENTARY

11 διότι ἀπὸ ἀνατολῶν ἡλίου ἕως δυσμῶν τὸ ὄνομά μου δεδόξασται ἐν τοῖς ἔθνεσι,	διότι ἀπὸ ἀνατολῶν ἡλίου, καὶ ἕως δυσμῶν τὸ ὄνομά μου δεδόξασται ἐν τοῖς ἔθνεσι,	[Introduced with καὶ πάλιν after a quotation from Isaiah.]	(ὅτι ἀπὸ ἀνατολῶν ἡλίου μέχρι δυσμῶν τὸ ὄνομά μου δεδόξασται ἐν τοῖς ἔθνεσι, λέγει κύριος παντοκράτωρ)	
καὶ ἐν παντὶ τόπῳ θυμίαμα προσάγεται τῷ ὀνόματί μου καὶ θυσία καθαρά διότι μέγα τὸ ὄνομά μου ἐν τοῖς ἔθνεσι, λέγει κύριος παντοκράτωρ	καὶ ἐν παντὶ τόπῳ θυμίαμα προσφέρεται τῷ ὀνόματί μου, καὶ θυσία καθαρά· διότι μέγα τὸ ὄνομά μου ἐν τοῖς ἔθνεσι, λέγει κύριος παντοκράτωρ	μέγα τὸ ὄνομα αὐτοῦ ἐν τοῖς ἔθνεσι (Cod. 451 = ἐπὶ τοῖς ἔθνεσι) καὶ ἐν παντὶ τόπῳ θυμίαμα προσφέρεται τῷ ὀνόματί μου, καὶ θυσία καθαρά·	καὶ ἐν παντὶ τόπῳ θυμίαμα προσάγεται τῷ ὀνόματί μου, καὶ μέγα τὸ ὄνομά μου ἐν τοῖς ἔθνεσι, λέγει κύριος παντοκράτωρ.	μέγα τὸ ὄνομα αὐτοῦ ἐν τοῖς ἔθνεσι, καὶ ἐν παντὶ τόπῳ θυμίαμα προσφέρεται τῷ ὀνόματι αὐτοῦ, καὶ θυσία καθαρά.
12 ὑμεῖς δὲ βεβηλοῦτε αὐτό				ὑμεῖς δὲ βεβηλοῦτε αὐτό.	

CHAPTER 13: CONCERNING KEEPING THE SABBATH

Christian polemic against Sabbath observance is standard in the anti-cultic materials: Justin *Dial.* 21; Tertullian *Adv. Jud.* 4; *Barn.* 15.8. This section is not in the form of a TC, but rather a narrative explanation of the original reasons for the Sabbath, followed by several examples (not all scriptural) of situations in which complete Sabbath rest is not observed.

when Joshua (Jesus)...did he not rest on the Sabbath?: See the same argument in Tertullian *Adv. Jud.* 4 and *Alt. Sim.* 49.

How then is a boy circumcised on the eighth day?: Justin parallels this and Ps.-Gregory's following two arguments (*Dial.* 27.5; cf. further anti-Sabbath polemic in *Dial.* 21).

CHAPTER 14: CONCERNING SEALING WITH THE SIGN OF THE CROSS

Κατασφραγίζω can refer to sealing with the Holy Spirit (see already the connection of σφραγίζω with the Holy Spirit in 2 Cor 1:22; Eph 1:13; 4:30). See also the "sealing" (σφραγίζω) on the forehead in Rev 7:3-4, a text connected with Ezek 9:4.

Compare Cyprian's TC, "That in this sign of the cross is salvation for all people who are marked on their foreheads," which shares the Ezekiel texts with Ps.-Gregory (*Test.* 2.22: Ezek 9:4-6; Exod 12:13; Rev 14:1 [reference to the 144,000 sealed]; Rev 22:13-14).

Tertullian quotes the following version of Ezek 9:4, "The Lord said unto me, 'Go through the gate, through the midst of Jerusalem, and set the mark Tau upon the foreheads of the men'"; the Tau of course symbolizing the cross (*Marc.* 3.22.5; cf. also *Adv. Jud.* 11 and *Barn.* 9.8). Ps.-Epiphanius parallels this collection in his TC, "That even the mark on the forehead was foretold" (*Test.* 91; using Ps 59:6; Isa 8:16; Ezek 9:3-6). Ps.-Epiphanius's next TC is "That baptism in Christ was foretold" (*Test.* 92). See also *Alt. Sim.* 34-35. For detailed patristic evidence for the connection of the sign of the cross with baptismal rites (including a discussion of the term σφραγίζω), see Reijners, *Holy Cross*, 148-87. See also the use of κατασφραγίζω to refer to sealing during baptismal rites in *Apos. Con.* 8.8.4.

Given these parallels, and the likelihood that Ps-Gregory's *testimonia* source(s) follow(s) anti-cultic polemic with an emphasis on Christian practices (see Skarsaune, *Proof from Prophecy*, 166-74, 295-313), it is virtually certain that Ps.-Gregory refers here to the tracing of the sign of the cross (perhaps with oil) on a candidate's forehead as a part of the baptismal ceremony.

Yet God spoke about their sacrificing: This comment is apparently misplaced; it fits much better in Ps.-Gregory's anti-cultic chapter 12.

CHAPTER 15: CONCERNING THE GOSPEL

In this chapter, Ps.-Gregory connects two texts, Ps 67:12 and Isa 52:7, that share the word εὐαγγελίζω.

Isaiah 52:7 is applied to the preaching of the apostles (cf. Irenaeus *Epid.* 86; Tertullian *Marc.* 3.22.1; 5.2.5). Irenaeus and Tertullian also connect Isa 52:7 with the concept of the new law going forth from Jerusalem. On the role of Isa 52:7 in early Christian TCs grouped around εὐαγγέλιον and εὐαγγελίζω (including a discussion of pre-Christian Jewish roots), see Falcetta, "Theory of James Rendel Harris," 175–88.

CHAPTER 16: CONCERNING THE UNBELIEF OF THE JEWS, AND CONCERNING THE CHURCH OF THE NATIONS

This extensive TC is a rather haphazard collection of anti-Jewish texts with corresponding "pro-Gentile" passages. Again, the logic is that God has turned away from the Jewish people and has chosen the Gentiles.

Several texts in this chapter are quoted elsewhere in Ps.-Gregory's document, often in different versions—evidence that Ps.-Gregory is drawing on a discrete *testimonia* source in this chapter.

Mal 1:11: See the Commentary on chapter 12 for a comparison of the different versions of this passage quoted by Ps.-Gregory.

Mic 4:1–2: Skarsaune has shown that the parallel to this passage, Isa 2:2–3, was a central text in Justin's "kerygma source," serving to prove that Christ was the "new law" coming out of Jerusalem, replacing the Jewish law (see summary, *Proof from Prophecy*, 166–182). Justin further links the "new law" with the kerygma of the disciples coming from Jerusalem (see *1 Apol.* 39.1–3; *Dial.* 109.1; cf. Irenaeus *Haer.* 4.34.4). See also its use in Cyprian, "That a new law was to be given" (*Test.* 1.10); Lactantius *Inst.* 4.17.3.

kingdom of the Adversary: The phrase ὁ ἀντικείμενος often refers to the devil in patristic literature (e.g., *1 Clem.* 51.1; Origen *Cels.* 6.44).

Ps 17:44–46: Psalm 17:44–45 forms part of Justin's anti-cultic *testimonia* (*Dial.* 28.6); *Barnabas* includes Ps 17:44 in an anti-circumcision TC (9.1). Skarsaune sees further evidence here that *Barnabas* and Justin share a *testimonia* source (*Proof from Prophecy*, 129). Tertullian follows the same tradition, applying the passage to the Gentiles as the "new people" of God who follow the "new law," since the old law has been superceded (*Adv. Jud.* 3). Cyprian includes the passage in his TC, "That the Gentiles should rather believe in Christ" (*Test.* 1.21).

Gen 12:3: The text is key in Paul's thought on Israel's relationship with the Gentile nations (Gal 3:8). Genesis 12:1–3 is quoted in Cyprian's TC, "That the Gentiles should rather believe in Christ" (*Test.* 1.21).

Deut 32:20–21: Paul quotes Deut 32:21 in his scriptural reflection on why Israel has not accepted the gospel (Rom 10:19); Irenaeus employs it to prove that God has abandoned the Jews and turned to the Gentiles (*Epid.* 95). Justin includes Deut 32:20b several times in his anti-cultic *testimonia* (e.g., *Dial*. 20.4, 27.4; Deut 32:16–23 is quoted in *Dial*. 119.2). See also Eusebius *Dem. ev.* 2.3 (79).

Isa 53:9: Ps.-Gregory previously included a long quotation of Isa 53:4–9 (sect. 6.2; reading with the LXX). This passage is standard in the passion *testimonia* literature (e.g., Justin *Dial*. 97.2). The function of the passage in this particular section of Ps.-Gregory's *Testimonies* is not transparent; possibly Ps.-Gregory understands "the Jews" as the wicked—the thought may be that God gives them up in "exchange" for the death of the righteous one, Jesus.

Isa 65:1: Ps.-Gregory quotes this text in *Test*. 2.4; see comments there.

Ps 21:23: Quoted in *Barn*. 6.16.

Isa 52:5b: Quoted in Rom 2:24. This is a standard passage in the polemical literature against the Jews: Justin *Dial*. 17.2; Tertullian *Marc*. 3.23.2; 4.14.16. The author of 2 Clement has a non-polemical application of this passage to Christians (13.2–4; cf. Ignatius *Trall*. 8.2 and Polycarp *Phil*. 10.3).

Mal 1:10b–11: This is Ps.-Gregory's second quotation of the passage in this chapter, and his third of four times overall. Here Ps.-Gregory divides the quotation into three parts, varying in details both from the LXX and from his version in chap. 12. See the Commentary on chapter 12 for a synoptic comparison.

Ps 2:8: Ps.-Gregory quotes Ps 2:7–8 in sect. 1.7; see comments there. In that section, the focus was on the relationship between Father and Son in the Godhead; here the focus is on the role of the "nations."

Uncertain quotation: Zacagni comments that Ps.-Gregory refers to the sense of Exod 32:10, but not to the exact words. Compare also Deut 9:14.

Isa 1:13b–16: Ps.-Gregory quotes Isa 1:11–16 in chap. 12 (essentially LXX); the version here differs markedly.

COMMENTARY

Ps.-Gregory *Test.* 16	LXX Isa 1:13b–16
Τὰ Σάββατα ὑμῶν, καὶ <u>τὰς νεομηνίας</u> μισεῖ ἡ ψυχή μου· καὶ τὰς εὐχὰς ὑμῶν οὐ προσδέξομαι· λούσασθε, καθαροὶ γίνεσθε· αἱ χεῖρες ὑμῶν μεμολυσμέναι <u>αἵματι</u>.	13 οὐ προσθήσεσθε· ἐὰν φέρητε σεμίδαλιν, μάταιον· θυμίαμα βδέλυγμά μοί ἐστι· <u>τὰς νουμηνίας ὑμῶν καὶ τὰ σάββατα</u> καὶ ἡμέραν μεγάλην οὐκ ἀνέχομαι· νηστείαν καὶ ἀργίαν 14 καὶ τὰς νουμηνίας ὑμῶν καὶ τὰς ἑορτὰς ὑμῶν <u>μισεῖ ἡ ψυχή μου</u>· ἐγενήθητέ μοι εἰς πλησμονήν οὐκέτι ἀνήσω τὰς ἁμαρτίας ὑμῶν 15 ὅταν τὰς χεῖρας ἐκτείνητε πρός με, ἀποστρέψω τοὺς ὀφθαλμούς μου ἀφ' ὑμῶν, καὶ ἐὰν πληθύνητε τὴν δέησιν, οὐκ εἰσακούσομαι ὑμῶν· <u>αἱ γὰρ χεῖρες ὑμῶν αἵματος</u> πλήρεις. 16 λούσασθε, καθαροὶ γένεσθε

Ps.-Gregory's quotation involves an extensive reworking of the original:

Ps.-Gregory *Test.* 16	Quotation techniques
Τὰ Σάββατα ὑμῶν, καὶ τὰς νεομηνίας μισεῖ ἡ ψυχή μου	Combines elements from Isa 1:13–14; reads νεομηνίας for νουμηνίας
καὶ τὰς εὐχὰς ὑμῶν οὐ προσδέξομαι	Paraphrase of v. 15a
λούσασθε, καθαροὶ γίνεσθε	Direct quotation from v. 16
αἱ χεῖρες ὑμῶν μεμολυσμέναι αἵματι	Slight variation of v. 15b

as to the law clearly directing: On the law providing clear directions (διαγορεύω) see 1 Esd 5:48 and Sus 62 (o'). See also Ps.-Gregory's use of the same verb in his discussion on circumcision (*Test.* 11).

Zeph 2:11b: Eusebius quotes this passage in the context of his discussion of the destruction of the Jerusalem Temple; he follows with a quotation of Mal 1:10–11 (*Dem. ev.* 1.6 [19]).

Isa 65:15–16: Irenaeus applies the passage to those saved in God's name (*Epid.* 88; see also Clement of Alexandria *Paed.* 1.14.5). Cyprian includes Isa 65:13–16a in a TC with the unusual heading, "That the Jews should lose while we should receive the bread and the cup of Christ and all his grace, and that the new name of Christians should be blessed in the earth" (*Test.* 1.22). Cyril of Jerusalem applies the verse to the new name of "Christians" (*Cat.* 10.16).

Isa 11:9: The messianic passage Isa 11:1–10 is widely quoted by the early Christians (see sect. 2.9 above).

Ps 21:28–29: Cyprian includes this passage under the heading, "That he [Christ] will reign as king for ever" (*Test.* 2.29). Eusebius quotes Ps 21:28–32 as part of his long series of prophecies that God would bless "the nations" (*Dem. ev.* 2.1 [46]).

Matt 21:43: Ps.-Gregory makes Matt 21:43 into an explicitly anti-Jewish statement.

nation of Christians: The notion of Christians as a separate "nation" or "race" was sometimes expressed as the idea of Christians as a "third" race distinct from Jews and Greeks, see, e.g., the *Preaching of Peter* frg. 2d (*apud.* Clement of Alexandria *Strom* 6.5.39–41); Aristides *Apol.* 2.1; 14.1).

Yet the blameless one confesses: Ps.-Gregory picks up on the word ἐξομολόγησις in Ps 110:3, reflecting the traditional Christian belief in Jesus' sinlessness.

Ps 109:1 and Isa 45:1:

Psalm 109:1 is the most oft-quoted scriptural passage in the NT and is used heavily in early Christianity in general; see David M. Hay, *Glory at the Right Hand: Psalm 110 in Early Christianity* (SBLMS 18; Nashville/ New York: Abingdon, 1973); Albl, *Early Christian Testimonia*, 216–36.

The combination of Ps 110:1 and Isa 45:1 is well attested in the *testimonia* literature: *Barn.* 12.10–11; Irenaeus *Epid.* 48–49; Tertullian *Prax.* 11.7–8; Novatian *Trin.* 26.7; Lactantius *Inst.* 4.12.17–18.

In quoting Isa 45:1, several authors, read Κυρίῳ ("to the Lord") for Κύρῳ ("to Cyrus"), although this is nowhere attested in the Greek versions of Isaiah: *Barn.* 12.11; Irenaeus *Epid.* 49; Tertullian *Prax.* 11.8, 28.11; *Adv. Jud.* 7.2; Novatian *Trin.* 26.7; Cyprian *Test.* 1.21; *Alt. Sim.* 13. For further references, see Robert A. Kraft, "*Barnabas*' Isaiah Text and the 'Testimony Book' Hypothesis," *JBL* 79 (1960): 342; idem, "Christian Transmission of Greek Jewish Scriptures: A Methodological Probe," in *Paganisme, Judaïsme, Christianisme: Influences et affrontements dans le monde antique: Mélanges offerts à Marcel Simon* (ed. A. Benoît, M. Philenko, and C. Vogel; Paris: Boccard, 1978), 214, 216 n. 3.

Ps.-Gregory reads Κύρῳ ("to Cyrus"), but his comments that the passages following Isa 45:1–3 fit not Cyrus but rather Christ indicate his familiarity with the variant reading.

Isa 49:6: A passage from the similar Isa 42:6, εἰς διαθήκην γένους, is inserted into this quotation of Isa 49:6 (witnessed also in the versions and patristic witnesses). The texts are linked by the catch-phrase "light of the nations" (φῶς ἐθνῶν). See also Ps.-Gregory's quotation of Isa 49:6–9 above (chap. 4) and the commentary there.

Ps.-Gregory Test. 4	Ps.-Gregory Test. 16	LXX Isa 49:6	LXX Isa 42:6b–7
Ἰδοὺ τέθεικά σε εἰς διαθήκην γένους, καὶ εἰς φῶς ἐθνῶν, τοῦ καταστῆσαι τὴν γῆν, καὶ κληρονομίαν ἐρήμου, λέγων τοῖς ἐν δεσμοῖς, Ἐξέλθετε· καὶ τοῖς ἐν τῷ σκότει, Ἀνακαλύφθητε.	καὶ τέθεικά σε εἰς διαθήκην γένους, εἰς φῶς ἐθνῶν, τοῦ εἶναί σε εἰς σωτηρίαν ἕως ἐσχάτου τῆς γῆς.	καὶ εἶπέ μοι Μέγα σοί ἐστι τοῦ κληθῆναί σε παῖδά μου τοῦ στῆσαι τὰς φυλὰς Ιακωβ καὶ τὴν διασπορὰν τοῦ Ισραηλ ἐπιστρέψαι· ἰδοὺ τέθεικά σε εἰς φῶς ἐθνῶν τοῦ εἶναί σε εἰς σωτηρίαν ἕως ἐσχάτου τῆς γῆς.	ἔδωκά σε εἰς διαθήκην γένους, εἰς φῶς ἐθνῶν, ἀνοῖξαι ὀφθαλμοὺς τυφλῶν, ἐξαγαγεῖν ἐκ δεσμῶν δεδεμένους καὶ ἐξ οἴκου φυλακῆς καθημένους ἐν σκότει.

Isaiah 49:6 is quoted in Acts 13:47 as a proof-text for turning away from the Jews to preach to the Gentiles.

See also the use of Isa 49:5–6 in Irenaeus *Epid.* 50–51 and Isa 42:6–7 in Tertullian *Adv. Jud.* 12.2; Cyprian *Test.* 2.7 ("That Christ our God should come, the Enlightener and Savior of the human race"; Isa 42:6–8).

CHAPTER 17: THAT BEFORE THE SECOND *PAROUSIA* OF THE LORD ELIJAH WILL COME

Mal 4:4–5: Ps.-Gregory refers to the belief that Elijah would come in the eschatological age (e.g., *Sib. Or.* 2.187–189); in the Gospel tradition, Jesus is recorded as identifying John the Baptist with Elijah (e.g., Matt 11:14; Mark 9:11–13). Justin sees the passage as a sign of the second *parousia* (*Dial.* 49.2–3; cf. Tertullian *Res.* 22.10).

CHAPTER 18: THAT WE WILL BE CALLED "CHRISTIANS"

A collection in Ps.-Epiphanius (*Test.* 90) bears the same title and reads word for word the same (LXX-deviant) forms of the first two quotations of Ps.-Gregory's TC (Isa 62:2 and Is 65:15b–16a).

Isa 65:15b–16a: Ps.-Gregory also quotes Isa 65:15–16 in chap. 16 (see comments there).

Hosea, "And in the end his name": The source of this quotation is unknown. Resch suggests a connection with Hos 14:10: εὐθεῖαι αἱ ὁδοὶ τοῦ κυρίου, καὶ δίκαιοι πορεύσονται ἐν αὐταῖς (*Agrapha*, 332; Logion 58). Williams suggests a combination of Mal 1:14 and Isa 2:2–3 (*Adversus Judaeos*, 130).

Chapters 19–22: These chapters are lacking in Codex 451 and Sifanus. The latter notes that his exemplar is quite corrupt at this point, witnessing material that does not correspond with the heading. Williams thinks it probable that these chapters were added by a later copyist (*Adversus Judaeos*, 125 n. 1). Yet Codex 451 and Sifanus do in fact include the heading of chapter 19 and the beginning of the accompanying proof-text from Jeremiah, so the lack of these chapters in Codex 451 and Sifanus is more likely to be attributed to textual corruption rather than to a shorter original text.

CHAPTER 19: THAT HEROD WILL BE TROUBLED, AND ALL THOSE WITH HIM

The title is an apparent allusion to Matt 2:3: "When King Herod heard this, he was frightened, and all Jerusalem with him." The title of the TC and the version of Jer 4:9 correspond exactly with Ps.-Epiphanius *Test.* 19 (except Ps.-Epiphanius reads ’Ιερεμίας λέγει. (In the Ps.-Epiphanius text, ἡ καρδίαν is an apparent misprint.)

CHAPTER 20: CONCERNING BAPTISM

Barnabas applies passages from Ezek 47 to baptism (11.10–11). Ps.-Epiphanius, in his TC, "That when he is baptized, he would sanctify the waters," reads the same non-LXX summary (with only minor variations) of Ezek 47:8–9 (*Test.* 27b). Jer 29:20 is apparently understood as a reference to John's baptism of Jesus in the Jordan; Ps.-Epiphanius includes the text under the heading, "That he would ascend from his baptism gloriously" (*Test.* 28).

CHAPTER 21: CONCERNING THE DESCENT
OF THE LORD INTO EGYPT

Eusebius interpets Isa 19:1 as a reference to the infant Jesus' flight into Egypt with his family; the "light cloud" refers to the physical body of Christ and the "shaking of the idols" to the reaction of the Egyptian demons (*Dem ev.* 6.20 [296–297]; 8.5 [413–415]; 9.2 [421–423]; see Matt 2:13–15).

Ps.-Epiphanius has the same two texts under the heading, "That the Christ would go down into Egypt" (*Test.* 25). Ps.-Epiphanius also reads the same LXX deviations (except Ps.-Epiphanius reads Φοβηθήσονται οἱ Αἰγύπτιοι τὸν κύριον for Ps.-Gregory's Φοβηθήσονται Κύριον).

Athanasius provides the same interpretation in his TC on the incarnation of Christ (*Inc.* 33.5).

CHAPTER 22: CONCERNING THE HOLY SPIRIT

This TC collects a variety of references to God's spirit. Of particular interest are several summaries of OT passages instead of the usual direct quotation (Joel 2:28; Isa 11:2–3; Exod 31:3–11; 4 Kgdms 2:9–11).

Ps.-Gregory shares several *testimonia* with Ps.-Basil's *Adversus Eunomium*. Common texts are underlined.

Ps.-Gregory *Test.* 22	Ps.-Basil *Eunom.* 161	Ps.-Basil *Eunom.* 191–192
Isa 48:16, Num 11:16–17, Ps 50:12–14, Ps 138:7a, Job 33:4, Job 32:8, Job 27:2–3, Hag 2:4–5, Wis 1:7, Isa 63:10, Mic 2:7, Joel 2:28 [3:1] (cf. Acts 2:17), Isa 61:1, Isa 11:2–3 (allusion), Isa 62:14, Exod 31:3–11 (summary), 4 Kgdms 2:9–11 (summary), Isa 57:16, Isa 42:1 (cf. Matt 12:18), Isa 30:1, Isa 34:15b–16, Ps 103:29–30	Ps 138:7–10, Wis 1:7, Isa 11:2–3, Zech 4:10, Jer 23:24, Hag 2:4–5	Joel 2:28 (3:1), Isa 34:15–16, Isa 57:16, Ps 50:13, Ps 50:12, Ps 142:10, Ps 50:14, Job 33:4, Job 32:8, Ps 103:30, Ps 138:7, Isa 30:1, Isa 11:1–3, Isa 61:1

Ps.-Basil also employs other "Spirit" TCs: *Eunom.* 131: Job 33:4 with Ps 32:6 and other texts in a TC proving "That the spirit is the creator"; *Eunom.* 180: Ps 32:6; Ps 142:10; Ps 50:12, 14; Wis 1:7; and many NT texts; *Eunom.* 195: Job 27:2–3 and many NT texts.

Isa 48:16: See Basil *Spirit* 49.

Ps 50:12–14: Ps.-Gregory's version is carefully edited to focus on its references to "spirit." The passage is used often in patristic literature to refer to the Holy Spirit, e.g., Irenaeus *Haer.* 3.17.2; Ps.-Basil *Eunom.* 191.

Hag 2:4–5: The passage is falsely attributed to Zechariah. Ps.-Gregory quotes a markedly different form of this passage earlier in his composition (see sect. 1.8.2 and comments there).

Ps.-Gregory Test. 1	Ps.-Gregory Test. 22	LXX Hag 2:4–5	Ps.-Epiphanius Test. 5.17
Ἴσχυε, Ζοροβάβελ διότι		καὶ νῦν κατίσχυε, Ζοροβαβελ, λέγει κύριος, καὶ κατίσχυε, Ἰησοῦ ὁ τοῦ Ιωσεδεκ ὁ ἱερεὺς ὁ μέγας, καὶ κατισχυέτω πᾶς ὁ λαὸς τῆς γῆς, λέγει κύριος καὶ ποιεῖτε· διότι	
ἐγὼ μεθ' ὑμῶν εἰμι,	Ἐγώ εἰμι ἐν ὑμῖν,	μεθ' ὑμῶν ἐγώ εἰμι, λέγει κύριος παντοκράτωρ,	ἐγώ εἰμι μεθ' ὑμῶν, λέγει κύριος,
καὶ ὁ Λόγος μου ὁ ἀγαθός,			
καὶ τὸ Πνεῦμά μου ἐν μέσῳ ὑμῶν.	καὶ τὸ Πνεῦμά μου ἐφέστηκεν ἐν μέσῳ ὑμῶν.	καὶ τὸ πνεῦμά μου ἐφέστηκεν ἐν μέσῳ ὑμῶν·	καὶ τὸ πνεῦμά μου ἐφέστηκεν ἐφ' ὑμᾶς.

Joel 2:28: In the second half of the quotation, Ps.-Gregory simply summarizes the passage. Ps.-Gregory offers another version of this passage in sect. 1.8.2 ; see the Commentary above.

Isa 61:1: Ps.-Gregory quotes this passage earlier in his work (chap. 4); see comments there. The passage is applied generally to Jesus in the *testimonia* literature (e.g., Irenaeus *Epid.* 53; Cyprian *Test.* 2.10); specific applications to the Spirit are found in Novatian *Trin.* 29.13 (with Isa 11:2–3); Ps.-Basil *Eunom.* 192.

"**Seven spirits will come to rest upon him**": Ps.-Gregory alludes to a tradition locating seven works of God's spirit in Isa 11:2–3. The following authors attribute these gifts to Christ: Novatian *Trin.* 29.13; Tertullian *Marc.* 3.17; Irenaeus *Epid.* 9.

Isa 57:16: Irenaeus uses the passage to show a distinction between the "spirit" as a special gift given by God and "breath" which is common to all humanity (*Haer.* 5.12.2; cf. Tertullian *An.* 11.3; *Herm.* 32.3).

Isa 42:1 (cf. Matt 12:18): Passages from Isa 42:1–4 appear often in the *testimonia* literature, though they are generally applied to Jesus rather than the Spirit. For Justin's mixed use of the LXX and Matthew's version, see Skarsaune, *Proof from Prophecy*, 60–61. See also Tertullian *Prax.* 11.5; Cyprian *Test.* 2.13; Novatian *Trin.* 9.6; Ps.-Basil *Eunom.* 193.

Isa 30:1: Irenaeus quotes this passage in an anti-cultic TC (*Haer.* 4.18.3).

Ps 103:29–30: Ps.-Gregory also quotes Ps 103:30 in sect. 1.2 above, in a TC on God sending out his word and spirit. See comments there.

Appendix: Analysis of the Quotations

I. SEPARATE QUOTATIONS OF THE SAME PASSAGE

Ps 103:30 (chs. 1.2 and 22)
Ps 2:8 (chs. 1.7 and 16)
Hag 2:4–5 (chs. 1.8.2 and 22)
Joel 2:28 (chs. 1.8.2 and 22)
Bar 3:36 (chs. 2.1 and 4)
Isa 65:1a (chs. 2.4 and 16)
Isa 65:1b (chs. 2.4 and 16)
Zeph 2:11 (chs. 2.4 and 16)
Isa 40:9b-10 (chs. 2.6 and 16)
Isa 49:6 (chs. 4 and 16)
Isa 61:1 (chs. 4 and 22)
Isa 53:9 (chs. 6.2 and 16)
Ps 109:1 (chs. 9 and 16)
Two versions of Jer 7:22 (ch. 12).
Isa 1:11–16 (ch. 12) and Isa 1:13b–16 (ch. 16)
Mal 1:10b-11 (ch. 12 and 16 [3 times in ch. 16])
Isa 65:15–16 (chs. 16 and 18)

II. UNCERTAIN QUOTATIONS

Ch. 1.4: "You complete the years, O God, by your power."
Ch. 2.4: "You will see the great king"
Ch. 3: "Look! The heifer has given birth, and not given birth."
Ch. 7: "When the tree of trees is bent, and rises, and when blood drips from the tree"
Ch. 11: "Circumcise your heart, and not the flesh of your foreskin"

Ch. 16: "Let me destroy this people, and I will give you a nation that is great, and much more so than this one."

Ch. 18: "And in the end, his name will be manifest in all the earth, and many people will be called by his name, and those going along his ways will live in them."

III. FALSE ATTRIBUTIONS

Ch. 1.8.2: Codex 451 and Sifanus read "to Abraham" instead of "to Jacob" before Gen 31:13.

Ch. 2.6: Codex 451 reads "Zephaniah" before Isa 40:9–10.

Ch. 4: Ps.-Gregory reads "Jeremiah" before Isa 49:6–9.

Ch. 6.3: Ps.-Gregory attributes the conflated quotation in Matt 27:9–10 (Zech 11:12–13 and Jer 32:6–9) to "Zechariah."

Ch. 12: Ps.-Gregory reads "Isaiah" before Jer 7:22.

Ch. 18: Ps.-Gregory reads "Hosea" before an uncertain quotation.

Ch. 22: Ps.-Gregory reads "From Exodus" before Num 11:16–17.

Ch. 22: Ps.-Gregory reads "Zechariah" before Hag 2:4–5.

IV. OT QUOTATIONS (LXX-DEVIANT) INFLUENCED BY NT READINGS

Ps.-Gr. Test.	OT Quot.	NT Par.	Comment
1.4	Isa 40:13	Rom 11:34	Ps.-Gregory follows Paul's LXX-deviant quotation, adding γάρ before ἔγνω and reading ἤ for καί.
1.8.2	Deut 32:43	Heb 1:6	Ps.-Gregory follows the quotation of Hebrews, omitting the initial καί.
1.8.2	Joel 2:28 [3:1]	Acts 2:17	Ps.-Gregory follows the non-LXX text of Joel 2:28 [3:1] in Acts 2:17 (except reading Κύριος for θεός and reading ἐνύπνια for ἐνυπνίοις). He deviates from both Acts and the LXX in making αἱ θυγατέρες ὑμῶν the subject of ἐνυπνιασθήσονται.

2.2	Zech 9:9	Matt 21:5		Ps.-Gregory essentially follows the LXX over against Matthew's non-LXX readings. He omits (with Matt 21:5) the LXX's δίκαιος καὶ σῴζων αὐτός before πραΰς.
2.2	Mal 3:1/Exod 23:20	Matt 11:10		Ps.-Gregory follows Matthew precisely.
2.5	Mic 5:2	Matt 2:6		Ps.-Gregory follows the non-LXX reading of Mic 5:2 in Matt 2:6 with only minor variations (trans. σοῦ / γάρ; adds μοι before ἡγούμενος; and reads ὅς for ὅστις. Unlike Matthew, however, Ps.-Gregory does include the last phrase from LXX Mic 5:2, with some slight deviations (Ps.-Gregory omits αἱ before ἔξοδοι; reads ἀφ' ἡμερῶν αἰῶνος for the LXX's ἐξ ἡμερῶν αἰῶνος.
2.5	Deut 18:15–19/ Lev 23:29	Acts 3:22–23		Ps.-Gregory essentially follows the quotation in Acts 3:22–23 (itself composed of elements from Deut 18:15, 16, 19 and Lev 23:29); reads ὁ θεὸς ἡμῶν for Acts ὁ θεὸς ὑμῶν (ℵ* reads ἡμῶν); λαλήσει for λαλήσῃ; the last phrase reads καὶ ἔσται, ὃς ἂν μὴ ἀκούσῃ for Acts's ἔσται δὲ πᾶσα ψυχὴ ἥτις ἐὰν μὴ ἀκούσῃ; reads ἐξολοθρευθήσεται for ἐξολεθρευθήσεται.
3	Isa 7:14	Matt 1:23		Ps.-Gregory reads (with Matt 1:23) καλέσουσι for the LXX's καλέσεις. Ps.-Gregory reproduces the comment of Matt 1:23: ὅ ἐστιν μεθερμηνευόμενον μεθ' ἡμῶν ὁ θεός (although he reads ἑρμηνεύεται for Matthew's ἐστιν μεθερμηνευόμενον.

3	allusion to Exod 13:2, 12, 15	Luke 2:23	Ps.-Gregory follows Luke precisely
4	Isa 61:1	Luke 4:18	Ps.-Gregory follows the version in Luke 4:18 precisely (omitting the LXX's ἰάσασθαι τοὺς συντετριμμένους τῇ καρδίᾳ). Ps.-Gregory does not include Luke's additional quotations from Isa 58:6 and Isa 61:2a.
6.3	Zech 11:12–13; Jer 32:6–9	Matt 27:9–10	Ps.-Gregory follows the quotation in Matt 27:9–10 exactly.
7	Zech 13:7	Matt 26:31	Ps.-Gregory reads τὸν ποιμένα for τοὺς ποιμένας (= Matt 26:31, Mark 14:27); reads διασκορπισθήσονται τὰ πρόβατα for ἐκσπάσατε τὰ πρόβατα (= Matt 26:31, Mark 14:27); adds τῆς ποίμνης after τὰ πρόβατα (Matt 26:31).
8	Isa 28:16	1 Pet 2:6	Ps.-Gregory follows the quotation in 1 Peter, only reading ὁ πιστεύων εἰς αὐτὸν οὐ καταισχυνθήσεται for 1 Peter's ὁ πιστεύων ἐπ' αὐτῷ οὐ μὴ καταισχυνθῇ
15	Isa 52:7	Rom 10:15	Ps.-Gregory follows the non-LXX reading in Rom 10:15. He reads exactly a variant reading of Rom 10:15 (witnessed in ℵ^c and D; cf. also Nah 1:15), reading εἰρήνην for [τὰ] ἀγαθά.
22	Isa 42:1	Matt 12:18	Ps.-Gregory follows Matthew's version of Isa 42:1, except for reading ὁ ἐκλεκτός for Matthew's ὃν ᾑρέτισα.

V. DIRECT QUOTATIONS OF NT

Ps.-Gr. Test.	NT Passage	Comments
1.4	1 Cor 1:24	Ps.-Gregory adds δέ after Χριστός.

1.8.3	John 12:41	Ps.-Gregory reads ὅτε (with D) for ὅτι.
2.6	Gospel miracle stories (Matt 8:3 par.; Luke 7:14, John 11:43, Mark 4:39)	Precise quotation of these passages
16	Matt 21:43	Ps.-Gregory reads ἀπὸ τῶν 'Ιουδαίων for Matthew's ἀφ' ὑμῶν.

VI. ALLUSIONS TO NT AND OT PASSAGES

The following passages form part of Ps.-Gregory's commentary, and are clearly not intended as direct quotations. Precise parallels in wording, however, indicate specific allusions.

Ps.-Gr. Test.	NT Pass.	Allusion
1.1	John 1:1	"rather 'Word' is he who was with God in the beginning, since he is indeed God"
1.1	John 15:26	"Spirit" is from the mouth of God, "the Spirit of truth, who goes forth from the Father"
2.10	Heb 3:1	"For after becoming incarnate, he became 'high priest, and apostle of our confession.'"
8	Phil 2:8	"For he became like a helpless human, humbling his own flesh until the point of death, death on a cross."
8	Ps 117:22–23	For he became "the head of the corner," that is, clearly of another building near the church, "which is marvelous in our eyes."

VII. CONFLATED PASSAGES

The *Testimonies* include several conflated passages, listed below. (See also various conflations in quotations influenced by NT readings, noted above in sec. IV):

Ch. 1.7:   Ps 71:17b and 71:5
Ch. 4:   Isa 49:6b, 8b–9a, Isa 42:6b–7
Ch. 11:   Jer 4:3 and Deut 10:16
Ch. 16:   Isa 49:6 and Isa 42:6

Often Ps.-Gregory reads several passages together with no intervening comments or introductory formulas, giving the impression that he reads them as one quotation. See, for example, the string of Ps 83:8, Ps 117:27, and Mal 3:1b in sections 2.1–2.2.

VIII. NON-STANDARD PASSAGES

Several quotations differ sharply from the LXX or are heavily edited. These passages are often paralleled in other early Christian authors, thus suggesting the use of a common source. See the Commentary and notes for details.

Ch. 1.4:   Prov 8:27–30
Ch. 1.5:   Gen 1:26–27
Ch. 2.9:   Hag 2:4–5
Ch. 3:   Isa 9:5–6
Ch. 7:   Deut 28:66–67
Ch. 7:   Zech 14:6–7
Ch. 7:   Zech 13:7
Ch. 11:   Jer 9:26
Ch. 12:   Jer 7:22
Ch. 16:   Isa 1:13–16
Ch. 20:   Ezek 47:8–9
Ch. 22:   Num 11:16–17
Ch. 22:   Ps 50:12–14
Ch. 22:   Hag 2:4–5
Ch. 22:   Joel 2:28
Ch. 22:   Isa 11:2–3
Ch. 22:   Exod 31:3–11
Ch. 22:   4 Kgdms 2:9–11

Bibliography

DEAD SEA SCROLLS

Discoveries in the Judean Desert. Oxford: Clarendon, 1955-.

SEPTUAGINT

Academia Litterarum Gottingensis. *Septuaginta: Vetus Testamentum Graecum.* Göttingen: Vandenhoeck & Ruprecht, 1931-.
—— Vol. 1: *Genesis.* Edited by John William Wevers. 1974.
—— Vol. 2/2: *Leviticus.* Edited by John William Wevers. 1986
—— Vol. 3/1: *Numeri.* Edited by John William Wevers. 1982.
—— Vol. 3/2: *Deuteronomium* Edited by John William Wevers. 1977.
—— Vol. 8/1: *Esdrae Liber I.* Edited by Robert Hanhart. 1974.
—— Vol. 10: *Psalmi cum Odis.* Edited by Alfred Rahlfs. 2nd ed. 1967.
—— Vol. 13: *Duodecim Prophetae.* Edited by Joseph Ziegler. 3rd ed. 1984.
—— Vol. 14: *Isaias.* Edited by Joseph Ziegler. 3rd ed. 1983.
—— Vol. 16/2: *Susanna, Daniel, Bel et Draco.* Edited by Joseph Ziegler. 1954.
Origenis Hexaplorum quae supersunt. 2 vols. Edited by Frederick Field. Oxford: Clarendon, 1867, 1875. Repr. Hildesheim: Olms, 1964.

OT PSEUDEPIGRAPHA

The Five Fragments of the Apocryphon of Ezekiel: A Critical Study. Edited by James R. Mueller. Journal for the Study of the Pseudopigrapha: Supplement Series 5. Sheffield: Sheffield Academic Press, 1994.
The Old Testament Pseudepigrapha. Edited by James H. Charlesworth. 2 vols. New York: Doubleday, 1983.

NT APOCRYPHA

Les Actes de Pierre. Edited by Léon Vouaux. Paris: Letouzey et Ané, 1922 (*NTApoc* 2:285–317).

Evangile de Pierre. Edited and translated by Maria Grazia Mara. Sources chrétiennes 201. Paris: Cerf, 1973.

New Testament Apocrypha. Edited by Wilhelm Schneemelcher. Translated by R. McL. Wilson. Rev. ed. Cambridge: J. Clarke; Louisville, Ky.: Westminster/John Knox, 1991–1992.

APOSTOLIC FATHERS

The Apostolic Fathers. Edited and translated by Bart D. Ehrman. 2 vols. Loeb Classical Library. Cambridge, Mass.: Harvard University Press, 2003.

The Apostolic Fathers: A New Translation and Commentary. Volume 3: Barnabas and Didache. Translated by Robert A. Kraft. New York: Thomas Nelson, 1965.

Épître de Barnabé. Edited by Pierre Prigent. Translated by Robert A. Kraft. Sources chrétiennes 172. Paris: Cerf, 1971.

PATRISTIC TEXTS — COLLECTIONS

The Ante-Nicene Fathers. Edited by Alexander Roberts and James Donaldson. 10 vols. 1885–1887. Repr. Peabody, Mass.: Hendrickson, 1994.

Bibliotheca veterum patrum antiquorumque scriptorum ecclesiasticorum graecorum. Edited by Andreas Gallandi. 14 vols. Venice: J. B. Albritius Hieron Fil., 1765–1781.

Patrologia graeca. Edited by J.-P. Migne. 162 vols. Paris, 1857–1886.

Patrologia latina. Edited by J.-P. Migne. 217 vols. Paris, 1844–1864.

PATRISTIC TEXTS — INDIVIDUAL TEXTS

Apostolic Constitutions. Les Constitutions apostoliques. Tome III, Livres VII et VIII. Edited by Marcel Metzger. Sources chrétiennes 336. Paris: Cerf, 1987.

Athanasius. *De synodis.* Pages 46–67 in vol. 2/1 of *Athanasius Werke.* Edited by Hans-Georg Opitz. Deutsche Akademie der Wissenschaften zu Berlin. Kirchenväter-Kommission. Berlin: de Gruyter, 1935 (PG 26:736–40).

———. *Sur l'incarnation du verbe.* Edited by Charles Kannengieser. Corrected ed. Sources chrétiennes 199. Paris: Cerf, 2000.

Basil of Caesaria. *Sur le Saint-Esprit.* Edited by Benôit Pruche. 2d ed. Sources chrétiennes 17. Paris: Cerf, 1968.

Ps.-Basil. *Adversus Eunomium IV-V.* Translated by Franz Xaver Risch. Supplements to *Vigiliae Christianae* 16. Leiden: Brill, 1992 (PG 671–774).

Chrysostom, John. *Demonstration against Jews and Greeks that Christ is God.* PG 48:813–838.

Clement of Alexandria. *Paedagogus.* Edited by Miroslav Marcovich, with J. C. M. van Winden. Supplements to Vigiliae Christianae 61. Leiden: Brill, 2002.

———. *Stromate V.* Edited by Alain le Boulluec. Translated by Pierre Voulet. 2 vols. Sources chrétiennes 278, 279. Paris: Cerf, 1981.

———. *Stromate VI.* Edited and translated by Patrick Descourtieux. Sources chrétiennes 446. Paris: Cerf, 1999.

———. *Stromate VII.* Edited and translated by Alain Le Boulluec. Sources chrétiennes 428. Paris: Cerf, 1997.

Ps.-Clementine Homilies. Die Pseudoklementinen I: Homilien. Edited by Bernhard Rehm. Revised by Georg Strecker. 3rd ed. Die griechische christliche Schriftsteller der ersten drei Jahrhunderte. Berlin: Akademie, 1992 (*ANF* 8:223–346).

Commodian. *Carme apologetico.* Edited by Antonio Salvatore. Corona Patrum 5. Turin: Società Editrice Internazionale, 1977.

Cyprian. *Ad Quirinum; Ad Fortunatum.* Vol. 1 of *Sancti Cypriani Episcopi Opera.* Edited by R. Weber. Corpus Christianorum: Series latina 3/1. Turnhout: Brepols, 1972 (*ANF* 5:507–28).

Cyril of Alexandria. *Contre Julien.* Edited by Paul Burguière and Pierre Évieux. Sources chrétiennes 322. Paris: Cerf, 1985.

Cyril of Jerusalem. *Sancti patris nostri Cyrilli Hierosolymarum archiepiscopi opera quae supersunt omnia I-II.* Edited by W. C. Reischl and J. Rupp. 2 vols. 1848–1860. Repr. 2nd ed. Hildesheim: Olms, 1967.

———. *The Works of Saint Cyril of Jerusalem.* Translated by Leo P. McCauley and Anthony A. Stephenson. 2 vols. Fathers of the Church 61. Washington, D.C.: Catholic University of America Press, 1969.

The Dialogues of Athanasius and Zacchaeus and of Timothy and Aquila. Edited with Prolegomena and Facsimiles. Edited by Frederick C. Conybeare. Anecdota Oxoniensia. Oxford: Clarendon, 1898.

"The Dialogue of Timothy and Aquila: A Critical Text, Introduction to the Manuscript Evidence, and an Inquiry into the Sources and Literary Relationships." Edited by Robert Gerald Robertson. Ph.D. diss., Harvard University, 1989.

Epiphanius. *Panarion Haer. 65–80; De Fide.* Vol. 3 of *Epiphanius*. Edited by Karl Holl. Revised by Jürgen Dummer. Die griechische christliche Schriftsteller der ersten drei Jahrhunderte 37. 2nd ed. Berlin: Akadamie, 1985.

Ps.-Epiphanius. *A Pseudo-Epiphanius Testimony Book.* Edited by Robert V. Hotchkiss. Society of Biblical Literature Texts and Translations 4. Early Christian Literature Series 1. Missoula, Mont.: SBL/Scholars Press, 1974.

Eusebius. *De Demonstratio Evangelica.* Edited by Ivar A. Heikel. Vol. 6 of *Eusebius Werke*. Die griechische christliche Schriftsteller der ersten drei Jahrhunderte 23. Berlin: Hinrichs, 1913.

———. *Eclogae Propheticae.* Edited by Thomas Gaisford. Oxford: Academic, 1842 (PG 22:1018–1262).

———. *Gegen Marcell; Über die kirchliche Theologie: Die Fragmente Marcells.* Vol. 4 of *Eusebius Werke*. Edited by Erich Klostermann. Revised by G. C. Hansen. Die griechische christliche Schriftsteller der ersten drei Jahrhunderte. Berlin: Akademie, 1991.

———. *Livres 5–7.* Vol. 2 of *Histoire ecclésiastique*. Translated and annotated by Gustave Bardy. Sources chrétiennes 41. Paris: Cerf, 1955.

———. *Die Praeparatio Evangelica. Bücher IX.* Vol. 8 of *Eusebius Werke*. Edited by Karl Mras. 2 vols. 2nd ed. Die griechische christliche Schriftsteller der ersten drei Jahrhunderte. Berlin: Akademie, 1982.

———. *The Proof of the Gospel being the* Demonstratio Evangelica *of Eusebius of Caesaria.* 2 vols. Translated by W. J. Ferrar. London: SPCK, 1920.

Evagrius. *Altercatio Simonis et Theophili. Evagrii altercatio legis inter Simonem Iudaeum et Theophilium Christianum.* Edited by Edward Bratke. Corpus scriptorum ecclesiasticorum latinorum 45. Scriptores Ecclesiastici Minores Saec IV V VI; Vindobona: Tempsky; Lipsia: Freytag, 1904.

Gregory of Nyssa. *In illud: Tunc et ipse Filius.* Pages 3–28 of *Gregorii Nysseni Opera Dogmatica Minora Pars II*. Edited by J. K. Downing, J. A. McDonough, H. Hörner. Gregorii Nysseni Opera 3/2. Leiden: Brill, 1987.

Ps.-Gregory of Nyssa. *Selected Testimonies against the Jews.* Pages 288–329 of *Collectanea monumentorum veterum Ecclesiae.* Edited by Lorenzo Alessandro Zacagni. Rome: Sacred Congregation for the Propagation of the Faith, 1698.

———. Selected Testimonies against the Jews. Pages 315–331 of *Divi Gregorii episcopi Nysseni Opera.* Edited by Laurentius Sifanus. Basel: Per Nic. Episcopium iuniorem, 1562.

Hippolytus. *Contra Noetum.* Edited and translated by Robert Butterworth. Heythrop Monographs. London: Heythrop College, 1977.

———. *Contro Noeto.* Edited and translated by Manlio Simonetti. Biblioteca Patristica 35. Bologna: EDB, 2000.

Irenaeus. *Contre les hérésies.* Edited and translated by Adelin Rousseau et. al. Sources chrétiennes 100, 151, 152, 210, 211, 263, 264, 293, 294. Paris: Cerf, 1965–1982 (*ANF* 1:315–567).

———. *Démonstration de la prédication apostolique.* Edited and translated by Adelin Rousseau. Sources chrétiennes 322. Paris: Cerf, 1995.

———. *Proof of the Apostolic Preaching.* Translated by Joseph P. Smith. Ancient Christian Writers 16. Westminster, Md.: Newman; London: Longmans, Green, 1952.

Justin. *Apologiae pro Christianis.* Edited by Miroslav Marcovich. Patristische Texte und Studien 38. Berlin: de Gruyter, 1994 (*ANF* 1:163–87).

———. *Dialogus cum Tryphone.* Edited by Miroslav Marcovich. Patristische Texte und Studien 47. Berlin: de Gruyter, 1997 (*ANF* 1:194–270).

Lactantius. *Institutions Divines Livre IV.* Edited by Pierre Monat. Sources chrétiennes 377. Paris: Cerf, 1992 (*ANF* 7:9–223).

Ladder of Jacob. Translated, with introduction and notes, by H. G. Lunt. *OTP* 2.401–411.

Marius Victorinus. *Opera Pars I: Opera Theologica.* Corpus scriptorum ecclesiasticorum latinorum 83. Vindobonae: Hoelder, Pichler, Tempsky, 1971.

Melito. *On Pascha and Fragments.* Edited and translated by Stuart George Hall. Oxford Early Christian Texts. Oxford: Clarendon, 1979.

Novatian. Pages 1–78 of *Opera.* Edited by Gerard Frederick Diercks. Corpus Christianorum: Series latina 4; Turnhout: Brepols, 1972 (*ANF* 5:611–44).

Origen. *Commentaire sur Saint Jean: Tome I: Livres I–V.* Edited by Cécile Blanc. Sources chrétiennes 120. Paris: Cerf, 1966.

Philo. *Philo: Volume V.* Translated by F. H. Colson and G. H. Whitaker. Loeb Classical Library. Cambridge, Mass./London: Harvard University Press, 1929.

Rufinus. *A Commentary on the Apostles' Creed.* Translated by J. N. D. Kelly. Ancient Christian Writers 20. Westminster, Md.: Newman Press, 1955 (PL 21:335–86).

Tertullian. *Adversus Iudaeos: Mit Einleitung und kritischem Kommentar.* Edited by Hermann Tränkle. Wiesbaden: Steiner, 1964 (*ANF* 3:151–73).

———. *La chair du Christ.* Edited by Jean Pierre Mahé. Sources chrétiennes 216, 217. Paris: Cerf, 1975 (*ANF* 3:521–42).

———. *Contre Marcion.* Edited by René Braun. 4 vols. Sources chrétiennes 365, 368, 399, 456. Paris: Cerf, 1990–2001 (*ANF* 3:321–44).

———. *Contro Prassea.* Edited and translated by Giuseppe Scarpat. Corona Patrum 12. Turin: Società Editrice Internazionale, 1985 (*ANF* 3:597–627).

———. *De resurrectione.* Pages 919–1012 in Vol. 2 of *Tertulliani Opera.* Edited by J. G. P. Boreffs. Corpus scriptorum ecclesiasticorum latinorum 2. Turnholt: Brepols, 1954.

Theophilus. *Ad Autolycum.* Edited by Miroslav Marcovich. Patristische Texte und Studien 44. Berlin: de Gruyter, 1995 (*ANF* 2: 89–121).

SECONDARY SOURCES

Albl, Martin C. *"And Scripture Cannot Be Broken": The Form and Function of the Early Christian Testimonia.* Novum Testamentum Supplements 96. Leiden: Brill, 1999.

Attridge, Harold W. *The Epistle to the Hebrews.* Hermeneia. Philadelphia: Fortress, 1989.

Bardenhewer, Otto. *Geschichte der altkirchlichen Literatur.* 5 vols. 2nd ed. Freiburg: Herder, 1913–1932.

Brown, Raymond E. *The Birth of the Messiah: A Commentary on the Infancy Narratives in the Gospels of Matthew and Luke.* Updated ed. Anchor Bible Research Library. New York: Doubleday, 1993.

Bruce, F. F. *The Epistle to the Hebrews.* Rev. ed. New International Commentary on the New Testament. Grand Rapids: Eerdmans, 1990.

Collins, John J. *The Scepter and the Star: The Messiahs of the Dead Sea Scrolls and other Ancient Literature.* Anchor Bible Research Library. New York/London: Doubleday, 1995.

Crossan, John Dominic. *The Cross that Spoke: The Origins of the Passion Narrative.* San Francisco: Harper & Row, 1988.

Daniélou, Jean. "Bulletin d'histoire des origines chrétiennes." *Recherches de science religieuse* 44 (1956): 576–624.

———. *The Theology of Jewish Christianity*. The Development of Christian Doctrine before the Council of Nicaea 1. London: Darton, Longman & Todd; Chicago: Henry Regnery, 1964.

———. *Études d'exégèse judéo-chrétienne (Les Testimonia)*. Théologie historique 5. Paris: Beauschesne, 1966.

Dodd, C. H. *According to the Scriptures: The Sub-Structure of New Testament Theology*. London: Nisbet, 1952.

Falcetta, Alessandro. "The Logion of Matthew 11:5–6 Par. from Qumran to Agbar." *Revue biblique* 110 (2003): 222–48.

———. "The Testimony Research of James Rendel Harris." *Novum Testamentum* 45 (2003): 280–99.

———. "A Testimony Collection in Manchester: Papyrus Rylands Greek 460." *Bulletin of the John Rylands University Library of Manchester* 83 (2001): 3–19.

———. "Testimonies: The Theory of James Rendel Harris in the Light of Subsequent Research." Ph.D. diss., University of Birmingham, 2001.

Glasson, T. F. "'Plurality of Divine Persons' and the Quotations in Hebrews I.6ff." *New Testament Studies* 12 (1965–66): 270–72.

Harris, J. Rendel. *Testimonies*. 2 vols. Cambridge: Cambridge University Press, 1916–1920.

Hanson, R. P. C. *The Search for the Christian Doctrine of God: The Arian Controversy 318–381*. Edinburgh: T & T Clark, 1988.

Hay, David M. *Glory at the Right Hand: Psalm 110 in Early Christianity*. Society of Biblical Literature Monograph Series 18. Nashville/New York: Abingdon, 1973.

Kelly, J. N. D., trans. *A Commentary on the Apostles' Creed*. Ancient Christian Writers 20. Westminster, Md. Newman Press, 1955.

Kraft, Robert A. "*Barnabas*' Isaiah Text and the 'Testimony Book' Hypothesis." *Journal of Biblical Literature* 79 (1960): 336–50.

———. "Christian Transmission of Greek Jewish Scriptures: A Methodological Probe." Pages 207–26 in *Paganisme, Judaïsme, Christianisme: Influences et affrontements dans le monde antique: Mélanges offerts à Marcel Simon*. Edited by André Benoît, M. Philenko, and C. Vogel. Paris: Boccard, 1978.

———. "The Epistle of Barnabas: Its Quotations and Their Sources." Ph.D. diss., Harvard University, 1961.

Lindars, Barnabas. *New Testament Apologetic: The Doctrinal Significance of the Old Testament Quotations*. Philadelphia: Westminster, 1961.

Murray, Robert. *Symbols of Church and Kingdom: A Study in Early Syriac Tradition*. Cambridge: Cambridge University Press, 1975.

Norelli, Enrico. "Avant le canonique et l'apocryphe: Aux origines des récits de la naissance de Jésus." *Revue de théologie et de philosophie* 126 (1994): 305–24.

———. "Il dibattito con il giudaismo nel II secolo. *Testimonia*; Barnaba; Guistino." Pages 199–233 in *La Bibbia nell'antichità cristiana. I: Da Gesù a Origene*. Edited by Enrico Norelli. La Bibbia nella storia 15/1. Bologna: EDB, 1993.

———. "Due *testimonia* attribuiti a Esdra."*Annali di storia dell' esegesi* 1 (1984): 231–82.

———. "Il *Martirio di Isaia* come *testimonium* antigiudaico?" *Henoch* 2 (1980): 37–57.

Prigent, Pierre. *Justin et l'Ancien Testament: L'Argumentation scripturaire du traité de Justin contre toutes les hérésies comme source principale du Dialogue avec Tryphon et de la premiére apologie*. Études bibliques. Paris: Gabalda, 1964.

———. "Quelques testimonia messianiques: leur histoire littéraire de Qoumrân aux Pères de l'église." *Theologische Zeitschrift* 15 (1959): 419–30.

———. *Les testimonia dans le christianisme primitif: L'Épître de Barnabé 1–16 et ses sources*. Études bibliques. Paris: Gabalda, 1961.

Reijners, Gerardus Q. *The Terminology of the Holy Cross in Early Christian Literature as Based upon Old Testament Typology*. Graecitas Christianorum Primaeva Fascicle 2. Nijmegen: Dekker & Van de Vegt, 1965.

Resch, Alfred. *Agrapha: Aussercanonische Schriftfragmente*. Texte und Untersuchungen 30, 3/4; n.f. 15, 3/4. Leipzig: Hinrichs, 1906.

Richard, Marcel. "Quelques nouveaux fragments des pères antenicéens et nicéens." *Symbolae Osloenses* 38 (1963): 76–83.

Ruether, Rosemary Radford. "The *Adversus Judaeos* Tradition in the Church Fathers: The Exegesis of Christian Anti-Judaism." Pages 27–50 in *Aspects of Jewish Culture in the Middle Ages*. Edited by Paul E. Szarmach. Albany: State University of New York Press, 1979. Repr. pages 174–89 in *Essential Papers on Judaism and Christianity in Conflict: From Late Antiquity to the Reformation*. New York: New York University Press, 1990.

Schreckenberg, Heinz. *Die christlichen Adversus-Iudaeos-Texte und ihr literarisches und historisches Umfeld (1.–11. Jh.)*. 3rd ed. European University Studies, Series 23, Theology, Vol. 172. Frankfurt: Peter Lang, 1995.

Segal, Alan F. *Two Powers in Heaven: Early Rabbinic Reports about Christianity and Gnosticism*. Studies in Judaism in Late Antiquity 25. Leiden: Brill, 1977.

Skarsaune, Oskar. *The Proof from Prophecy: A Study in Justin Martyr's Proof-Text Tradition. Text-Type, Provenance, Theological Profile.* Novum Testamentum Supplements 56. Leiden: Brill, 1987.

Slusser, Michael. "The Exegetical Roots of Trinitarian Theology." *Theological Studies* 49 (1988): 461–76.

Smith, Joseph P., trans. *Proof of the Apostolic Preaching.* Ancient Christian Writers 16. Westminster, Md.: Newman; London: Longmans, Green, 1952.

Stendahl, Krister. *The School of St. Matthew and its Use of the Old Testament.* 2nd ed. Philadelphia: Fortress, 1968. Repr. Ramsey, N.J.: Sigler, 1991.

Strousma, Guy G. "From Anti-Judaism to Antisemitism in Early Christianity?" Pages 1–26 in *Contra Iudaeos: Ancient and Medieval Polemics between Christian and Jews.* Edited by Ora Limor and Guy G. Strousma. Texts and Studies in Medieval and Early Modern Judaism 10. Tübingen: Mohr-Siebeck, 1996.

Thunberg, L. "Early Christian Interpretations of the Three Angels in Gen. 18." *Studia Patristica* 7 (1966): 560–70.

Williams, A. Lukyn. *Adversus Judaeos: A Bird's-Eye View of Christian Apologiae until the Renaissance.* London: Cambridge University Press, 1935.

Wilson, R. McL. "The Early History of the Exegesis of Gen. 1.26." *Studia Patristica* 1 (1957): 420–37.

Index of Biblical and Other Ancient Sources

NOTE: Biblical passages clearly quoted in the *Testimonies* are in bold print.

A. OLD TESTAMENT (LXX)

Genesis
1   87
1:1   87
1:2   5
1:4   7
1:6   7
1:14-16   7
1:16-27   91
1:26   84, 88, 89, 91, 94
1:26-27   7, 88-90, 94, 142
3:22   7, 88, 89, 91
9:6   11, 94
11:7   9, 89, 91, 94
12:3   49, 127
17:11-25   121
18   90
18:1-3   7, 91
18:9-10   9, 91
19:24   9, 84, 89-91, 93, 94, 96, 102, 105
31:13   11, 94, 95, 138
49:10   21, 101
49:10-11   21, 100
49:11   97, 103

Exodus
Passim   90
False attribution   57, 138
9:5   11
12:13   126
13:2-15   107, 140
19:10-11   11, 94, 95
20:9-10   43
23:20   15, 98, 139
31:3-11   59, 133, 142
32:10   51, 128
34:4-6   11, 94, 95
35:30-35   82 n. 289

Leviticus
23:29   19, 99, 139

Numbers
Passim   90
11:16-17   57, 133, 138, 142
24:17   21, 100, 101
24:17-18   23

Deuteronomy
5:13-14   76 n. 197
5:28-29   99
9:14   51, 128
10:16   39, 41, 120, 121, 141
10:16-17   120
12:32   19
18:15   99
18:15-19   19, 99, 139
18:17-18   19
18:18-19   99
28:66   111-14

28:66–67 33, 142
30:15 110
32:1–43 95
32:16–23 128
32:20 128
32:20–21 49, 128
32:21 128
32:37–42 94
32:43 11, 94, 95, 138

2 Kingdoms (2 Samuel)

7 93
7:12–13 100
7:12–16 93
7:14 9, 93, 100

3 Kingdoms (1 Kings)

8:26–27 21, 100
8:27 100

4 Kingdoms (2 Kings)

2:9–11 59, 133, 142

1 Chronicles

17:11–14 21
17:13 63 n. 22

2 Chronicles

6:17–18 67 n. 79

Job

3:10–11 106
21:10 105
27:2–3 59, 133, 134
32:8 59, 133
33:4 57, 133, 134

Psalms

2:1 109
2:1–2 31, 93, 109
2:4 13, 96
2:7 93
2:7–8 9, 89, 93, 94, 102, 128
2:8 51, 128, 137
3:6 111
3:8 35
4:6 75 n. 190
4:7b 45
15:8–10 117
15:10 37, 117
17:44–45 128
17:44–46 49, 127
21 xv, 111
21:1 111
21:8 111
21:15 111
21:17 111, 112
21:17–19 33, 111, 112, 115
21:17–23 111
21:19 111
21:21 111
21:23 49, 128
21:28–29 53, 130
21:28–32 130
21:32 51
22:17 111
29:9 13, 96
32 84
32:6 3, 83–88, 90, 93, 134
40:10 29, 109
43:24 35
43:27 37
44 119
44:6–7 102, 105
44:7 119
44:7–8 23, 90, 93
44:10 39
46:6 37, 118
46:6–10 118
49 122, 124
49:1–6 97
49:2–3 15, 97
49:9–14 124
49:9–15 122
49:9 43

INDEX OF BIBLICAL AND OTHER ANC. SOURCES 155

49:13 43, 124
49:13–15 122
49:14 43, 122
50:12 133
50:12–14 57, 133, 134, 142
50:13 133
50:14 133
59:6 45, 126
64:2 51
67:7a 51
67:12 47, 126
68:9 49
68:21–22 35, 113, 116
68:22 111
71 92, 99
71:5 9, 92, 93, 141
71:6 17, 97, 98
71:17 9, 93, 141
79:2–3 17, 98
79:2c 98
81:8 37, 117
83:8 15, 142
85:17 45
86:5 29, 103, 107
87:5 37, 117
87:7 35, 113
88:4–5 21
96:7 95
101:20–22 13, 96
101:26–27 102
101:26–28 25, 102
102:28 86
103:29–30 61, 133, 135
103:30 5, 86, 133, 135, 137
106:20 5, 83, 84, 86
109 92
109:1 39, 53, 89, 90, 93, 94, 102, 105, 118, 119, 130, 137
109:3 9, 84, 92, 93
110:1 118, 130
110:3 53, 130
117:22–23 37, 118, 141
117:27 15, 142

118:120 111
131:11 19, 100
138:7–10 133
138:7a 57, 133
142:10 133, 134
147:4 86
147:7 3, 84, 86

Proverbs

8 83, 87, 88, 93
8:22 87, 93
8:22–30 87
8:22–31 84, 87, 88
8:22–36 87
8:23–25 93
8:27 87, 88
8:27–29 87
8:27–30 5, 87, 88, 142
8:30 87

Isaiah

False attribution 41, 100, 121–23, 138
1:2–3 27, 103, 106
1:3 106
1:10 51
1:10–14 124
1:11 122
1:11–12 122
1:11–14 41, 43, 122, 123
1:11–16 128, 137
1:13–14 124, 129
1:13b–16 51, 122, 124, 128, 129, 137, 142
1:16 43, 122, 124
2:2–3 127, 132
3:12–14 31, 109
3:13 109
3:13–14 109
3:14 109
7:10–15 104
7:10–17 104
7:13–14 103–5

7:14 25, 103–5, 139
7:14–16 103
7:15 25, 103–5
8:1–3 27, 103, 106
8:3 106
8:4 25, 103–5, 106
8:16 126
9:5 103–5
9:5–6 25, 103, 104, 142
9:6a 104, 106
10:33 101
10:33–11:5 23
11:1 100, 101, 103
11:1–3 101, 133
11:2–3 59, 133–35, 142
11:9b 51, 129
11:10 23, 100, 101
19:1 57, 133
19:21 57
28:16 37, 103, 118, 140
30:1 61, 133, 135
33:10–11 37, 117
33:14–17 98
33:17 17, 98
34:15b-16 61, 133
35:3–4 29, 108
35:3–6 108
35:4–6 108
35:5–6 29, 108
40:9b-10 19, 29, 137, 138
40:10 99
40:13 5, 87, 88, 138
42:1 61, 108, 133, 135, 140
42:1–4 135
42:6 107, 130, 141
42:6–7 55, 107, 108, 131, 141
42:6–8 131
45:1 53, 89, 94, 102, 130
45:1–3 53, 130
45:14–15 25, 102, 103, 105
48:8 47
48:12–16 90
48:16 57, 133, 134

49:1 106
49:1–2 27, 103
49:5–6 131
49:6 55, 107, 108, 130, 131, 137, 141
49:6–7 108
49:6–9 29, 107, 131, 138, 141
50:6 33, 110
50:6–7 111, 112
50:6–8 111
51:4–5 119
51:5 101
52:5b 49, 128
52:7 47, 126, 127, 140
52:10–54:6 '120
53 xv, 110, 112
53:1 13, 96, 102, 105
53:2–3 33, 111
53:4–9 31, 111, 128
53:5–7 111
53:7 111, 112
53:8 33, 103, 111
53:9 49, 71 n. 128, 128, 137
53:12 31, 110
57:16 59, 133, 135
58:6 108, 140
61:1 29, 59, 103, 108, 133, 134, 137, 140
61:1–2 108
61:2a 140
62:2 55, 131
62:10 35, 113, 115
62:10–63:6 115
62:14 59, 133
63:10 59, 133
65:1a 17, 49, 98, 128, 137
65:1b 17, 49, 128, 137
65:2 35, 111–13, 115
65:13–16 129
65:15–16 51, 55, 129, 132, 137
66:7 103

Jeremiah

False attributions   29, 31, 92, 97, 107, 113, 138
1:9b-10   47
4:3b   41, 120, 121, 141
4:3-4   120-122
4:4a   39, 41, 74 nn. 174 and 176, 120-22
4:9   57, 132
7:21-22   122, 123
7:21-25   122
7:22   41, 123, 137, 138, 142
7:22-23   124
9:25-26   120
9:26   39, 120, 121, 142
11:19a   33, 111-113
11:19b   33, 111-113
15:9   35, 113, 114
17:9   21, 100
23:5   100
23:18   5, 86
23:24   133
29:20   57, 132
32:6-9   33, 112, 138, 140
33:15   100
38 (31)   xv
38:31-32   39, 119, 120
38:32   123

Lamentations

4:20   31, 109

Ezekiel

9:2-6   45
9:3-6   126
9:4-6   126
9:4   45, 126
44:1-2   27, 103, 106
44:2   103
46:12   103
47   132
47:8-9   57, 132, 142

Daniel

2:34   103, 106
2:34-35   27, 103, 106
7   118
7:9   39
7:13   103, 118-19
7:13-14   39, 119

Hosea

False attribution   55, 100, 132, 138
5:15-6:2   117
5:15-6:3   37, 117
6:1-2   117
6:2   117
6:3   117
14:10   132

Joel

False attribution   100
2:28   11, 59, 133-34, 137-38, 142
2:28-29   96
2:28-31   94-95
2:28-32   95
2:31-32   13

Amos

4:11   13, 96
4:12b-13   21, 100
5:18-6:7   122
5:21   124
5:21-23   43, 124
8:9   33, 113, 114
8:9-10   113, 114
9:11   100

Micah

1:2-3   21
2:7   59, 133
4:1-2   47, 127
5:2   17, 99, 139

Nahum
1:15   76 n. 208, 140

Habakkuk
1:5   114

Zephaniah
False attribution   138
2:11   17, 51, 129, 137

Haggai
2:4-5   11, 59, 94-95, 133, 137, 138, 142
2:5   95

Zechariah
False attributions   59, 113, 134, 138
2:10-11   15, 97
3:1   97
3:1-2   17
3:1-5   98
3:6-8   17

4:10   133
7:10   124
8:17   124
9-14   xv
9:9   15, 97, 139
11:12   113
11:12-13   33, 112, 138, 140
13:7   35, 111, 113, 116, 140, 142
14:4   15, 97, 98
14:6-7   35, 113, 115, 142
14:7   114
14:20   35, 113

Malachi
1:10   49
1:10-11   43, 122, 124, 128, 129, 137
1:10-12   122
1:11   47, 49, 51, 127
1:12   51
1:14   132
3:1   15, 97, 98, 139, 142
3:1-2   97
4:4-5 (3:23-24)   55, 131

B. NEW TESTAMENT

Matthew
1:20-21   106
1:23   25, 103-5, 139
2:3   132
2:6   17, 99, 139
2:13-15   133
8:3   19, 141
11:10   15, 98, 139
11:14   131
12:18   61, 133-35, 140
21:5   15, 97, 139
21:43   53, 130, 141
26:31   35, 116, 140
27:9-10   33, 112, 138, 140
27:34   116

27:45   114
27:46   111
27:48   116

Mark
1:2   65 n. 50, 98
4:39   19, 141
9:7   99
9:11-13   131
14:27   72 n. 146, 116, 140
14:62   118
15:23   116
15:33   115
15:34   111
15:36   116

Luke

1:78   101
2:23   27, 103, 107, 140
4:18   29, 140
4:18–19   108
7:14   19, 141
7:27   65 n. 50, 98
21:37   98
22:37   110
23:36   116

John

1:1   3, 84, 90, 102, 105, 141
1:1–3   84, 86
1:1–4   84
1:1–5   83
1:3   83, 84
6:14   99
11:43   19, 141
12:15   65 n. 48, 97
12:38   96
12:41   13, 64 n. 41, 141
13:18   109
15:26   3, 84, 141
18:18   116
19:24   111
19:29   116

Acts

2:17   11, 59, 96, 133, 138
2:17–21   95
2:25–28   117
2:30   100
3:22–23   19, 99, 139
4:25–28   109
7:37   99
8:32–33   110
13:25   117
13:33   93
13:47   108, 131

Romans

2:24   128
9:33   118

10:15   47, 76 n. 208, 140
10:16   96
10:19   128
10:20   98
10:21   72 n. 140, 115
11:34   5, 138

1 Corinthians

1:24   5, 86–88, 140
2:16   62 n. 10

2 Corinthians

1:22   126
6:18   93

Galatians

3:8   127

Philippians

2:8   37, 141

Hebrews

1:5   93
1:6   11, 94, 95, 138
1:8–12   102
1:8–13   102
1:10–12   68 n. 91
3:1   23, 102, 141
7:14   101

1 Peter

2:6   37, 118, 140
2:7   118
2:22   110

Revelation

5:5   100
7:3–4   126
14:1   126
21:7   93
22:13–14   126
22:16   101

C. DEUTEROCANONICAL (APOCRYPHAL) REFERENCES

Baruch
3:36 29, 107–8, 137
3:36–37 96
3:36–38 15, 96, 97, 108
3:38 96

1 Esdras
5:48 129

Susanna
62 129

Wisdom
1:7 59, 133–34
2:20 112
8:19–20 25, 103

D. OT PSEUDEPIGRAPHA

Apocryphon of Ezekiel
Frg. 3 25, 103, 105

Ascension of Isaiah
11:12–14 104

4 Ezra
4:33 115
5:5 115

Sibylline Oracles
2.187–189 131
2.241–245 119

E. DEAD SEA SCROLLS AND PHILO

4QMidrash on Eschatology
(4Q174 and 4Q177) 93

4QPs.-Ezekiel (4Q385)
Frg. 2 115

4QTestimonia (4Q175)
Passim xv
5–7 99

Philo *On Dreams*
1.227–230 95

F. APOSTOLIC FATHERS

Barnabas
Passim xv, xvii, 119
2.5 75 n. 185
2.5–8 124
2.7 123
5.2 71 n. 127, 110

5.2–14 111
5.12 72 n. 146, 117
5.13 112
5.14 110
6.11–12 89
6.16 128

INDEX OF BIBLICAL AND OTHER ANC. SOURCES 161

7.3, 5   116
7.9   98
9.1   127
9.5   120
9.8   126
11.10–11   132
12.1   115
12.4   115
12.10–11   130
12.11   79 n. 255, 130
14.7   80 n. 260
14.7–8   107
14.7–9   108
15.8   125

1 Clement
8.4   75 n. 187
36.4   93
51.1   127

2 Clement
13.2–4   128

Ignatius *To the Trallians*
8.2   128

Polycarp *To the Philippians*
10.3   128

G. OTHER EARLY CHRISTIAN REFERENCES

Acts of Peter
24   103–6, 111

Apocalypse of Peter
6   119

Apostolic Constitutions
8.8.4   126

Aristides *Apology*
2.1   130
14.1   130

Athanasius *On the Councils*
27   85, 89, 94

Athanasius *On the Incarnation*
33.3–4   104
33.4   67 n. 84, 101
33.5   133
40.3   101

Basil of Caesaria *On the Holy Spirit*
38   84–85

49   134

Ps.-Basil *Against Eunomius*
Passim   xvii
131   134
161   95, 133
180   134
183   89, 91
191–192   133
192   81 n. 279, 134
193   135
195   134

Clement of Alexandria *Christ the Educator*
1.14.5   129
1.79.1   120
3.89–91   124

Clement of Alexandria *Exhortation to the Greeks*
79.2   100

Clement of Alexandria
    Miscellanies
5.14   100
6.5.39–41   130
6.92.1   119
7.94   105

Ps.-Clementine Homilies
3.55.3   99

Ps.-Clementine Recognitions
Passim   119

Chrysostom *Demonstration
    against Jews and Greeks
    that Christ is God*
3   99

Commodian *Apologetical
    Song*
269   111
270–276   112
333–334   113
371–372   97
405–410   104
518–519   113
772   113

Creed, First Sirmian
Anathema 8   85
Anathema 14   88–89
Anathema 17   94

Cyprian *To Quirinus:
    Testimonies against the
    Jews*
Passim   xiv
1.3   106
1.8   122
1.8–11   120
1.10   127

1.16   122
1.21   98, 127, 130
1.22   129
2.1   88
2.3   83, 86
2.4   96, 99
2.6   97, 102, 105
2.7   108, 131
2.8   104
2.10   100, 101, 108, 134
2.11   100, 101
2.12   99
2.13   110, 135
2.15   110, 112
2.16   106
2.20–22   112
2.20   71 n. 133, 111–15
2.21   105, 114
2.22   114, 126
2.23   72 n. 138, 113, 114
2.24   117
2.25   64 n. 33, 95, 117
2.26   117, 119
2.28   97, 117
2.29   97, 98, 130

Cyril of Alexandria *Against
    Julian*
1.28   89
8   67 n. 84
9   63 n. 27
26   91
28–29   89

Cyril of Alexandria
    Commentary on Jonah
Proem.   66 n. 66

Cyril of Jerusalem
    Catechetical Lectures
Passim   xvii
10.6   94
10.12   106

INDEX OF BIBLICAL AND OTHER ANC. SOURCES 163

10.16 129
11.10 85
11.15 97
11.16 106
12.8 99
12.8–11 97
12.9 99
12.10 97
12.17 99
12.20 99
12.23 100
13.7 109
13.10 113
13.12 109
13.13 110
13.19 112
13.24 115, 117
13.29 116
13.34 117
13.35 118
14.1 117
14.4 117
14.8 117
14.14 117
14.24 118
14.27–28 119
15.21 97
16.29 95

Dialogue of Athanasius and Zacchaeus

Passim xvii
3–12 89
7 83
11 85
12 89
13 87
36 71 n. 137, 114
47 67 n. 83
93–97 106
113–114 106
123 120–21
125 122

Dialogue of Timothy and Aquila

Passim xvii
5.6 68 n. 99, 104
12.9–12 124
19.26–20.6 106

Epiphanius *Refutation of all Heresies (Panarion)*

30.30.3 105
65.5 86
74.5.2 86
76.38.4 95

Ps.-Epiphanius *Testimonies*

1.2 88
2 89
2–3 88
3.2 83
4 86
4.3 108
5 96, 100
5.17 95, 134
5.18 97
5.21b 98
5.24 98
5.28 105
5.54 100
6.1 97
6.2 100
6.3 97
6.5 107
6.9 105
8 104
8–14 103
9 106
10 106
12.2 108
13a 106
14 105
19 132
25 133

25.2   81 n. 272
27b   132
28   81 n. 270, 132
33   108
37.3   97
41   109
41.1   109
43.2   109
45.2   113
48.3   110
51   112
51.2   110
51.5   111
53.1   116
55.3   110
57.1   113
61   114
62   111
63   110
71.2   110
74.1   117
74.6   117
85.1   117
86.1   118
87   108
89.3   119
90   131
91   126
92   126
92.1   124
94.5   119

Eusebius *Against Marcellus*
1.1.4   84
2.2.9   84
2.2.41   88

Eusebius *Ecclesiastical History*
5.17.3   83

Eusebius *Preparation for the Gospel*
7.12   84

Eusebius *Proof of the Gospel*
Passim   xvii, 88
1.3   101
1.6   129
2.1   130
2.3   101, 128
3.2   100, 101
4.16   100
5.4   106
5.5   84
5.5–18   90
5.17   63 n. 27, 95
5.26–28   97
5.28   97
6.2   118
6.3   97
6.12   100
6.18   116
6.20   133
6.21   108
7.1   68 n. 99, 101, 104, 107
7.2   99
7.3   98, 100
8.5   133
9.2   133

Eusebius *Prophetic Selections*
Passim   xvii
4.24   106

Evagrius *Dialogue of Simon and Theophilus*
Passim   xvii
7   95
9   93
10–11   86
13   130
15–16   104
25   122
28   112, 115
34–35   126

INDEX OF BIBLICAL AND OTHER ANC. SOURCES 165

38–39   117
39   114
40   118
42   119
44   105
44–46   99
49   125
49–51   124

Gospel of Ps.-Matthew
14   106

Gospel of Peter
5.16   116
15   113

Gregory of Nyssa *In illud: Tunc et ipse Filius*
8   105

Gregory of Nyssa *Life of Moses*
2.270   xviii n. 14

Hippolytus *Against Noetus*
2–4   106
2.5   97
5.1   97
12   98
12.3–4   86
13.2–3   86

Irenaeus *Against Heresies*
Passim   xvii
1.3.4   107
1.22.1   83
3.6.1   63 n. 23, 93, 94, 97, 98, 102
3.8.3   83
3.9.2   66 n. 74, 100
3.9.3   108
3.10.2   110

3.11.8   98
3.16   107
3.17.2   134
3.18.3   100
3.19.2   65 n. 48, 100
3.21.4   105
3.21.7   106
3.24.2   83
4.10.2   101, 113
4.16.2   122
4.17.1–4   124
4.17.1–6   122
4.17.5   124
4.18.3   135
4.20.1   88
4.20.3   87
4.20.4   96
4.33.1   65 n. 48
4.33.1, 12   97
4.33.11   100, 106, 108, 111, 118
4.33.11–12   96
4.33.12   110, 113–16
4.34.4   127
5.1.1   88
5.12.2   135
5.18.3   113

Irenaeus *Proof of the Apostolic Preaching*
Passim   xvii
5   83
9   135
36   93, 100
43   87, 92
44   94
44–46   90
47–49   102
48–49   130
49   93, 130
50–51   131
53   108, 134
53–57   103
55   105

55–56   104
56   104, 105
57   101
57–59   100
58   101
63   99
64   100
65   97
67   108
68   110
68–70   110
70   111
71   110
74   109
76   117
79   112, 113, 115
79–80   111
81   113
82   116
85   119
86   126
88   129
92   98
95   128
97   96

Jerome *Commentary on Ezekiel*

13   106

Ps.-Jerome *Commentary on Mark*

15:33   115

Justin I *Apology*
Passim   xv, xvii
32   100
32.1   101
32.12   101
34.1   99
35.2   104, 105
35.3   115
35.3–5   111

36.2   87
37   123
38.1–6   111
39.1–3   127
40   109
48.1–3   108
50–51   110
50.2   110
51.1   111
52.3   110
53.11   121
55.5   109
59.3   62 n. 11
64.3   62 n. 11

Justin *Dialogue with Trypho*
Passim   xv, xvi
10–29   119
11–47   123
13–23   122
13.4   71 n. 131
15.7   122
15.7–16.1   120
16.2   xx, 122
17.2   128
19.3–4   122
20.4   128
21   125
22.6   123
22.7–10   124
26.2   80
26.3   115
27.4   128
27.5   125
28.2   120, 122
28.6   127
31–32   118
34.2   106
34.3–6   99
36–37   118
41.1   123
41.2   124
42.2   96

43.5–6   104
45.4   92
49.2–3   131
52   97
53.3   65 n. 48
53.6   116
56–60   89, 93, 95
56.12–15   93
58.5   95
61–62   87
62   88
62.1–3   89
62.3   88
63.1–3   111
66.2–3   104
69.5   108
71–73   xvi
72–73   112
72.2   112
74   113
76–77   93
76.1–2   111
76.1   106
76.7   92
78.1   99
86   112
86.2–3   106
87.6   95
88.8   93
89.3   110
97.1–3   111
97.2   128
100.4   106
106.4   67 n. 84, 101
109.1   127
113   98
114.2   96
115.4   98
116   98
118.2   93
118.4   96
119.2   128
119.4   98

120   xvi
121.4–122.6   108
121.4–123.2   107
122.3   80
122.6   93
126.1   106
130.1   95

Lactantius *Divine Institutes*

4.12.4   104
4.12.17–18   130
4.13.7   106
4.13.8   97
4.13.9   102
4.13.10   100, 101
4.16.14   99
4.17.3   127
4.18.16   110
4.18.21–30   112
4.18.24   110
4.19.8   117
4.19.9   117

Ladder of Jacob

7.2   115

Marius Victorinus *Against Arius*

2.5   86

Melito *On Pascha*

61   113
62   109
64   110
94   71 n. 137

Novatian *On the Trinity*

9   101, 108
9.5   113
9.6   104, 135
9.8   115, 117
12.4   108
17   91

17–19   90
18.5   96
26   94
26.3–7   89
26.7   130
28   107, 111
28.10   115
28.11   116
29.2   95
29.13   108, 134, 135

Origen *Against Celsus*
6.44   127

Origen *Commentary on John*
1.3 [17]   83

Preaching of Peter
Frg. 2d   130

Protevangelium of James
22.2   106

Rufinus *Commentary on the Apostles' Creed*
Passim   xvii
9   106
19   109, 110
20   109, 113
21–22   110
23   112
24   115
26   116

Tertullian *Against Hermogenes*
28.9   100
32.3   135

Tertullian *Against the Jews*
2.12–14   122

3   xx, 122, 127
4   125
5   122
5.6   124
7.2   130
9   103
9.1   104, 105
9.21   98
9.30   108
10.4   116
10.12   112
10.15–16   110
10.17   72 n. 138, 113
11   126
11.9   113
12.2   131
13.2   99
13.10   115
13.14   114
13.23   117
14   110
14.6   100, 111
14.7   98
14.12–13   93

Tertullian *Against Marcion*
1.20   122
3.6.6   100
3.6.7   110
3.7   96, 110
3.7.6   98, 100, 111
3.12–13   104
3.13.3   105
3.18–19   112
3.19.3   112
3.20.6   100
3.20.9   93
3.22.1   126
3.22.5   126
3.23.2   128
4.13.6   107
4.14.6   128
4.22.10   99

INDEX OF BIBLICAL AND OTHER ANC. SOURCES

4.39.19 98
4.40 109
4.40.2 113
4.40.3 112
4.42.2 109
4.42.4 110
4.42.5 114
4.43.1 117
5.2.5 126
5.4.6 124
5.9 92
5.9.10 98

Tertullian *Against Praxeas*
6.1 87
7 87
7.2 93
7.3 83
7.3–6 84
11.3 93
11.5 135
11.5–6 108
11.7–8 130
11.8 130
11.9–10 87
13.1 102
13.2 102, 105

13.3 96
14.10 110
16.1 91
16.2 63 n. 23, 91, 94
19.2 88
19.2–3 87
27.5, 10 107
28.9 100
28.11 130

Tertullian *The Flesh of Christ*
23 105, 107

Tertullian *The Resurrection of the Flesh*
20 109, 110, 113
22.10 131

Tertullian *The Soul*
11.3 135

Theophilus *To Autolycus*
1.7.3 83
2.10.6–10 87
2.18.2 88

Index of Modern Authors

Albl, M. C. xiii, xv n. 6, xvi n. 12, 101, 102, 105, 106, 111, 112, 118, 124, 130
Attridge, H. W. 95

Bardenhewer, O. xvii n. 14
Brown, R. E. 99, 106
Bruce, F. F. 95

Collins, J. J. 100
Conybeare, F. C. 121
Crossan, J. D. 109, 110, 114, 116

Daniélou, J. xv n. 9, xviii n. 14, 109, 112–15
Dodd, C. H. xiii n. 3, xv and n. 7

Falcetta, A. xiii n. 4, xiv n. 5, xvi and n. 11, 92, 101, 104, 106, 108, 113, 115, 118, 127

Gallandi, A. xviii
Glasson, T. F. 102

Harris, J. R. xiii and n. 4, xiv and n. 5, xv, xvi and n. 11, 92, 101, 104, 106, 113, 115, 118, 127
Hanson, R. P. C. 86
Hay, D. M. 130

Kelly, J. N. D. 106
Kraft, R. A. 115, 124, 130

Lindars, B. xv

Murray, R. 101

Norelli, E. xvi, 103, 104, 112

Prigent, P. xv n. 9, 101, 112, 113

Reijners, G. Q. 112, 115, 126
Ruether, R. R. xix nn. 16 and 17

Schreckenberg, H. xix n. 16
Segal, A. F. 102
Sifanus, L. xviii and n. 15, xix, 63 n. 24, 63 n. 28, 64 n. 41, 65 n. 58, 66 n. 63, 66 n. 65, 66 n. 67, 66 n. 71, 66 n. 72, 66 n. 74, 67 n. 81, 67 n. 83, 67 n. 84, 67 n. 85, 67 n. 86, 67 n. 87, 68 n. 90, 68 n. 99, 68 n. 100, 68 n. 102, 69 n. 103, 69 n. 104, 70 n. 113, 70 n. 114, 70 n. 115, 70 n.125, 70 n. 126, 71 n. 127, 72 n. 142, 72 n. 147, 73 n. 152, 73 n. 154, 73 n. 155, 73 n. 157, 73 n. 161, 73 n. 164, 74 n. 170, 74 n. 179, 74 n. 184, 75 n. 190, 75 n. 191, 75 n. 192, 75 n. 194, 76 n. 198, 76 n. 201, 76 n. 203, 76 n. 204, 76 n. 205, 76 n. 209, 77 n. 217, 77 n. 225, 78 n. 230, 78 n. 232, 78 n. 236, 79 n. 244, 79 n. 248, 79 n. 249, 79 n. 251, 79 n. 255, 79 n. 256, 79 n. 258, 79 n. 259, 80 n. 262, 80 n. 267, 132, 138
Skarsaune, O. xv n. 9, 87, 90, 92–94, 96–98, 100–2, 104, 107, 108, 110, 111, 115, 119, 120, 122, 123, 126, 127,135
Slusser, M. 87
Smith, J. P. 92, 111
Stendahl, K. 116
Strousma, G. xx n. 18

Thunberg, L. 90

Williams, A. L. xvii and n. 14, xix n. 16, 132

Wilson, R. McL. 89

Zacagni, L. A. xviii, xix, 63 n.17, 63 n. 24, 63 n. 25, 65 n. 58, 67 n. 78, 67 n. 82, 68 n. 88, 68 n. 92, 68 n. 98, 69 n. 104, 69 n. 108, 70 n. 111, 73 n. 156, 73 n. 163, 75 n. 191, 76 n. 198, 77 n. 216, 78 n. 232, 79 n. 248, 79 n. 250, 80 n. 269, 81 n. 274, 98, 128

www.ingramcontent.com/pod-product-compliance
Lightning Source LLC
Chambersburg PA
CBHW020759160426
43192CB00006B/378